The Catholic
Homeschool Companion

The Catholic Homeschool Companion

Selected and Edited by
Maureen Wittmann and Rachel Mackson

SOPHIA INSTITUTE PRESS®
Manchester, New Hampshire

Sophia Institute Press®
Box 5284, Manchester, NH 03108
1-800-888-9344
www.sophiainstitute.com

Library of Congress Cataloging-in-Publication Data

The Catholic homeschool companion / selected and edited by Maureen Wittmann and Rachel Mackson.
        p. cm.
Includes bibliographical references.
ISBN 1-933184-16-7 (pbk. : alk. paper)
1. Home schooling — United States. 2. Catholic Church — Education — United States. 3. Christian education — Home training — United States. I. Wittmann, Maureen. II. Mackson, Rachel.

LC40.W58 2005
371.04′2 — dc22   2005028870

05 06 07 08 09 10 9 8 7 6 5 4 3 2 1

To my first-born child, Christian,
who has shown me how to be
a home educator, a mother,
and a Christian.

Maureen Wittmann

To my father, Gregory New,
who made this book a possibility;
to my beloved husband, Dave;
and to my cherished children:
Philip, Grace, and Emily.
In loving memory of my grandmother,
Teresa New, and my mother, Susan.

Rachel Mackson

Contents

Chapter One
Core Subjects

Chapter Two
Enrichment Subjects

Chapter Three

High School

Chapter Four

Homeschooling Styles
and Strategies

Chapter Five

Children with Special Needs

Chapter Six

Homeschooling in Unique Circumstances

Chapter Seven

The Father's Perspective

Chapter Eight

Finding Inspiration

Chapter Nine

Homeschooling Community and Support

Chapter Ten

Home Management

Chapter Eleven
Homeschool Students and Graduates

Appreciation

The authors who contributed essays to *The Catholic Homeschool Companion* have our warmest thanks. They took valuable time from their families and their homeschooling endeavors to share their stories, but their contributions do not stop with the publication of this book. They have inspired us to be better homeschoolers and better mothers. We hope they will inspire you as well.

Many others donated their time and talent, especially Nancy Carpentier Brown, who spent her Christmas vacation proofing the manuscript and finding all of those little errors that somehow missed many layers of editing. We are indebted to her.

The list does not end there. Sue Crawford and Sheila Pohl graciously offered their secretarial skills in transcribing several essays from audiotapes. Without them, we would have been lost.

Several Catholic publishers provided review copies of books and texts, so that we, in turn, could share them with you. We are especially grateful to Bethlehem Books, Neumann Press, Catholic Heritage Curricula, and Laura Berquist.

Alicia Van Hecke stepped in and helped verify the resource information found in the appendices. Her time and Internet savvy are fully appreciated.

We would also like to express our gratitude to those who offered their advice, support, and prayers, including the Aquilina Family,

Patrick Baker, Dawn Smith, Joan Stromberg, the Wissner Family, and the members of the Catholic Writers' Association.

For help with our websites — www.catholictreasury.com and www.homeschool.mackson.org — Maureen owes a great debt to Michael Aquilina III and Kaleb Nation, and Rachel would like to thank her brother, Jay Riley, Jr.

But no appreciation would be complete without a mention of our families: Maureen's husband, Rob, and her children, Christian, Mary, Laura, Joseph, Gregory, Margaret, and Brendan; Rachel's husband, Dave, and her children, Philip, Grace, and Emily. We are grateful for their patience, their support, and their love.

Most important, we give thanks to God for the grace necessary to be writers and editors, in addition to wives and mothers.

Foreword

Bishop Carl Mengeling

As you pursue your God-given responsibility for the education of your children, allow me to offer some encouragement.

You have made a choice, you have a right to make that choice, you believe in that choice, and you are committing yourself to that choice: to be homeschoolers of your children. Others do not make that choice, and that is their business, but you have made the choice and you are proud of it, and the Church is also proud.

That choice was made by today's saint, Thomas More. If you know his life, you know that he was a homeschooler in every sense. At the heart of his family was nothing but the total education of the human person centered, above all, in religion. As one of the great leaders in Europe, he brought to his home a great renaissance of learning and a renaissance of faith. He taught his daughters languages. He taught them political science. He taught them music. He taught them, above all, religion. That is why the choice he made, when put to the test by King Henry VIII, ultimately recalls the fullness of Scripture.

You and I must never expect that what happened to Jesus is not going to happen to us. We, too, are going to be put to the test. We are being put to the test now, and the Church has always been put to the test. The Lord separates the goats from the sheep. He summons us in these times of trial and testing to measure up and to rise higher and higher. This is the time, as it was five hundred years ago in Europe, when we need saints. Saints are the solution. That is the Church's solution to everything, and that is what you want. You want your children to become saints.

Education has a twofold objective. Number one is to become citizens of the kingdom of heaven. Number two is to become effective citizens here, while that kingdom is taking shape in this world. Citizens of this world, citizens of the next: that is our vision.

I do want to stress something very important, and that is the absolute centrality of religion in the entire education program. Without that, it is merely preparing people for what they are going to do in this life. That is important, but secondary. Far more important, my dear Catholics, is not what we are going to do, but who we become; that we become men and women of God and saints of God, the presence of Christ in this world. That is the object of education: who we become. You and I are not done with it. That is why we keep coming to the Eucharist. That is why we keep going to Confession, because we are not yet the person we can become by God's grace.

Maria Montessori said that the whole essence of her educational program lay in two words: *milk* and *honey*. You may not have thought of it that way, but Augustine, who died in the year 430, said that the milk stands for all the fundamental needs we have in this life — the need for food, shelter, and clothing. Augustine said that is important, but the milk is not enough by itself.

Today, as you well know, most Americans are drowning in milk. We have too much milk, and yet we want more milk; we want more junk, more stuff. We are drowning in milk, and education today, for the most part, is to prepare people to get more milk. Yes, we need the milk, and we need education that gives us the knowledge and the skills to build all the factories and the automobiles and to provide food and everything else, and in no way do I denigrate that, but it is not enough. We are more than that. What is missing in the lives of so many people is the *honey*.

What is the honey? The honey is what gives meaning and purpose and destiny to my life and ties it all together and gives meaning to all this milk stuff. Think of it, my dear Catholics, how sweet it is to be a believer. How sweet it is, like honey, to see myself the way God does: born in the image and likeness of God, with the capacity to know and love God and to know and love one another. To see myself as the Lord Jesus on the Cross sees me, worthy enough that he died for me. Oh, how sweet it is to be so loved. How sweet it is to have faith, to see the whole picture, not just a fourth of it, or a half of it. Not just in terms of this world, but in terms of eternity and the kingdom of God, which gives meaning to all of this. How sweet it is to have the faith, the mind and heart that God reveals in Jesus humanly, so that we can grasp it. How sweet it is to see everyone else the way God sees them. To see that every person has value and meaning, that everyone is worthy, that everyone is to be loved and given a break and saved.

Yes, that is the honey: to be a believer, a person of hope and optimism and enthusiasm, no matter what is going on. It isn't always easy; it's tough. You say how great it is to be a Catholic. It's *tough* to be a good Catholic. But it's worth it.

John Paul II said so beautifully when he challenged university professors in 1988, "Education is an act of love of man toward man, of parents toward children, of teachers toward students, and adults toward minors." He calls it an act of love. Think about it. That is precisely what you are motivated by in the choice that you have made as homeschoolers: an act of love that requires tremendous sacrifice, a tremendous dedication and patience and perseverance to educate your own children and others with you in the environment you have chosen. That is an act of love. Education is not a job. It is not a profession. We can look at it that way, but that is not enough. Educators, parents, are gifts for their children.

How sweet it is when our children know what it means to be honest, to be truthful. How sweet it is when other people know that what they say or what we say can be relied on as truth. How sweet it is when we have a deep sense of respect for others. How sweet it is to have patience and endurance, never to give up on anybody, to know that no one is waste or garbage, and that everyone counts. How sweet is chastity. How sweet that decency, how sweet it is to integrate the sexual reality of who we are in the reality of love. How sweet it is to have a mind that is pure and chaste and a voice that speaks decency.

That, my dear Catholics, has to be taught. That has to be experienced in the home. It is a battle today to find role models, because we are surrounded with pornography, and yet at the same time you and I roll up our sleeves and we keep on striving for that which is right and good. How sweet it is to respect other people's property. That whole gambit of acquisition and taking becomes more for us who are giving. Yes, the choice between being a giver or a taker.

My dear Catholics, the whole reality of our religion is the honey. The whole of the Gospels is the honey. The teachings of Jesus, the eight Beatitudes, are the honey. That is where the meaning of education lies. Take the honey away, and all we have left is the milk, and that does not give you a reason to live. It does not give you a destiny. It does not give you a purpose. All of the things that prepare us for that — and they are important: mathematics and science, the language arts, and all the other subjects — do not give you a reason to live. They are just tools. Faith, hope, and love are what give you a reason to live.

In the Eucharist, we celebrate the love of Christ, the risen Lord, who is present to draw us in. You hear in the Mass, "This is my body given up for you," and "This is my blood poured out for you." The body given up, the blood poured out — total gift. The world hates that. The world is against that. The world is always attracting us to be takers — me, me, me, take, take, take, milk, milk, milk. The Lord Jesus, on the other hand, is just the opposite: the Giver and the Honey in which the milk finds its meaning.

So, my dear homeschoolers, you are on the right track. You're doing the right thing, and I know it isn't easy. A lot of people don't like you for it, and some people criticize you for it. You're in good company. Jesus, they said, was possessed by the Devil. They couldn't wait to kill him. So we're in good company. Amen.

+Bishop Carl Mengeling
Feast of St. Thomas More

Blessed are those who have not seen and yet believe.
John 20:29

Introduction

Like *A Catholic Homeschool Treasury*, *The Catholic Homeschool Companion* addresses a wide variety of topics and provides an insight into the homes of real-life Catholic homeschoolers. However, my children and Rachel's were young when we compiled and edited the first book, and therefore it's heavy on grade-school information. With *The Catholic Homeschool Companion*, Rachel and I have taken great care to include a chapter exclusively on high school instruction. Additionally, we devote entire chapters to topics such as home management and learning disabilities.

We're also excited to have more fathers contributing to *The Catholic Homeschool Companion*. If you look at *A Catholic Homeschool Treasury*, you'll see that Dad has a prominent place on the cover. That was very important to Rachel and to me, as fathers are too often overlooked in homeschooling circles. In producing this book, we made a special effort to seek out male authors. This book is not just for mothers; homeschooling fathers will find that this is their book, too. (You'll even find several essays of interest to your older children.)

We encourage husbands to assist their wives in the education of their children. This often leads to better communication between spouses and mutual commitment, and therefore leads to stronger marriages. Assistance can include teaching a course, providing wives with the tools necessary for success, taking little ones for a weekly night out so that wives can plan the school week, and providing moral and spiritual support. In this way, homeschooling becomes much more than an educational model; it becomes a way of life for the family. Education is not a place or system; it's an experience.

Just as schoolteachers refer to themselves as professional educators, so should homeschooling parents. Professionals keep up to date in their fields by reading all the right books, subscribing to professional journals, joining professional organizations, and attending conferences. As home educators, we benefit greatly when we follow this example. For this reason, you'll find an extensive Catholic resource section in the appendices of this book. The information there will give you a step up in taking on the attitude of a professional educator.

Rachel and I do not presume to be homeschooling experts with all the answers. We presume to be experts only in the Mackson and Wittmann homeschools. You are the expert in your homeschool. No one person knows your children better than you and your spouse do, and through the sacrament of Marriage you have the grace necessary to teach your own children.

The Church teaches us that parents are the primary educators of their children (CCC, 2221-2231). This is not a teaching to be taken lightly, and as home educators, we take that teaching to heart. Most important, we're responsible for the formation of our children's souls in addition to their intellect.

There are many ways to homeschool. This is why *The Catholic Homeschool Companion* presents a wide range of family situations and solutions. It's my hope and prayer that you'll be able to learn from the writers of the following essays, taking the ideas and recommendations that will work in your home.

Ultimately, if parents want to be successful homeschoolers, they must have a burning desire to take their children's education into their own hands. If they have that desire, and they prayerfully look for God's will in making the decision, everything else will fall into place. I've seen, firsthand, parents overcome great obstacles in order to homeschool, and you will, too, in reading the following pages.

The Catholic
Homeschool Companion

Chapter One

Core Subjects

*"Apply your mind to instruction
and your ear to words of knowledge."*

Proverbs 23:12

Phonics and Beyond

Linda Bromeier

Many years ago, at the end of my first year of teaching in a public school, I anxiously awaited my students' reading achievement test scores. The students in my learning-disabilities and remedial-reading classes were teenagers reading three to six years below grade level. We had spent the year memorizing sight words, completing worksheets (not phonics, which was frowned upon by my supervisor), and reading as much low-level material as I could find. This was how I had been instructed by university professors to teach reading, and I thought that was the way to do it.

When the reading scores finally arrived, I was stunned. Many of my students scored only a few points higher than their reading scores from the beginning of the year. I wondered what I had done wrong.

Instinctively, I decided to teach reading using phonics: the study of the sounds in a language, the symbols (letters of the alphabet) for those sounds, and how to blend those sounds into words. Phonics was the method by which I had learned to read as a child, but it was out of vogue in many public schools. Most schools taught a little phonics in first grade, but for the most part, students were expected to learn to read by memorizing sight words that often did not follow any particular phonetic pattern or rules (e.g., *one*, *find*, *could*). Students with memory problems or attention problems simply could not memorize enough words to keep up and eventually ended up in learning-disabled classrooms like mine, completely confused.

To my great satisfaction, my students showed much better progress the next school year, after using the phonics-based Merrill Linguistic Readers and phonics workbooks from Modern Curriculum Press (MCP). I continued to teach phonics for several more years in the classroom and through private tutoring.

When I began homeschooling my children, phonics was naturally the choice of reading method to use.

Intensive Phonics

How exactly do you teach reading using phonics? Teach it *intensively*. Intensive phonics means: teaching *all* the phonograms, or letter-sounds, in the English language; teaching in a systematic and orderly manner; and teaching until the student has thoroughly mastered each phonogram.

When I teach intensive phonics, I follow four basic steps to make sure the student learns each phonogram thoroughly:

• *First*, I introduce the new phonogram by pointing to the letter(s), I pronounce the sound, and I name pictures that begin with that sound.

• *Second*, I have the student perform daily word drills in which he practices reading a list of words containing that phonogram. The word drills are absolutely essential, because they help the child learn the phonogram so well that he knows it instantly.

• *Third* (after a day or two of word drills), I have the student read phonetic stories containing an abundance of words with that phonogram.

• *Finally*, I have the student complete phonics worksheets or workbook pages that provide further practice in writing and reading that phonogram.

Games, projects, and other creative methods of teaching the phonogram can make learning fun. When the child can read the phonetic word lists quickly and accurately, and can read the stories with comprehension, I know he has mastered that phonogram.

Which phonograms need to be taught, and when? There are forty-three speech sounds in English, represented by twenty-six alphabet letters or letter combinations. The simplest phonograms to teach are consonants, which usually only make one sound. After a student knows some consonant sounds, he can be taught the short vowels (*a, e, i, o,* and *u* as in *cat, bed, pin, dog,* and *bug*). The next step is to start reading actual words by pronouncing each letter sound and blending those sounds into a word. Beginning readers usually find this sounding-and-blending process to be difficult at first, but after a few weeks of practice, they improve.

From then on, new phonograms are introduced at the pace of about one per week, until all have been learned. It is best to introduce new phonograms in a logical order, so that the student can see the regularity in the English language. For example: long vowels with silent *e* as in *rake, kite, hope,* and *mule* should be taught close together, so that the "silent *e*" rule becomes apparent to the student. Irregular sounds and spellings should be taught last, after the student has a firm mastery of the regular phonograms.

Most children are ready to begin reading instruction around age six and can learn all the phonograms by the middle or the end of second grade.

Phonics Materials

When I began homeschooling in 1988, I searched in vain for a Catholic phonics series. There simply were none. I used a little of everything: homemade flash cards and *Professor Phonics* for word drill, the plaid-cover MCP phonics workbooks, stories from *Primary Phonics* (Educators Publishing Service) and Merrill Linguistic Readers (SRA), plus some of my own teaching materials. My children learned to read, but it was difficult to coordinate everything, because the publishers didn't always present phonograms in the same order, and I was skipping around in the books. Besides that, there was nothing Catholic or Christian about any of the stories.

In frustration I began writing my own phonetic stories and worksheets to go with them. These materials evolved into the Little Angel Reader® Catholic phonics program, published in 1997 (see Stone Tablet Press in Appendix A). The Little Angel Readers have made it a lot easier to teach phonics, because everything is included in one well-organized series. The readers have phonograms, word lists, and phonetic stories, with the bonus of Catholic content and color illustrations. Four workbooks and a teacher's manual are coordinated with the readers.

What Next?

After your child completes the intensive phonics instruction, take him to the library. Find a list of "Great Books" appropriate for his age, and let him read the wonderful tales that have delighted children for generations. With my children, I have insisted on a certain number of books to be read from a "classic" list each year. Along with the library books, my children read from a Catholic reader or saint book at least two days a week. We are fortunate to have original copies of the Faith and Freedom Readers (currently reprinted by Seton Media), and also books from Neumann Press and other Catholic publishers.

After my child finishes reading a book or story, I check his comprehension with oral questions or written exercises from the book, or by having him retell the story in his own words or in a written book report. If your child groans at the thought of writing a book report, let him occasionally make a poster, diorama, or other creative interpretation of the book instead. Catholic reading-comprehension workbooks (Seton Media or Catholic Heritage Curricula are good sources) can also be used once or twice a week for comprehension exercises.

Reading widely and often will naturally develop your child's vocabulary, because he will encounter new words in the stories he reads. However, most schools teach vocabulary directly, because having a large vocabulary improves reading comprehension and helps students achieve higher scores on standardized tests. In our homeschool, we use Wordly Wise workbooks to teach new vocabulary words. Another method is to take six to eight unfamiliar words from the story the student is currently reading, and have him write the definitions and use them in a sentence of his own. This involves extra preparation work for busy homeschooling mothers, so it may be impractical unless your reading text or curriculum provides a list of words to use.

In addition to comprehension and vocabulary, there are other advanced word-structure skills typically taught in the middle and upper grades. These include contractions, prefixes, suffixes, verb inflections (-s, -ed, -ing), homonyms, synonyms, and antonyms, Latin and Greek root words, and rules for dividing words into syllables. We use MCP phonics and word-study workbooks in grades three through six for a review of phonics as well as teaching these advanced skills. Many of the same skills are also included in the Voyages in English series.

As your child moves into high school, the emphasis will be almost entirely on reading comprehension and critical analysis. High school literature classes typically use an anthology, or collection of stories, as a textbook. Full-length novels may be read if there is sufficient class time. One of the best ways to make literature more meaningful to the high school student is to link the literature selections to the period of history being taught that year. For example, read *Gilgamesh* when studying ancient Sumeria in World History, or one of Nathaniel Hawthorne's stories when studying the American colonial period, or a work by Dostoyevsky when studying pre-Revolutionary Russia. A good guide to historical fiction is *Let the Authors Speak*, by Carolyn Hatcher (available from Emmanuel Books; see Appendix A). Kolbe Academy (see Appendix B) also has a well-developed history/literature program for the high school student.

The result of all this reading instruction should be a skilled reader with a lifetime love for great books.

"For the moment all discipline seems painful
rather than pleasant; later it yields the peaceful fruit
of righteousness to those who have been trained by it."

Hebrews 12:11

Grammar Phobia

Nancy Carpentier Brown

gram•mar pho•bia (gra′-mər fO′-bE-ə) n, 1. general, the fear of Language Arts, 2. specific, the fear of grammar, 3. school, the fear of English class, 4. homeschool, the fear of teaching one's offspring Language Arts.

Language arts, the mechanics of writing, is one of those subjects that homeschooling mothers seem to either love or hate. At one time, I hated English class and everything that was related to it. I never learned to diagram a sentence. I couldn't see any practical reason ever to use such knowledge.

I hated English as a subject so much in high school that when I chose my college major, nursing, I asked my guidance counselor, "Will I have to take English?" He didn't think I would. Later that summer, as I looked over the freshmen class requirements, I breathed a sigh of relief when I didn't see any English courses.

You can imagine my shock when I went to the campus bookstore to buy my books and learned that "Modes of Discourse I" was an English class. I don't know what I thought it was, but I remember being alarmed to find out that it meant English.

Here it is, twenty years later, and I'm trying to teach my children a subject I had no love for when I was a student. Older and wiser, I realize my fear and hatred were unfounded. Further, I have no intention of passing my personal phobias on to my children. When my oldest daughter was of the age to learn grammar, I did what any self-respecting homeschooling mother would do: I signed myself up for a grammar course. I had to overcome my grammar phobia, and I had to do it quickly. My nine-year-old daughter knew more about prepositional phrases than I did, and I was uncomfortable with that.

Being a busy mother, I looked for an online course I could take. I found a great course at www.timelineorkshops.com. The main thing I learned was that the mechanics of writing — the part I was so afraid of — is basically the *science* of writing. With my nursing background, I knew I could handle science. I made my way through the year-long class, my confidence level building and my grammar phobia subsiding.

My first word of advice in teaching grammar is to get comfortable with it yourself. With math, science, Greek, and theology, there are textbooks and answer keys. However, when our children write papers, compositions, or book reports, it's up to us as their parents and teachers to correct and advise them on their writing. This means that our grammar and language mechanics skills must be within us. If we're not familiar with some aspect of grammar, we need to study it so that we can be familiar with it.

If you seriously doubt that you can help your children with their writing, find someone who can, or find an online course for your children to take. Ask the people in your homeschooling community if anyone has an expertise in writing, English, or language arts. Perhaps someone knows a retired teacher or a community-college professor who'd be willing to spend time with your children.

The other option is the online courses available for children, such as WriteGuide.com (see Appendix A). The Institute for Excellence in Writing (see Appendix A) offers video courses for students and parents and is a wonderful resource.

There are different methods for teaching grammar. One that you can use with very young children is the Language of God series, available through Catholic Heritage Curricula (see Appendix A). Using this series alone, my sixth-grader tested at the twelfth-grade level in grammar. Needless to say, I've been very happy with this series.

There are fun ways to teach grammar as well. I recommend the video *Grammar Rock,* produced by the School House Rock series (www.school-house-rock.com). The catchy tunes help the younger students (older ones, too!) remember what conjunctions, adverbs, interjections, and other parts of speech are. School House Rock also publishes *Grammar Rock* as an interactive CD-Rom for children who like to learn on the computer.

Back in my early days, when I feared grammar, I had purchased a book that came highly recommended to me as the best writing book for homeschooling parents: *Any Child Can Write*, by Harvey Wiener. In this book are many ideas for helping your child to grow in his writing ability and skill. The author suggests starting when children are young. Have them help write out grocery lists and other simple tasks. Wiener also suggests helping the reluctant older writer by providing computer time to assist with writing. This book is good if you need ideas to help your child write more.

Recently, another homeschooling mother told me of an interesting series of books that she came across in the library. The series, called Persona, is out of print; however, you may be able to obtain them through your library. The idea is this: take a situation from the past or the present, and help your child to look at it from many perspectives. The child then writes several stories based on the differing viewpoints.

For example, in one of the stories, the child reads a newspaper advertisement from the "gold rush" days of Alaska. The newspaper ad asked for miners to come up and join a group of gold diggers to strike it rich. There are five lessons, one for each day of the week. On Monday, the student pretends he's the newspaper-man, reading the ad in his newspaper and thinking about all the men who might answer the ad. The student writes a story based on the newspaperman's life in Alaska. On Tuesday, the student imag-ines he's a man in Chicago reading the ad in the paper and then writes in answer to the ad. On Wednesday, the student is the man who placed the ad in the newspaper, and he writes a story about his hopes and dreams of making it rich in the gold rush. And so forth. The student learns to look at a situation from many points of view, and in an interesting way, writes stories based on different perspectives. If you have a lively imagination, you can make up your own stories and do this exercise with your children without the book.

Spelling is another important component of language arts. I had always thought of myself as a poor speller. As with English gram-mar, I didn't want to pass along my low spelling self-esteem to my children. The most exciting thing I've learned in helping my chil-dren with their spelling lessons is that there are spelling *rules*. (Ei-ther I've never learned spelling rules as a child or I was thinking about something else during those lessons.) I've used My *Catholic Speller*, published by Catholic Heritage Curricula (see Appendix A) exclusively. I'm sure there are other spelling programs that work well, but when I find something I like, I stick with it. One thing I like about My *Catholic Speller* is that the examples are from Church teachings or lives of the saints, reinforcing everything else that I teach the children about our Faith.

One thing I think is particularly important about teaching spelling is that you can't just rely on workbooks. The children must hear the words spelled and must hear themselves repeat back the correct spelling of the words. They'll learn to memorize the letters in a row, and that will help them spell well all their lives. As you may have heard before, the more senses involved, the better children learn. If you rely only on workbooks for spelling, children will get only visual reinforcement. With verbal practice and study, they get the hearing and the memory involved.

There are several good computer spelling programs that I like, including *Spelling Blaster* and *Spelling Jungle*. Playing games, such as Hangman, also helps reinforce spelling in a fun way. Repeat the spelling rules often ("*i* before *e* except after *c*"), so that they will stick in your child's brain.

Writing, grammar, and spelling tend to progress and improve together, along with reading. I suggest waiting to introduce writing, grammar, and spelling until your little one has at least a rudimentary grasp of reading. Reading progress is an individual thing. For some, it means kindergarten, for others, it means second, third, or fourth grade. Reading is a developmental, as well as a disciplinary, skill. Once those skills are mastered, the disciplines of writing, grammar, and spelling will be easier to establish.

———————

"There are two ways of dealing with nonsense in this world.
One way is to put nonsense in the right place; as when people
put nonsense into nursery rhymes. The other is to put nonsense
in the wrong place; as when they put it into educational addresses,
psychological criticisms, and complaints against nursery rhymes."

G. K. Chesterton

Using Saxon Math Effectively

Maureen Wittmann

Not all parents choose Saxon Math for their homeschool, but so many do that I think it's important to share with you how we implemented it in our home.

We use Modern Curriculum Press (MCP) Math K through 3, then move to Saxon in the fourth grade. I choose not to use Saxon in the earlier grades, as it relies heavily on manipulatives and requires a lot of time on the part of the parent/teacher. Every family is different, and I know of families who use Saxon Math effectively in the early years; but it's not for our family. As a mother of seven children, I simply don't have a lot of spare time, nor am I organized enough to keep track of manipulatives.

I'm sure, too, that there are math texts available that are more colorful than MCP and Saxon, but my children don't seem to mind the lack of flashy graphics. What's most important to our homeschool lessons is consistency. Yes, there might be math programs available that do this or that a tad better, but constancy in our method is one thing that has helped my children to excel in math (another is perhaps my personal love for the subject). They're not confused by sudden changes in teaching style, and they don't have large educational gaps caused by frequently changing programs that teach concepts in differing order.

We usually skip Math 54 and start with Saxon 65 in the fourth grade, but I don't think that we're the norm. To determine where your child should start, go to Saxon's website (www.saxonpub.com) or call 800-284-7019 for the placement test.

Because MCP and Saxon are two completely different programs, we don't go straight from the last page of MCP to the first page of our Saxon textbook. My children are able to start somewhere in the middle.

Finding where to start does take a little work. There is a test for every five lessons in the Saxon texts. I give one of these tests, beginning with the first, to my child each day. We go over any missed answers. If mistakes are not simple miscalculations, then we review the missed concept. Once they answer four or more questions incorrectly on the test, we stop there and begin using the text as instructed.

In site-based schools, there's an enormous amount of regurgitation. This is most likely due to the three months of summer vacation, where large chunks of learning can be forgotten. In our homeschool, we can forgo this problem by continuing to homeschool, albeit on a much lighter schedule, through the summer. This allows us to avoid going back and spending months reviewing. This is not an exaggeration; my public-schoolteacher friends confirm that they spend the first two to three months of each school year reviewing. For this reason, we have been able to skip Saxon Algebra ½ and go right to Saxon Algebra 1. Some families skip Saxon 87 and go straight to Algebra ½.

As the parent/teacher, you know best your child's abilities and limitations. If your child is in need of review and he can whiz through 87 instead of struggling through Algebra ½, he may gain some much-needed self-esteem, or "math esteem." Just be careful that he doesn't become too bored. Using the aforementioned placement test is vital in helping you choose the right textbook for your child.

In MCP, I allow the children to skip problems when the lesson is easy. I might have them do only the even problems or the first ten. With Saxon, a different approach is called for, since the problem sets test the children on much more than their knowledge of the current lesson. When a lesson is particularly easy in Saxon, we skip the entire problem set and move to the next lesson.

Drill tests are provided to begin each class. These drills involve sixty-four to a hundred problems per test. The first tests are simple addition and subtraction. They then become more difficult: multiplication, division, simplifying fractions.

When we first began, I didn't follow the instructions properly. I would give my son a hundred problems and then would time how long it took him to complete the entire page. This created all kinds of frustration, as the drill test would run into twenty to twenty-five minutes. And this was before the day's lesson had even begun.

Once I reread the instructions, I spent only five minutes on the drill test and then marked how many problems were completed correctly. After several weeks, my child gained proficiency and was able to complete the entire test in just five minutes. Once this occurred, I moved to the next level of drill.

Since I refer to the answer key at least once a day, it gets worn out quickly. I recommend three-hole-punching the answer keys and putting them all together in one three-ring binder. This way all your answer keys are in one place, and you won't find yourself searching for this or that answer key as you move from child to child. You might have to take the answer key to the office store, as a commercial hole punch is needed.

Saxon does provide help in setting up and implementing the math program. If you email info@saxonhomeschool.com or call (580) 338-4477, you can request assistance from veteran Saxon teachers. They'll even help when you and your child get stuck on an individual problem.

My learning-disabled son didn't take to Saxon right away. He often became overwhelmed by the problem sets. So I took a lesson from our spelling program, Spelling Power. I had him do one problem at a time; then I would check his work. Checking one problem at a time takes a lot of time from the parent, but we do what is necessary. It eased my son into Saxon, after three years of MCP workbooks. It built up his math esteem, and soon he was able to work on his own — requiring very little effort on my part.

One tip from a fellow homeschooler that has helped us tremendously is the use of graph paper. I noticed that my children were making many errors due to sloppy work. In MCP the children write directly in the workbook. With Saxon the problems are copied from the textbook. Neatness suddenly counts. By giving the children graph paper, they are able to line up arithmetic problems easily. It also helps them in drawing geometry problems.

Although it's cheaper to buy used Saxon texts, there's an advantage to purchasing the newer editions. In the newer texts, each problem includes a notation showing the lesson number where that individual concept is taught. This makes it very easy to go back and review when problems are answered incorrectly. Also, Math 87 has been rewritten and greatly expanded for the second edition.

The home-study kit contains the textbook, answer key, and test book. This is what is needed for homeschooling families. It's cheaper to buy the home-study kit than to purchase the necessary books separately, and all three books are necessary. Starting with Algebra ½, Saxon sells a solutions manual in addition to the home-study kit. Unlike a simple answer key, the solutions manual demonstrates how each problem is worked out step by step. I highly recommend it. I only wish that it were part of the home-study kit.

I've heard concerns from other Saxon users that there is no separate geometry course in the Saxon math program. Instead, it's integrated throughout the entire course. A student completing Algebra 2 and Advanced Mathematics can be given credit for one full year of Euclidean geometry. If you, for whatever reason, desire to supplement with a geometry program, Cathy Duffy recommends *Key to Geometry* (Key Curriculum Press).

The only thing left to say is to keep math fun. Don't be afraid to add in biographies of mathematicians or tie math into your other studies, such as history, science, and even religion. I schedule four days each week for Saxon and one day for fun puzzles from Mensa Publishing or Critical Thinking Press. Plus, we're always reading math literature simply for enjoyment (see below). For more ideas, read Rachel Mackson's essay "Math in the Home," found in *A Catholic Homeschool Treasury*.

I hope this is helpful to you in implementing Saxon in your homeschool and in building math esteem.

Math Literature

It is my prayer that the following list will help you in using literature more extensively in teaching mathematics. If you find that your library doesn't carry a lot of these books, take the initiative to make a purchasing suggestion. Most libraries welcome patron suggestions. You can usually do this in one of two ways: ask for a patron request form when you visit the library, fill it out, and return it to the library clerk; or visit your library's website and email your request.

I save time by using the Internet. I can check my library's card catalog online. I can also put books on hold at the library website. All I have to do then is run into the library, return the previous week's books, and pick up the books that I have on hold. If I'm really busy, I have my husband pick up my books on his way home from work. If you haven't already, see if your library offers similar services online.

Preschool

Anno's Magic Seeds, by Mitsumasa Anno: a neat book that teaches thrift as well as math.

Grandfather Tang's Story: A Tale Told with Tangrams, by Ann Tompert: tangrams are ancient Chinese puzzles and would be a great tie-in if you like to use math manipulatives.

Marvelous Math: A Book of Poems, edited by Lee Bennett Hopkins and Rebecca Davis, illustrated by Karen Barbour: a new way to look at math — through poetry!

Pigs in a Blanket: Fun With Math and Time, by Amy Axelrod, illustrated by Sharon McGinley-Nally: the abstract concept of time is made delightfully fun here as the Pig family races the clock to get to the beach.

A Remainder of One, by Elinor Pinczes: an easy introduction to the concept of remainders.

The Sir Cumference Series, by Cindy Neuschwander, illustrated by Wayne Geehan: a fun play on words, these books tie together the legend of King Arthur and math concepts.

Grade School

Anno's Mysterious Multiplying Jar, by Masaichiro and Mitsumasa Anno: a very neat book that visually explains factorials.

The Dot and the Line: A Romance in Lower Mathematics, by Norman Juster: a humorous tale about a straight line in love with a red dot, and the line's attempts to woo her away from a slothful squiggle.

G Is for Googol: A Math Alphabet Book, by David Schwartz, illustrated by Marissa Moss: not all ABC books are for preschoolers; this book is definitely for the older child. Presents complicated math concepts in a fun, colorful way.

The History of Counting, by Denise Schmandt-Besserat, illustrated by Michael Hayes: beautifully illustrated, this book traces the invention of number systems. Easy to tie into your history studies.

The Librarian Who Measured the Earth, by Kathryn Lasky: an eye-catching picture book about the Greek who was able to estimate the circumference of the earth without modern technology. Fascinating.

One Grain of Rice, by Demi: tells the story of a selfish Raja in India and the village girl who outsmarts him using math skills. The Raja learns an important lesson about selfishness as well as a lesson about the power of doubling. As with all of Demi's books, the illustrations are beautiful.

What's Your Angle, Pythagoras? A Math Adventure, by Julie Ellis: great fictional story of Pythagoras's childhood. Presents the Pythagorean Theorem through an appealing story. Easy for grade-school children to understand.

Middle School

Fractals, Googols and Other Mathematical Tales, by Theoni Pappas: a treasure trove of stories that make mathematical ideas come to life with an unusual cast of characters. Explores mathematical concepts and topics such as real numbers, exponents, dimensions, and geometry in both serious and humorous ways.

The Man Who Counted: A Collection of Mathematical Adventures, by Malba Tahan: takes place in thirteenth-century Baghdad. A well-written novel that introduces the reader to complex math puzzles in an interesting setting.

A favorite of the Wittmann children. Presents a great opportunity to discuss Islam.

A Gebra Named Al: A Novel, by Wendy Isdell: written by a seventeen-year-old girl who takes you on a journey through the Land of Mathematics.

The Number Devil: A Mathematical Adventure, by Hans Magnus Enzensberger, illustrated by Rotraut Susanne Berner, translated by Michael Henry Heim: I'd prefer if it were *The Number Angel,* but this is still a great book and loved by my children. Although it doesn't resemble a textbook in any way, shape, or form, it does teach math skills.

The Phantom Tollbooth, by Norman Juster: a classic! More logic than arithmetic. Every child with math phobia should read this fun book about a boy who goes on an adventure that's filled with number and word puzzles.

The Snark Puzzle Book, by Martin Gardner: based on Lewis Carroll's nonsense poem *The Hunting of the Snark.* Who says you can't tie math into poetry? The puzzles are challenging.

High School

The Cartoon Guide to Statistics, by Larry Gonick: although a comic book, this is a title for the teen or advanced student.

Euclid's Elements: Euclid's famous thirteen books. Start with the definitions before going to the introduction. For advanced students.

Flatland: A Romance of Many Dimensions, by Edwin Abbott: in addition to being a novel that introduces the concepts of second, third, and fourth dimensions, this is a funny satire on society and class distinctions of Victorian England (first published in the1880s).

The Parrot's Theorem: A Novel, by Denis Guedj: part murder mystery, part math history, this is an amusing introduction to mathematical discoveries.

Pensées, Christianity for Modern Pagans, edited by Peter Kreeft: Blaise Pascal was a great seventeenth-century mathematician. Catholic author Kreeft adds his commentary to Pascal's famous apology.

The Sand Reckoner, by Gillian Bradshaw: historical fiction based on the life of Archimedes. Not a lot of mathematics, but instead a great story about a man who loved mathematics.

Adult

Mathematical Apocrypha: Stories and Anecdotes of Mathematicians and the Mathematical, by Steven G. Krantz: a collection of anecdotes about the practice of mathematics that range in tone from humorous to celebratory. The anecdotes are arranged under sections devoted to great foolishness, great ideas, great failures, great pranks, and great people.

Men of Mathematics: The Lives and Achievements of the Great Mathematicians from Zeno to Poincaré, by E. T. Bell: originally written in 1937, parts of this book are outdated, but still an interesting read.

Uncle Petros and Goldbach's Conjecture: A Novel of Mathematical Obsession, by Apostolos Doxiadis: a fictional story of a mathematician who becomes obsessed with solving Goldbach's Conjecture. A good read whether you love or hate mathematics.

For even more math-literature recommendations to accompany your textbook studies, see my book *For the Love of Literature* (Ecce Homo Press).

---

*"For God did not give us a spirit of timidity
but a spirit of power and love and self-control."*

2 Timothy 1:7

Learning to Love Science

Nancy Stine

As a homeschooler, I've found science to be one of the toughest subjects to teach. However, when I take the time, it's also one of the most enjoyable.

Say the word *science*, and many people will think of any one of a broad range of topics that make up science. It's such a huge topic that sometimes I think that its mere size is the reason we give it so little attention in our curricula. I know I *think* a lot about teaching it, but doing so is another story. What is science? Why should we teach it? What should I be teaching? These are the questions whose answers should make science a larger part of our curricula.

First, what is science? Webster defines it first as:

• Possession of knowledge as distinguished from ignorance or misunderstanding.

• Knowledge attained through study or practice.

Under these definitions, we can place just about anything we study in science. However, farther down in the definition it gets more to what the general population would describe science as:

• Knowledge concerned with the physical world and its phenomena: natural science.

In the classical curriculum, science in this last sense would fall under the category of astronomy in the quadrivium. Science also involves the scientific method: the organized way in which scientists gather information.

There are many reasons to take this huge body of knowledge and pass it on to our children. The primary reason comes out of Scripture: "The heavens are telling the glory of God" (Psalm 19:1). What better way is there to impress upon our children the wonder of our God than to show them the order of the universe? They also see the variety of creation and begin to understand how marvelous God is. On a more practical note, science has become a necessary vocabulary in our everyday lives. Next time you sit down to read the newspaper, take note of all the articles that are scientific in nature: articles covering global warming, extinction, cloning, earthquakes, and so on. All of these topics require some knowledge to make informed decisions. There's also the old report that students in the United States have fallen behind other industrial nations in science. The more science knowledge our children obtain, the better citizens they can be.

Homeschoolers often spend a lot of time improving subjects such as math and writing, but we spend little time on science. Yet this is one of the areas where homeschooling can really make its mark. We have the ability to focus on the subject, as well as raise godly men and women in an arena that affects us all.

Another reason to teach science stems from the nature of the subject. Science itself is a discipline, and, as such, it teaches thinking and problem-solving skills. The process of scientific discovery is seen in the scientific method — that is, the skills of observing, classifying, measuring, generalizing, controlling, and hypothesizing. As children take in these skills and learn how to use them, they'll find that these apply to other areas in life.

These process skills cannot be separated from the content. Content skills are the easiest to teach. A *National Geographic* or

Magic School Bus video teaches a tremendous amount of the content in a wonderful way.

Some people prefer the Basal Science series approach. The drawback to these texts is that, for instance, a fourth-grade text tries to convey the information at a fourth-grade reading level. This can leave the text bland and the content dull. I prefer the wealth of information at the library, where books in any given subject vary in reading level. Some are books that a child can read to himself, and others are great candidates for reading together while curled up on the couch. The library also provides books at adult levels so that a parent can read up on the subject, too.

Now to the next hurdle: homeschooling on more than one grade level. I look at science as the one subject I can teach at all levels at the same time. One of the things I remember from my scientific-methods course in college is that science is taught in a circular way. Just as in math, we return to a certain type of problem and then teach the next step; science builds on what it has taught before. Many science texts have eight or nine science units to cover in a year, each one building on the year before. Each year, however, adds only a small bit of information. I've found with my own children that if I teach a given unit well the first time, I don't have to return to it again for a few years. Hence, I'd rather cover only three units during the year and really cover the information well.

Case in point: all my family loves *Star Trek*. In fact, there was a time when we attended 9 a.m. Mass so we would be home in time to watch the 11 a.m. showing. Because of this tradition, when the time came to teach science in first grade, I decided to begin with astronomy. We read many books about the planets, the moon, and other phenomena. The children soaked in all the details with no effort. Memorizing the order of planets was a five-minute task. I was truly amazed. Even today, in grade 4, they can reiterate information about the moons of Jupiter that I might not recall.

We'll come back to astronomy again in the next year or so. The next time, we'll review the previous lessons for the sake of the younger children and then build on the knowledge of the older ones by adding experiments to help them understand phases of the moon and other things in a concrete way. Again, I won't use a text, but will check out the section in the library and rent videos. A visit to a planetarium would round out the unit nicely. If an eclipse or a meteor shower is expected, I might even schedule the unit to coincide with it.

My experience with astronomy taught me one thing: if you can capture the students' interest, they'll learn. As I approach each unit of study, I try to find some fun things to do. Since I'm not trying to cover eight topics during a year, the fun part is an easy task to handle. I scour the shelves at the library for experiments and also hit the teachers' store. I have some texts from college that help a lot. I might check out a college bookstore some semester to see which text is being used for the scientific-method course in the school of education.

I also go online. There are many science-related websites. My favorite is the Core Knowledge website, which is a companion to the book series (www.coreknowledge.org). This site includes lesson plans that correlate with the book series. Although I never use every experiment given, the many suggestions invariably give me many choices that suit my mood and available materials, and capture the interest of my children.

The curriculum to teach science can be broken down into three-year cycles: first through third, fourth through sixth, and seventh through ninth. High school science traditionally spends a year each on biology, chemistry, and physics. As each subject is repeated the second and third time, new information is added. Always review the basics to make sure they have been retained; then go to the next level. One of the reasons science is taught in these cycles is that as children develop cognitively, they're able to grasp concepts at a different level. Still, it's important to use experiments at each level. One good experiment can cement a concept in the brain forever, and, again, it teaches that valuable process skill.

The science topics can be broken down this way: life sciences (plants, animals, the human body), physical sciences (matter, energy, chemistry), and earth sciences (weather, the earth, astronomy). If you choose one topic from each area per school year, put yourself on a rotation to repeat each topic three times for each child. The children might get subjects at different grade levels, but you'll do a better job and enjoy the subject more. As far as content goes, I recommend the *Core Knowledge* series. Find out what information is recommended for any given subject at each grade level, and teach that. You'll find the material in these books short and to the point, and very helpful, keeping in mind that it's a secular series.

Science was always one of my favorite subjects in school and at home. I've always enjoyed learning about the world around me. Today, I'm still drawn to *National Geographic* specials and their copycats. I love to walk in the woods and point things out to my children or stay up late to look at the stars. Although I'll never be a rocket scientist, I'll pass my love of science on to my children in the hope that they might achieve success in a scientific field. And if I do it right, I'll pass on to them those valuable problem-solving skills of the scientific method that will give them an edge in all fields.

*"Nothing in life is to be feared;
it is only to be understood."*

Madame Curie

History as God's Plan

Marcia Neill

History is storytelling. We began sharing history when we told our children a story beginning with "When I was little . . ." Our first-grade students need to know about creation, the beginning of man, and the Fall of Adam and Eve. They need to know about the promise of a Redeemer to prepare them for First Communion in the second grade.

The link between the past and the present and the eternal God would be lost if we had no memory of our history. With a God-centered approach, certain lessons emerge. When we look at the broad span of history, we see the Church under attack from Roman persecutors, heretics, barbarians, Byzantine emperors, power-hungry noblemen, schisms, Protestant revolutionaries, and modern materialists and atheists. Yet the Church still stands. The Church is built on a rock, and the gates of Hell will not prevail against it (Matthew 16:18-19). We know this is true through faith. Perhaps the strongest evidence history can give us that the Church will always stand is that it has survived attacks that would have destroyed any merely human institution. History confirms our faith. Without this God-centered approach, we would have missed a great source of understanding of who we are and of how we all fit into the history of salvation.

When you teach, it can be useful to present history from three perspectives: the social, the economic, and the political. As you move through time, it's also important to be objective and not attempt to rewrite history from our twenty-first-century perspective. To avoid this pitfall, and for help in finding the perspective of each particular period, immerse your family in an era by studying the leading people of the day and the governmental structure. Read the literature of the time, view the art, and listen to the music. Include research on the clothing, the living conditions, the tools, the weapons, the transportation, the geography, and the inventions of the period.

Start from early history and progress through time, thereby allowing your child to gain insight into the causes, remote and immediate, of successive major events. A remote cause might be a country's long-time desire for access to a waterway, whereas the immediate cause for a war might be the mobilization of an army across boundaries.

There are three sources of history (knowing what happened centuries ago).

• *Oral tradition:* stories and legends passed on by word of mouth.

• *Relics:* weapons, tools, works of art, ruins of buildings, and so forth.

• *Written records:* inscriptions, manuscripts, printed books, accounts, reports, and narratives of all kinds left us by past generations.

One of the goals of education, particularly with the young, is *sequencing.* Use of a timeline will help put whatever portion of history is being studied into perspective. I'm a visual learner. I need to write, draw, or graph information in order to see it. So my response to my daughter Stephanie's question, "When was Moses and when was Lincoln?" was, "Let's put up a timeline, and we'll see when they lived." After using timelines over the years, my children are able to look at the figures placed on our timeline and recall much of our previous studies.

The order of presentation is important, as are content and the labeling of each event. Consider this secular timeline: the Middle Ages, the Reformation, and the discovery of America. Even though it isn't chronological, it corresponds with a worldview of "progress" outlined over and over again in secular histories. The chronology for this same period in the Old World and in America in Catholic texts is:

1. Middle Ages (better known in Catholic circles as the High Middle Ages or the Glory of Christendom)

2. Discovery and exploration of the Americas

3. Reformation (Protestant revolt or the "Cleaving of Christendom")

This order is important, not only because it is chronological, but also because it reflects an important point to Catholics. God's providential hand was actively protecting his Church by opening up new lands in which to spread and preserve the true Faith before and during the revolutions that tore apart Europe. At the same time that Protestants and Catholics were fighting in Europe, Our Lady of Guadalupe was appearing to Juan Diego, and the Indians were converting to the Catholic Faith by the millions.

Strive to counter the "myth" of progress that exists in our modern mind set. History is sometimes a story of retrogression or falling back, instead of continuous advancement. Everything that is new is not always better.

Take advantage of the flexibility homeschooling affords by supplementing history texts with reading of living history books, classical writings, and original texts; use field trips, hands-on activities, and research and writing to develop a rich, fun history program. Add in lively family discussions, and you'll make for truly lasting comprehension of history as God's plan.

"History is the witness that testifies to the passing of time; it illumines reality, vitalizes memory, provides guidance in daily life, and brings us tidings of antiquity."

Cicero

Teaching American Catholic History Through Genealogy

Joan Stromberg

How important were Catholics in the shaping of this country? Can you think of more than a handful of statesmen, founding fathers, or presidents who were Catholic? Should we conclude that because there were so few prominent Catholics in our secular history books that Catholics were unimportant in shaping this country? Unfortunately, many of our history books don't show the whole picture. Perhaps we should rely on our memory books and photo albums for a more complete view of American history.

DeWitt Clinton, the governor of New York who was famous for pushing through the legislation to build the Erie Canal, wasn't Catholic. But thousands of workers who dug the ditch through swamplands, solid rock, and virgin forests were Irish and German immigrants and mostly Catholic. The powerful railroad owners such as J. P. Morgan who mined and shipped the coal that fueled the country into the modern age weren't Catholic. But the men who descended into the mines, risking life and limb to bring the black gold to the surface, oftentimes were. Sitting Bull and Geronimo, the great Indian chiefs who are mentioned in our history books, weren't Catholic. But the great tribes they left behind were clothed, fed, and educated by Catholic nuns such as St. Katharine

Drexel. Neither Robert E. Lee nor Ulysses S. Grant was Catholic, but legions and brigades of the men who fought to keep the Union intact were.

American history books are full of heroes: presidents, generals, statesmen, and chiefs. But I believe there are more important heroes in American history whom our textbooks don't mention by name. These heroes are our ancestors who traveled to this country and worked in it, toiled for it, and even died in it to build the America we have today. These people's stories are not in the history books; they're in our memories, kept alive by the families who cherish their stories and their heritage.

As a child, I never wearied of hearing how my great-great-great-great-grandfather lost an arm in the Battle of Gettysburg or how my great uncle died after the armistice was signed in World War I, because the Germans, evacuating the island that his submarine crew had just taken over, poisoned all the food before they left.

These stories are interesting because they're about ordinary people, just like me. And they're my family; their blood flows through my veins and the veins of my children. They're part of us in a way that presidents, generals, and statesmen could not be. They might not have been great enough to have their names in history books, but their contributions to the building of this country are far greater than the political hero's because, by their sheer number, determination, and fortitude, they shaped American history.

This country was built on the backs of immigrant labor, much of it Catholic. The dogged determination and strong work ethic of those Catholic immigrants were part and parcel of their Catholic identity. To make history come alive in our homeschools, we want to make our ancestors come alive. Children are more naturally interested in the social history of those everyday Americans than in that of the larger-than-life statesmen and generals. Children can transport themselves to another time and place more easily if they study how ordinary people lived their everyday lives.

Chances are some of your Catholic forbears were involved in one of the categories mentioned previously: factory worker, coal miner, railroad- or canal-builder, or soldier. Use a unit-study approach to incorporate your relative into a school lesson. Here's an example of how we did it in our own homeschool:

Great-great-great-grandfather Smith lost an arm in the battle of Gettysburg. He's in our family album book with pieces of official documentation, such as marriage certificates, medical release from the army, pension papers, and so forth. We took the few items we knew about one individual soldier and fleshed them out by asking questions: Why was the Civil War fought? What was the outcome? Where is Gettysburg? Why was this battle important? We make a diorama of the battle, using toy soldiers, one labeled with Grandfather Smith's name and missing an arm. Why would they cut off his arm? What was medicine like at that time? If he were shot in the arm, what would the gun look like? What were the firearms of the period? How did an average "Billy Yank" live, eat, and drink during the Civil War? Which regiment was Grandfather Smith in? What other battles did that regiment fight?

Another example: in researching my book *Kat Finds a Friend: A Saint Elizabeth Ann Seton Story*, we found out about another ancestor who was a shoemaker. He bartered shoes for tuition so his children could attend Catholic school. We started to ask questions about how the bartering system would work in the early nineteenth century in a rural setting. How was a shoe made? Where did the materials come from, and what kinds of tools were used? What other roles did the shoemaker play? (We found out he was often the dentist and sometimes the barber, too.) What other craftsmen would be needed in this setting? From there, we could visit a pioneer village and see a shoemaker or another craftsman at work, or actually make a shoe or practice other early-American crafts.

What makes this kind of history study real for the children is that they're studying their grandfathers, grandmothers, aunts, and uncles. Show them on a family tree where they belong in the great scheme of things. If children have a sense of history, they can more easily recognize their own value and how they're part of a much larger picture.

When you look at your family tree, try to find those very special relatives: nuns, priests, and other religious. They don't have any direct relations, so they count on you to carry on their stories. Perhaps a "Touched by a Saint" memory book would be a good start in keeping their stories alive. When you add them to your timeline, put a halo around their names to show how special they are to your family. Kat Walter became Sr. Theodosia. Her older brother, John, is our direct ancestor, but it was Kat who was personally touched by Mother Seton to devote her life as a bride of Christ.

Who in your family history could have met a saint? Did your family settle in the Midwest? Perhaps they were touched by St. Rose Philippine Duchesne, Fr. DeSmet, or Bl. Francis Seelos, who was stationed in Detroit for many years. Could someone have met Mother Cabrini as she visited her congregations in Denver, Seattle, or Chicago? Could a relative have been ministered to by St. John Neumann as he traveled through his parishes in Pennsylvania, Maryland, or New York? Name an area of the country, and it has probably been touched by an American saint or *beatus*.

Perhaps you have the special blessing, and the challenge, of being a convert, and you don't think you have any Catholic ancestors. Maybe you actually do, and you just need to look a little deeper. My mother-in-law is a convert to Catholicism. When she gave us the Walter genealogy book, I was surprised and thrilled to see that most of her ancestors were Catholic. It wasn't until the generation before hers that they stopped practicing the Faith.

If you're a convert, another possibility is to research the anti-Catholic bigotry in American history. Perhaps your relatives lived in Philadelphia during the anti-Catholic "Know Nothing" riots.

This would make a great unit study. Maybe your relatives knew of Maria Monk, who spread lies about the Catholic Church through most of the nineteenth century. Maybe your Protestant ancestors were touched by Catholics. The Walters' genealogy was intertwined with the Eby family, a stanch Lutheran family of the same area. In fact, there was a Lutheran seminary right across the state border from Emmitsburg, in Gettysburg. The give-and-take of the Lutheran seminary and Mount Saint Mary's would be a great study in American Catholic history.

We know what we're looking for, so now we need to find it. Fortunately, the information available to family genealogists is vast. Computer programs, websites, magazines, and genealogy classes are all available for the beginning genealogist. Many of us busy homeschooling parents might not have the time to devote to this, but perhaps an older teen could do it as a school assignment. Maybe someone in your family is already doing a genealogy, and you could simply tap into their work for your own family's study. My parents keep the genealogy for the family and share it with us every time we visit. My mother-in-law's cousin put together the Walters' genealogy many years ago, before the work could be done on the Internet. That was diligence!

Don't forget the special benefits of oral history. Older relatives might be a wealth of information and might love a visit from children interested in listening to them talk about their lives. What a great way to teach note-taking and interviewing. The personal connection from one generation to the next is also very important. The elderly grandmother, aunt, uncle, or cousin is the best source for firsthand social history. Retirement homes for priests and nuns are bursting at the seams, so consider tapping into their memory cache of truly American Catholic history.

When I learned American history in school, we always began with Christopher Columbus and progressed linearly and chronologically through the centuries to the present day. That was fine when reading a textbook, but I thought that my children would lack a sense of the larger picture. To solve this problem, we use a custom timeline (see www.catholictreasury.com for a free template to download) with great political events listed along the bottom and American saints listed along the top (at present, there are five American saints: Frances Xavier Cabrini, Elizabeth Ann Seton, John Neumann, Rose Philippine Duchesne, and Katharine Drexel). Then we fill in our ancestors as we study them. Here our children can see where things connect and relate.

The Catholic Church in America is an exciting, growing, living thing, just like history itself. Every day, as Catholic Americans, along with our family, we can make history. Teaching our little saints-in-progress about the struggles, joys, and sufferings of their own relatives will show them that the Body of Christ is one family of the past, present, and future.

"Homeschooling is in the best interests of America,
because it can only be good to raise up a new generation
committed to living in harmony with God's will. Homeschooling
is intensely patriotic because it trains up future leaders of this
country who will not be afraid to proclaim that the eternal
law of the universe must also be the law of our land."

Dr. Mary Kay Clark, *Catholic Home Schooling*

Chapter Two

Enrichment Subjects

"Man is created to praise, reverence, and serve
God our Lord, and by this means to save his soul.
All other things on the face of the earth are created for
man to help him fulfill the end for which he is created."

St. Ignatius of Loyola

Handwriting:
Making the World a More
Beautiful Place, One Letter at a Time

Monica Sohler

In my mother's day, the 1920s, penmanship was taught in schools, and taught systematically. Before they learned to form their first letter, children spent time on penmanship warm-up exercises, such as drawing rows of circles, angles, and slanted lines.

When I was in parochial school, penmanship was still taught. It wasn't stressed as much as in my mother's day, but I remember being told how a letter was made. I remember being issued a "slant sheet" to put under my loose-leaf page. The slant sheet had lines slanted at "just the right angle," so my letters would be uniformly slanted as I learned to write in cursive.

It's uncommon to find penmanship as a graded subject in school these days. In college in the 1980s, I majored in early-childhood education (pre-K through third grade), yet I received no instruction on how to teach penmanship. It was out of vogue. People said that such rigorous exercises stifled a child's natural creativity. After all, what does it matter if a child slants or not? As long as the writing is legible, what does it matter how the letters are formed? Sometime between my mother's day, my day, and today, penmanship lost its importance. And that is a shame.

Why? Does it really matter how letters are formed? Yes and no. (The longer I homeschool — indeed, the longer I live — I find "yes and no" to be an answer to many things.) Or to translate differently: "It depends."

As the pendulum swung away from structured penmanship, not only was training in legible writing lost, but a good form of overall discipline and training of the will was lost. Another loss, not only in penmanship, but overall, is a healthy pride in beauty.

Does it matter if letters are formed beautifully? Yes and no. It certainly isn't a moral fault to have poor penmanship. But why not try to make the world a little more beautiful, by taking care to make a letter beautiful? By training ourselves and our children to make letters beautiful, we train ourselves and our children to care for little things, and to find God in the tiniest event.

Of course, there's an unhealthy extreme. Training the will, and trying to craft a beautiful letter, doesn't have to mean boot camp. There are basics that are common to most handwriting methods, but using rigid rules, such as requiring a 45-degree slant or forcing a left-handed child to write with his right hand, can be excessive.

So we understand that penmanship does have importance, and teaching penmanship has a place in our homeschools. Now we must determine how to go about it, and which aspects are important and which are not. There are many penmanship programs available. I've used a number of them and can share my own experience with what was helpful to my children.

As I've homeschooled four children, I've found that a middle ground in teaching penmanship works best. There's wisdom in past methods of making scribbles and circles and angles and lines in a book before training in letter formation begins. In fact, there's evidence that such exercises aid students in other subjects as well, helping them "warm up" the mind as well as the hand. There's wisdom in correct posture. There's wisdom in starting letters at the top and forming them in a certain direction. Penmanship isn't something a child can learn purely by copying something someone else wrote. It needs to be taught. It also helps to learn ways to avoid writers' cramp. Too much painful penance should not be part of this discipline.

Within that framework, there are many ways to make it work. The result is legible writing, and a hand that doesn't go into muscle spasms after writing a few lines.

Some basics are common to most programs. Having children sit up straight, but comfortably, at a desk or at a table that's suited to their size will help them form letters without tiring quickly. Using a pencil small enough for tiny hands is also helpful. Certain grips are less likely to cause cramps as children learn to write, although I have two children who persist in using a "wrong" grip and appear to be doing fine.

Most programs stress the importance of starting manuscript (printing) letters from the top, and working down. This is important because, although it is slower to write this way in the beginning, as a child becomes proficient in letter formation, it becomes much easier to write quickly if he writes from the top down, and not up and down or from the bottom line up.

Try this: make several rows of vertical lines of uniform size. Writing slowly, write a row from the top down. Then write a row where you alternate, one from the top down and the next from the bottom up. Then write a row where you start at the bottom and go up.

All the lines probably look good. Now do the same thing, but quickly. You will find the lines made from the top down look much straighter, while the lines made the other ways are wobbling all over the place. This is why it is helpful to start at the top.

Even those basics aren't written in stone, but most methods share them. We've used four penmanship methods, with varying results.

• *The Palmer Method.* This is the classic cursive method. My children suffered as much as I did when learning it; trying to copy all those twirls and slanting at the correct angle was difficult. The result was not legible, beautiful writing. Some people find this a fine method, but it didn't work for us.

• *Italic Handwriting.* This program from Portland University Press is popular among homeschoolers. I found their printing program to be attractive, easy to teach, and easy to learn. My son took to it right away, and at age seventeen, he still forms his manuscript letters in this attractive yet simple printing. Our experience with Portland's cursive program wasn't as good. It wasn't always clear and easy to read, although my son still prefers it for cursive. Most of the time, however, he prints, and his printing is always clear.

• *The Reason for Writing.* This program is a modified Palmer method and offers several advantages. One is that the children learn a Scripture verse each week, as that is what they use to practice their letters. After all, we need a *reason for writing,* and if it were not for the monks writing Scripture and preserving it through the Dark Ages, we wouldn't have our Bible today. Children start each week learning letters and words, and by the end of the week, they're copying a verse, which uses the newly learned letters. The final page usually has an attractive design or illustration, which the children then color, making their own "illuminated manuscript." I like this because it ties in the idea I mentioned earlier: we study penmanship in part to learn to create something beautiful. This program also has a teacher's manual that gives tips on helping children understand how to form their letters, which letters rise above the line, which hang below it, and so forth.

• *Handwriting Without Tears.* I currently use this program with my children, and it's the one with which I'm happiest.

The teacher's manual is chock-full of tips on teaching penmanship. In fact, it contains many of the lost tools for teaching this art, which my mother's teachers knew well. It shows correct posture and has fun ways to get the child to sit correctly. It has manipulatives to help very little ones form letters and uses some clever tricks to avert the dreaded letter flipping so common in young children's printing. The cursive program also has something I like very much: nonslanted cursive. It's hard enough for some children to learn the cursive letters, let alone learning to slant at the same time. This program teaches a clear, attractive, simple cursive, which lends itself to slanting if the child turns out to be a "slanter." Some people are, and some are not. My own adult cursive is straight up and down, but my daughter, who learned cursive through this method, has chosen to slant, after learning a clear and neat letter formation without slanting. It was easier for her to learn one thing at a time — letter formation first, then slanting.

These programs are only a few of the many available. Whichever program you choose, remember: penmanship can be a spiritual tool. We learn to make something beautiful, or try to, because God's creation is beautiful, and ours can be, too. We learn some discipline and some training of the will, in striving to make these letters. We learn to communicate clearly, because witnessing to God requires clear communication.

———————

"Meek correction is desired by our Lord!
Therefore, we must guard against an angry tone
that betrays an absence of self-control;
this does more harm than good!"
St. Alphonsus Liguori

Art Appreciation:
Recognizing Symbolism in Religious Art

Pattie Kelley-Huff

My husband teases me that we run a resort for birds. Our house is surrounded by many large trees that make good homes for them. It isn't unusual for us to awaken on days when the weather is mild and hear the sweet sounds of singing and chirping. We've positioned the bird feeders in the backyard so that they can be easily seen from either the kitchen or the dining room. From our cozy, comfortable spots, we can glance out the window and see an assortment of wild birds.

It's a fun family hobby. We purchase basic birdseed, mix it with black-oiled sunflower seeds, cracked corn, peanuts, and sunflower kernels and then regularly supply the ground feeder. We plant large sunflowers in the summer and watch for long periods as the birds work at freeing the seeds from the heads of the flowers. We have special feeders with suet for the woodpeckers, thistle seeds for the finches, and, when the weather is warm, red nectar for the hummingbirds. God has blessed us with a wide variety of types and colorings of birds. They're a real treat.

This lesson about the goodness of God's creation is not lost on our household. The enjoyment we receive from these creatures will always be a vicarious one. We must enjoy them at a distance;

we can't hold them or touch them. Even attempting to pursue them means they will fly away. This is a wonderful lesson for the children. We show our love for some things by patiently watching from a distance, never attempting to overpower or overwhelm. Yet generously, and with no expectation of reward, we nurture and feed the birds we admire.

This past year Christmas Day fell on a Monday, so we were treated to a long weekend with Daddy. We were finishing our last-minute wrapping and baking, relishing our time together, when my oldest daughter, Amanda, noticed a purple finch clutching the mesh of the sliding screen door from the back patio into the dining room. She walked closer to the inside glass door for a better view and was surprised that the bird didn't fly away. Both of its eyes were matted shut, and it swayed in the bitter cold breeze. Knowing that Amanda had already decided to become a veterinarian, I realized that I would have to investigate further before she would be satisfied.

I soon found myself out in this miserable weather, in a wind chill of 40 degrees below zero, watching this wild but immobile bird. He fluttered a bit, flew a few feet away, and then flew right back within easy reach of where I was standing. It was pretty clear that this bird wasn't well, and I wondered if he would die soon. His feathers were tattered, and frankly he was a mess. By now I had attracted an audience and all eyes were on me, wondering what I intended to do. Then it hit me: I'll try to catch it; it will fly away, and the problem will be solved.

I sent one of the children to prepare a plastic cage for the bird, and another to fetch the butterfly net. Making an elaborate show, I slowly moved the net near the bird to nudge him. To my surprise he was still in the same spot. Without a fight, he stepped onto the edge of the net and was in the net in a second. Wondering if this was a glimpse of God's sense of humor, I took the bird in the house and placed him in the cage. Is this what we mean when we say that homeschoolers should be flexible? I wondered, *Just what are we going to do with a half-dead purple finch two days before Christmas?*

I gave my children the lecture you might expect, about the probable fate of the bird, and put a little dish of water and some thistle seeds in the cage. He huddled in the corner for almost an hour and then jumped to his feet and slowly made his way to the water. We found a quiet place for him where he would avoid further stress while I went about the business of finding out where I could take him. Since the wildlife refuge was closed until the day after Christmas, we would have to keep "Noel" for a couple of days.

In the next twenty-four hours, Noel drank three bowls of water and ate two bowls of food. Slowly, one eye and then the other opened, and his feathers smoothed. His general appearance and demeanor improved significantly, and it was clear from his fluttering that he was winning the uphill battle for recovery. He was so beautiful, his colors so awesome, that the children would watch him intently for long periods. We were all fascinated by him and could hardly believe that we were graced with such a close view of one of God's elusive creatures.

After we had attended Christmas Eve Mass and arrived home, our dear Noel was still fluttering about his cage. I had set him near the window, where he could see the familiar outdoors. It seemed as though his only desire was to rejoin nature. Both of his eyes were clear; his feathers looked good. He soon became much too feisty to keep in this small cage for two more days. We held a quick family meeting and, with the agreement of our "resident vet," decided it would be best to return Noel from whence he came. I carefully carried the cage out onto the back patio and opened the top. In a moment, our beautiful little visitor flew away. He landed on a branch in the Japanese maple tree, pecked a bit at the snow and then flew out of sight. We have a regular visitor now at the thistle feeder who looks suspiciously like Noel. We can only hope.

That evening, we carried on our many family rituals for Christmas Eve. There were cookies for Santa, carrots and magic reindeer food, lighting the candles for evening prayers, and a final check of our little makeshift wooden crib that we had prepared for Baby Jesus. After much excitement, all the children were finally tucked into their beds. Scott and I began our final duties of the day before retiring. I like to include religious items among the many gifts that my children receive to help them keep the true meaning of Christmas in proper perspective. I had, therefore, purchased some very nice antique holy cards for the occasion.

I was looking them over to decide which cards to place in each child's stocking when I came across one entitled "Madonna of the Goldfinch." Mary is holding baby Jesus, who has a beautiful goldfinch perched on his left index finger. After our recent adventure,

I was fascinated by the connection: first the purple finch, then our Blessed Mother with a member of the finch family. I had never seen Our Lady under this title before and wondered what to make of the coincidence. Little did I know what a serendipitous event our encounter with Noel would turn out to be.

I have long yearned to understand art symbolism and the work of the great masters. I had been delighted by a wonderful book published by Dorling Kindersley (DK) called *Annotated Art*. It offers explanations and insights for many of the finest works of art. Yet, while I could begin to see and understand the symbolism used by the artists, I found it inadequate. It stirred my interest for more, rather than satisfying me.

Never needing much of an excuse to visit a bookstore, I took the visit of the purple finch as an occasion to go down to my favorite used bookstore to dig around in the art section. I hoped to gather enough information from several used books to round out my knowledge of symbolism in art. I started systemically searching the stacks and was eventually rewarded by a book entitled *Signs & Symbols in Christian Art; With 350 Illustrations*, by George Ferguson. I opened the cover and began to read the foreword: "My seven-year-old daughter was looking at a color reproduction of Tiepolo's *Madonna and the Goldfinch*. . . . She asked, 'What's the goldfinch in the child's hand mean?' This question, which my daughter asked several years ago, was the beginning of this book. . . . No thorough work which included the entire field of religious symbolism had been attempted for many years."

I didn't know which excited me more: that I had finally found the keys to the religious symbolism I had yearned for so long, or that I was about to find out the meaning of the goldfinch in the *Madonna and the Goldfinch*. The price for this wonderful discovery was only $3.24. I quickly thumbed through the pages until my eyes rested on the entry *Goldfinch* in the middle of page 19: "The goldfinch is fond of eating thistles and thorns, and since thorny plants have been accepted as an allusion to Christ's crown of thorns, the goldfinch has become an accepted symbol of the Passion of Christ. In this sense, it frequently appears with the Christ Child, showing the close connection between the Incarnation and the Passion."

I had finally found the answer. The mystery of what to make of our little visitor at Christmastime was a mystery no longer. Just as the wood of the crib at Christmas foreshadows the wood of the Cross on Calvary, our little Noel had come to foreshadow one of the most profound and meaningful theological realities for all of mankind, the marvelous and miraculous connection between the Incarnation and the Passion. Just as the image of the goldfinch has come to symbolize this salvific connection, a real goldfinch graced our Christmas with its presence.

I can only interpret the event as a magnificent gift from God to our family, to accentuate our desire and confirm our embrace of the true meaning of the Christmas celebration. In many ways, it is the same lesson we learn from our little makeshift crib about the deeper meaning of the wood. In a way that only God in his magnificence could achieve, our Christmas season was coupled with a living symbol of the Incarnation and Passion. We should never forget that the true reason to celebrate Jesus' birth is to acknowledge the gift we receive as a result of his dying. The gift offers us the opportunity for salvation and redemption.

Needless to say, I became even more inspired to seek out the deeper meaning in religious art. What a joy this realization has brought to me. I can only hope that by sharing a small portion of what I have discovered, I can help you share some of the same joy with your family.

Symbols in Religious Art

There are some basic symbols that you'll view in many paintings. Let me offer a primer on symbols in religious art. Foremost is the aureole, usually portrayed as a field of radiance and splendor encircling the body or the head and appearing to emerge from it. It is reserved for the representation of Divinity or Persons of the Trinity, although some artists extended its use to representations of the Blessed Virgin. The aureole usually is white, blue, or gold. Many artists wanting to suggest a divine or sacred quality of certain personages would place a halo or nimbus behind the head of a person. These were generally represented by a circle, a square, or a triangle.

You may notice various letters included in some of the paintings. Here are a few of the more commonly used symbols and their meanings:

> A and Ω: The first and last letters of the Greek alphabet, used in reference to Revelation 1:8: " 'I am the Alpha and the Omega,' says the Lord God. . . ."

> T or Θ: The first letter in the Greek word $\Theta\varepsilon o\varsigma$ (*Theos*), meaning "God."

> IHS, IHC: A shortened version of the Greek word for "Jesus," Latinized as *IHSOUS* or *IHCOUS*.

> INRI: Four initial letters of the Latin, *Iesus Nazarenus Rex Iudaeorum* ("Jesus of Nazareth, King of the Jews"). Pilate commanded that a sign bearing this inscription be hung on the Cross, above Christ's head.

> XP: Two Greek letters *Chi* and *Rho*, the first two letters of the Greek word for "Christ."

> IC XC NIKA: The symbol for "Christ the Conqueror." I and C are the first and last letters of the Latinized Greek word for "Jesus"; X and C are the Latinized first and last letters of the Greek $X\rho i\sigma \tau o\varsigma$ (*Christos*) meaning "Christ"; and $Ni\kappa\alpha$ (*Nika*) is the Greek word for "conqueror."

Like the use of liturgical colors in the Church, an artist's use of color can point to a deeper meaning in his painting. The following will give you a sense of the religious symbolism of most colors:

> *Black* is the symbol for death, the underworld, mourning, sickness, or negation.
>
> *Black and white* together symbolize humility and purity of life. They're a common combination for the habits of some religious orders.
>
> *Blue* is the color of the sky, which represents heaven and God's love. It's also the color of truth, as the blue sky remains when the clouds move on.
>
> *Brown* can represent spiritual death and degradation. It also symbolizes renunciation of the world. Again, in some religious habits, it symbolizes another kind of movement away from life in this world and a turn toward God and a contemplative life.
>
> *Gray* symbolizes mourning and humility, sometimes the immortality of the spirit after the death of the body.
>
> *Green* represents life, deriving from the green of plants and vegetation. It also represents the season of spring.
>
> *Purple or violet* is often associated with royalty and power. It can also represent sorrow and penitence.
>
> *Red*, the color of blood, is often associated with the emotions of love and hate. It's the Church's color for martyrdom and also symbolizes fire, which can be seen as a symbol of Pentecost.

White or silver is symbolic of innocence of soul, purity, and holiness.

Gold and yellow vary in what they represent, depending on their hue. A golden yellow suggests divinity and a sacredness of that which is depicted; a symbol of revealed truth. Pale yellow can suggest infernal light, degradation, jealousy, treason, or deceit.

When you view a painting, questions can arise about whether many of the objects are included for some symbolic meaning. Perhaps the artist painted them more randomly, as the accessories and elements that would normally be found in such a setting. Determining the purpose of objects in a painting usually comes with a little practice; as you view more and more paintings, you'll learn to interpret the meaning of the objects more accurately. Here are the more commonly used objects with symbolic meaning:

Anchor: Hope and steadfastness.

Armor: Spiritual weapon.

Banner: With a cross, symbolizes victory.

Book: In the hands of the Evangelists or Apostles, it represents the Bible. In the hands of saints, it indicates that they're known for their writing or learning.

Bow: War and worldly power.

Bread: Sustaining life, the Eucharist.

Gates: Can represent death and departure from this life; can also signify a barrier between the righteous and the damned.

Gate, enclosed structure, or room: Reference to Mary's unblemished virginity.

Glass: Purity.

Globe: Power and sovereignty, attributed to God; sometimes suggests humankind or the peoples of the earth.

Nail and hammer: Symbols of the Passion and the Crucifixion.

Ax: Destruction.

Keys: Keys to Heaven.

Lance, knife, or spear: Instruments of martyrdom; sometimes refers to the lancing of Christ's side on the Cross.

Ladder: Descent of Christ's body from the Cross.

Lamp or light: Represents wisdom and piety.

Money or rope: Both symbols commonly associated with the Passion and Judas's betrayal of Christ.

Musical instruments: With angels, represents eternal praise.

Pillar or scourge: Symbols of the Scourging and the Passion.

Plane, rule, or saw: Carpenter's tools; accessories of St. Joseph.

Ring: Eternity.

Balance scales: Equality and justice, weighing the souls of the departed.

Ship: Symbolic of the Church of Christ; sometimes represents Noah's Ark.

Veil: Modesty and chastity.

Rainbow: Union, reconciliation, or pardon.

Salt: Strength and superiority.

Smoke: Suggests vanity and all that is fleeting, shortness of life; can also depict God's anger and wrath.

Star: Divine guidance or favor.

Water: Symbol of cleansing and purifying.

Many animals used in paintings have symbolic meaning. There are too many to list, but a few of the more common ones are:

Cow, ox, or ass: Humblest and lowliest of animal creation. Despite their lowliness, their presence suggests a certain awareness of God in their presence.

Birds: Winged souls; certain species have come to have a more specific meaning.

Eagle, butterfly, or phoenix: Resurrection.

Goat: The damned, separated from righteousness.

Dove: The Holy Spirit; purity and peace.

Dragon or serpent: The Devil.

Egg: Hope and resurrection.

Fish: Christ; occasionally a symbol of Baptism.

Lamb: Christ.

Lion: Strength, majesty, courage, and fortitude.

Peacock: Immortality.

Pelican: Great love, self-sacrificing like Christ.

Sparrow: Considered a lowly bird, represents God's love and protection of all, even the lowliest.

Swallow: Incarnation of Christ.

There are also many flowers, trees, and plants used in paintings with symbolic meaning. Again, I've included just a few of the more common ones:

Apple: Evil and forbidden fruit from the Garden of Eden. In the hand of Mary, however, it alludes to salvation.

Clover: The Trinity.

Wheat or grain: The Eucharist.

Grapes: Wine and the Blood of Christ in the Eucharist.

Lily: Purity.

Olive branch: Peace.

Palm: Victory; used with martyrs for their triumph over death.

Red rose: Martyrdom.

White rose: Purity.

Garland of roses: The Blessed Mother and the Rosary.

Wreath of roses: Heavenly joy.

Thorn or thistle: Grief, tribulation and sin; also the crown of thorns and the Passion.

Tree: Depending on the condition of the tree, can symbolize either life (healthy and strong) or death (poorly nourished and withered).

Vine: Expresses the relationship between God and his people.

There are a few other elements that can cause confusion or uncertainty for the viewer, such as when an artist paints two persons who lived during different periods. This technique is called "compressed time." The artist's intention to emphasize a particular point might best be achieved by combining related representations from two times. For example, in some paintings of the Crucifixion, you'll see either a skull or a figure depicting Adam at the foot of the Cross. Adam wasn't present at the Crucifixion, but the artist takes the liberty of showing him there to emphasize the relationship between the Fall from grace and the restoration of redemption.

Knowing the purpose for which a work was commissioned can help you identify and interpret the symbolism, particularly if the painting was intended for private devotion. Often the purpose is explained in a commonly available description of the painting. A religious order, for instance, might have commissioned the work to be hung in the monastery. Some triptychs (paintings with three panels) will include the founder of the order in one panel, patron saint(s) of the order in another panel and Mary or Jesus, or both, in the third panel. This type of painting serves as a visual reminder to the community that they're connected to Jesus and Mary, and their work within their order is the way in which they will gain heaven.

Works commissioned for self-promotion or for political purposes often demonstrate complex symbolism that can be a possible source of confusion. A great example of this kind of baffling depiction can be seen in the painting that was commissioned by King Richard II of England for his coronation. The painting includes not only King Richard but also King Edmund, King Edward, and Richard's patron saint, St. John the Baptist. A map of the British Isles suggests that heaven is giving Richard the right to rule. It's also interesting and puzzling that Richard is painted in the posture in which one might see Christ (with his hand extended), not in a humble gesture of folding his hands. It's clear that this painting was intended as political self-promotion, to convince the viewer that Richard's reign was divinely sanctioned.

Now, armed with a basic knowledge of interpreting religious art symbols, let's look at a few pieces of art together. All of the paintings I refer to can be found in one of the first two books in the resource list at the end of this essay. I've also included an Internet resource that will allow you to view the paintings on a larger scale and in color.

• *The Adoration of the Magi*, by Fra Angelico and Fra Filippo Lippi. Notice the goat with its back turned away from the Nativity, suggesting the separation of the damned from Christ. In a very prominent position atop the stable, you can see two peacocks (immortality). Notice the Magi and their expensive gifts, gifts suitable for a king; not typical gifts that someone might give an ordinary infant. Did you notice the halos around the heads of Jesus, Mary, and Joseph?

Pat yourself on the back. That wasn't so difficult. You're well on your way to gaining a much deeper understanding of those beautiful worlds of art by the Masters. There is a rich heritage in the treasures awaiting you.

• *The Annunciation*, by Fra Angelico. Notice the humility of Mary symbolized by her crossed arms. I mentioned time compression earlier. Notice in the upper left-hand corner of the painting that Adam and Eve are expelled from the garden, highlighting the contrast between the Fall and the Annunciation, with its hope for salvation through Jesus' birth. Mary is in an enclosed structure representing her virginity. The image of the man just above the post nearest to Mary is the prophet Isaiah. Mary appears to be reading a passage from the Bible, Isaiah 7:14, about a young woman bearing a son. Notice the dove (the Holy Spirit) and the white roses (purity), the gold halos (divinity, sacredness), and the palm tree (victory) in the back on the left.

The next two paintings are of a very different style than that of Fra Angelico, who lived and painted in the 1400s. In the late 1600s, another artist would choose similar subjects for his paintings. Jan Vermeer is an interesting individual to study apart from his paintings. He converted to Catholicism as an adult. He's one of my favorite artists because most of his paintings seem, at first glance, to be a study of the individual he depicted. Yet upon closer inspection, you realize that he has included many subtle elements that suggest a theological truth he's trying to convey.

• *A Woman Holding a Balance*, by Jan Vermeer. Notice the diffused sunlight helping to illuminate the scene, suggesting the light

of Christ as the Enlightenment casting clarity and understanding on the subject. Vermeer is famous for including a painting within a painting, and in this case, he has included the Last Judgment in the background. The visual association between the woman holding the balance and the Last Judgment suggests a thematic parallel — namely, to judge is to weigh. The juxtaposition suggests an irony as well, that God's judgments are eternal, while the woman's are temporal or *of this world*. Also notice the very dark quality of the picture with the exception of the light shining through the window. The color and light here suggest the light of Christ shining forth in an otherwise dark world.

I want to point out two other details. First, the woman appears to be noticeably pregnant, and I wonder if this suggests a hopeful aspect for humanity amid the ever-present and inevitable judgment we will all experience. Second, although it's difficult to make out, there's a mirror on the left side of the painting directly across from the woman's head. This could further extend the theme of judgment with an opportunity for self-examination.

• *Allegory of Faith*, by Jan Vermeer (opposite page). This is one of my favorite paintings. It's so clear that Vermeer included elements that have significant symbolic meaning. Perhaps that's why I like it so much; it's so straightforward and easy to interpret. Again, we see a painting within a painting — in this case, the Crucifixion. So many images jump right out that it's difficult to settle on any one particular aspect. This work is considered less of a piece of art and more an example of iconography. That is, the images have no intrinsic value other than their symbolic references. Vermeer intended this painting as a clear statement of his Catholic faith.

The woman wearing the blue and white dress trimmed with gold is very reminiscent our Blessed Mother. We see the woman, much like Our Lady of Grace, with her foot on top of the world (humanity) while a dead snake (the Devil) lies crushed beneath

her feet. Again, we see the curtain on the left enclosing the room suggesting Mary's virginity and the clear globe above her head suggesting her purity. The table on the right with its crucifix, chalice, and book (Bible) suggests an altar used during Holy Mass. The triangular composition of these items, along with the Mary figure and the painting in the background, suggests the connection between Christ's birth, death, and continued presence in the world during Mass and in the reception of the Eucharist. Notice the floor tiles; black and white together is the symbol of humility and purity. Again, we see the use of very dark tones with the lighter contrast cast on the Mary figure.

It must have been great fun for the artists to select and paint those symbolic elements that would further enhance and reinforce the central theme of the painting. What a treat, and what a gift we have in understanding the religious symbolism used in art. We begin to understand the mind and thoughts of artists by studying their work. We can't see them or speak to them, but in a way that transcends time, we can share in the same faith.

That faith does not pass away with the passing of the artists. They have captured a faith that offers its grace-filled salvific opportunity to us, who admire their art. It's a faith that offers to share the heavenly reward with generation after generation since that moment when Jesus, our beloved Lord and Savior, hung on the Cross and offered his life for our benefit. We owe a great debt of gratitude to the masters who have kept alive our deposit of faith in a great feast for the eyes. They have preserved our history as a believing people who seek to do the will of God.

May you and your family enjoy great graces, and may God bless you with a deeper spirituality as you gaze upon these vast treasures of the Masters in their timeless and constant message.

☞

Resources for Further Study

Signs and Symbols in Christian Art, by George Wells Ferguson (Oxford University Press)

Annotated Art: The World's Greatest Paintings Explored and Explained, by Robert Cumming (DK)

Art through Faith, by Mary Lynch and Seton Staff (Seton Media; see Appendix A)

Art Masterpieces: A Liturgical Collection (Catholic Heritage Curricula; see Appendix A)

Theology of the Icon, by Leonid Ouspensky (St. Vladimir's Seminary Press)

Renaissance (Eyewitness Book), by Andrew Langley (Knopf)

Sister Wendy's Story of Painting — Set of five VHS tapes
   (BBC Video)
Sister Wendy's Story of Painting (second edition), by Sr.
   Wendy Beckett (DK)
Sister Wendy's 1,000 Masterpieces, by Sr. Wendy
   Beckett (DK)
Vermeer: The Complete Works, by Arthur Wheelock, Jr.
   (Harry N. Abrams)
Illustrated Lives of the Saints, by John McNeill
   (Crescent Books)
Carol Gerten-Jackson's website:
   http://sunsite.dk/cgfa/index.html.

Usually one or two of the national museums offer an Advent calendar that includes miniature copies of religious masterpieces. Search for such Advent calendars on the Internet or contact the National Gallery of Art (www.nga.gov; (800) 697-9350) or the Art Institute of Chicago (www.artic.edu; (888) 301-9612).

"There is a certain truth to the adage 'we are what we eat.' When we eat healthy foods, we are healthier, because our bodies receive the kind of nutrition that enables them to grow and develop. When we eat junk food, the opposite happens; our bodies are starved for real nutrients. This is also true on a spiritual level. We are what we read and what we see and what we hear. Our imaginations are furnished by these objects. If this furniture is noble and beautiful, the faculty of imagination will be strengthened and ordered."

Laura Berquist, *Designing Your Own Classical Curriculum*

Basic Piano:
Providing a Foundation for
the Universal Language of Music

Lynne Cimorelli

After spending sixteen years teaching private piano lessons and earning a master's degree with a concentration in piano performance, I couldn't wait to work with my own children. Music is a universal language, and from birth all of my eleven children have loved it. Even without previous experience, you, too, can give your children some basic piano lessons.

The first step in teaching your children music is to provide exposure to it from birth. Research shows that classical and baroque music (Mozart, Beethoven, Bach, Handel, Vivaldi) stimulates the brain more positively than other types of music at all ages. In a study, students taking tests while listening to Mozart scored higher than while listening to other styles of music or listening to nothing at all. Another study compared the IQ levels of young children in three groups: those who were given music lessons, those who were given computer lessons, and those who had neither. The musicians tested the highest. So set your radio dial to your local classical station, and play it as much as possible.

The next step is to dance with your youngster. This will help develop a sense of rhythm. Step to the beat, clap to the beat, read rhythmic poetry aloud, clap out rhythms that your child can echo back to you.

Sing to your child, and encourage him to sing along; this helps develop a sense of pitch.

Allow free access to the piano. At our house, the only rule regarding the piano is, "Only fingers on the piano." In other words, no banging toys on the keys. Encourage your child to try to make the piano sound like various things (birds chirping, a big bear, a waterfall, fireworks, a cat chasing a mouse, bells, and so forth.) This is the beginning of improvisation. Take this opportunity to introduce the concepts of high and low (the high sounds are on the right end of the keyboard), loud and soft, and fast and slow.

Point out that the black keys are arranged in groups of twos and threes. Have your child play all the pairs of black keys up and down the keyboard, then do the same with the groups of three. Teach him that the white keys have names: A, B, C, D, E, F, and G, and show him that D always falls right in the middle of each group of two black keys. Find all the Ds, then teach C and E. Next are F and B, which are on the outsides of the groups of three black keys, and finally G and A. To avoid confusion, teach C, D, and E one day, F and B another day, and G and A on a third day. Learning the keys in this order will help your child to be able to identify the keys instantly from the visual cues of where they lie in relation to the black keys.

For learning actual notation, most piano-method books teach quarter notes, half notes and whole notes first. Personally, I prefer the system Zoltan Kodaly developed in Hungarian music classrooms in the early twentieth century; it introduces quarter notes, eighth notes in groups of two, and sixteenth notes in groups of four before moving on to half and whole notes. I've found that not only is it easier to understand, but it develops a much stronger sense of rhythm, and it's also more fun. Basically, the quarter note, which is usually the beat, is given the syllable "ta," groups of two eighth notes are called "ti-ti," and groups of four sixteenth notes are called "tiki-tiki."

I have flash cards made up with one of the groupings on each one. (It's fun to make them on colored felt, foam, or heavy card stock.) I lay them out in patterns of four or eight cards (because the most common meter has four beats in every measure), and the child speaks the rhythm back to me (for example, ti-ti ta, tiki-tiki ta). You can also speak a rhythm and then let the child pick out the correct symbols and lay them out in sequence. You can clap the beat and speak the rhythm or just clap the rhythm.

These simple games are an enormously fun and effective way to learn rhythm, which for most people is the most complicated aspect of reading music, and they lay a solid foundation with just a few short and easy lessons.

After learning to read basic rhythm, the student learns his finger numbers (thumbs are 1, pointers are 2, and so on), and then he starts playing what is called *directional music*. This is printed music that has notes moving up and down without being on a staff (a staff is the set of five lines on which music is written). The finger numbers are written under every note, and the student is given the starting key. The student soon understands that notes moving up the page equate to keys on the piano moving to the right (the higher sounds) and notes moving down are played as keys to the left (the lower sounds).

Next, the notes are placed on the staff, and the student learns that the notes tell him which keys to play on the piano. The clefs (treble and bass) are usually taught using the landmarks of G (the loop on the treble clef goes around the G line), F (the dots of the bass clef surround the F line), and middle C (it's drawn on its own separate ledger line between the two staves). It's a good idea to learn both clefs simultaneously. Students who are taught treble clef first and play treble clef music exclusively for too long end up being poor bass-clef readers. (Bass clef is used mostly for the left hand).

While your child is learning the basics of rhythm and notation, continue to encourage improvisation. This develops the habit of listening to the piano. Often when children are learning to read music, they concentrate so hard on the reading part that they're almost oblivious to the actual sound they're making. Improvisation also helps the child to begin to think like a composer. Just as creative writing helps a child to develop a deeper understanding of the English language and a better appreciation of great literature, so improvisation and composition enhance the study of music.

One improvisation game you can play is to take a rhythmic pattern that your child made up with his flash cards and play it on the piano using any keys he wants; black or white or any combination of the two. Try using four rhythm cards and repeating the pattern four times; this exercise will give the composition a nice rhythmic structure.

The most important thing to stress in this exercise is that there are no wrong answers. The student is experimenting with sound and learning how to put it into a simple structure. This is improvisation. If he finds a particular pattern of notes that he likes and wants to put into a fixed form (by recording it or writing it down in some rough format), it has become a composition. A simple way to start is to use only black keys as any note played will sound good. (It will have a Far Eastern flavor because the black keys make up what is called a pentatonic scale, which is used extensively in music from the Far East, especially in Japan.)

Playing by ear can be learned simultaneously with note-reading, or it can be started with children as young as two or three years old (note-reading seems to work best when the child is at least five and a half years old; it can be done earlier, but the child will move much more slowly). I've found that "Peter, Peter, Pumpkin Eater" is the easiest song to teach by ear because it's played solely on black keys, it uses only one finger on each hand, and it alternates hands. It uses mostly large-muscle movement as opposed to the finer-muscle movement of pieces that use all the fingers, and is thus ideal for a young child. Some other easy pieces to teach by ear are "Old MacDonald" on black keys (start on F-sharp), "Jingle Bells" (start on E), and "Mary Had A Little Lamb" (start on E, A, or B).

Teach your child three or four notes at a time (if you can't figure them out by ear, buy yourself a simple book of nursery rhymes set to music, and you'll find most of them in there). Before long, he'll be able to pick out the melody to any piece by himself. Next he'll be able to start adding left-hand parts by ear.

Transposing is an important and easy skill to teach at this point. Transposing simply means playing the piece in another key. Once your child has learned "Mary Had a Little Lamb" starting on E, have him play it starting on A, then again starting on B. He'll also be able to play it easily on black keys, starting on the black key to the left of B (B-flat). Once he sees how this works, have him transpose every piece he learns by ear. Eventually, he'll learn how to transpose by sight as well.

When people find out that I'm a pianist, they often tell me that they took lessons as a child for many years, only to quit out of frustration or boredom, or both. Many times they regret having quit, to this day. I believe that this experience is widespread because students aren't always taught sight-reading skills. Sight-reading refers to the skill of being able to pick up a piece of music and play it with a minimal number of mistakes the first time through. The importance of this skill can't be emphasized enough. Because piano-playing is such a complex activity, just progressing normally through a method book isn't enough to develop sight-reading skill.

For this reason, it's not only possible, but all too common, for a person to take piano lessons for ten years and still not be able to play anything without spending hours of practice on it first. This is akin to being given Shakespeare to read and having to sound out the words. No wonder people get frustrated and quit.

We can prevent frustration by practicing sight-reading from the very beginning. Have the child play through some new music every day (generally on a slightly easier level than the repertoire pieces that are usually assigned) to develop this skill. Even with as little as one line of new music per day, he will have sight-read 365 lines of new music by the end of the year. The best approach is for the child to study the music for a few minutes before actually playing it. He should name the notes out loud, clap out the rhythm, and look for details such as dynamics (loud and soft), tempo (speed), any repeated patterns, and any accidentals (added sharps, flats, and naturals). Don't ask him to play the piece over and over; three or four times is sufficient. If you have a child who is already playing fairly advanced pieces, a hymnal is a great resource for sight-reading practice.

One of the tricks to becoming good at both sight-reading and transposing is to learn to read music by interval and pattern as well as by the names of the notes. An interval is the distance between two notes. On the keyboard, two white keys next to each other are said to be a second apart (e.g., C and D are a second apart). Two notes a second apart are written on the staff as a note with a line going through the middle of it (a "line note") touching a note filling the adjacent space either above or below that line (a "space note"). A third is two white keys that have one white key between them (e.g., C and E).

There are also fourths, fifths, sixths, sevenths, and eighths. (They go on beyond that, but these are the most commonly used intervals, especially for the beginner.) Once the student recognizes written intervals, he should begin to look for patterns on his printed music. These take the form of repeated "motives." A motive is a short grouping of notes that's used many times throughout the piece. Very often a piece will have a melodic motive (e.g., CDEC, that is, up two seconds and down a third) or a rhythmic motive (e.g., ti-ti ta ti-ti ta) or both. The motive will be used throughout the piece, either directly repeated or sequenced (that is when it starts on a different key). Recognizing a pattern of repeated or sequenced motives is akin to the recognition of words in reading the English language. It makes the reading go so much faster than having to sound out each letter.

After learning intervals, the student should start learning scales and chords. The concepts of intervals, scales, and chords will be more thoroughly understood if they are seen, played, written, used in short improvisations and compositions, and sung. Sight-singing is a separate skill that isn't usually addressed in piano methods, but it's essential to becoming a well-rounded musician. The easiest way to incorporate it is to have your child sing everything he's learning to read and play, starting with scales and intervals. You can use either numbers or the traditional solfège syllables (do, re, mi, fa, sol, la, ti, do). A second (C-D) would be sung either "1-2" or "Do, re". A third would be sung either, "1-3" or "Do, mi," and so on.

Ear-training ties in directly with sight-singing. As the student learns a new concept (seconds and thirds, for instance), have him listen to the two intervals with his eyes closed until he can identify them by sound. Do the same with all the intervals, major and minor scales, and major, minor, augmented, and diminished chords as they are introduced in the method book you're using.

Being able to recognize these concepts by sound signals a full understanding of them. It is this ability that allowed the major composers to scrawl down their masterpieces hurriedly, away from their instruments. Franz Schubert, for instance, was the classic absent-minded professor. In the middle of teaching his class, a beautiful song would come to him, and he'd go to his desk and write it down immediately on whatever scrap of paper he could find. He could do this because he understood the sound in the same way we understand the written word. If a story line or a grocery list comes to mind, we can scrawl it down immediately; we don't have to wait until we get near a dictionary to find the right letters and words.

From Theory to Practice

We've been discussing theory, which helps the child understand the form and structure in music. Ideally, every concept learned in theory (intervals, scales, chords, three-part song form, and so on) is put into practice immediately by playing it, reading it, writing it, singing it, hearing it, improvising and composing with it, and identifying it in the pieces that are assigned to be played. We now turn to technique.

Technique encompasses two main areas: proper position and movement of the hands, arms, and body; and the exercises that build strength and evenness in the fingers. The student should sit up straight at a height and distance from the piano so that his arms form right angles when his hands are on the keys. In general, the fingers should be slightly curved but not rigid. (Place your hand on the crown of your head to get the right amount of curvature.) The wrist should be straight, not drooping nor raised, but again, not rigid.

As the student gets more advanced, he'll learn that in long scale passages, the elbow leads the way, and in repeated broken chords, the hand moves in circles. These types of motions keep the hand and wrist from building up muscle tension, which can cause not only unevenness in the playing, but even repetitive motion injuries in an advanced player.

There are some helpful videos that show proper technique. *Freeing the Caged Bird,* by Barbara Lister-Sink, a series by Nelita True on piano technique, and anything by the Taubman Institute can help develop a healthy playing technique. Your local music store should be able to order the first two for you; the third is available directly from the Taubman Institute: www.taubman-institute.com; (800) 826-3720.

Technical exercises are generally based on scales and arpeggios, and they're essential for strengthening the fingers. *The Virtuoso Pianist*, by Hanon, for example, is a collection of exercises that has been considered a standard for over a hundred years. There are also many collections of études (exercises) at every level that will help build technique. As important as études are, however, they can't supplant the learning of the scales and arpeggios in every key. These are essential to mastering the instrument.

Arguably the most important part of piano playing is the actual sound produced. No matter how blazing and precise the technique is, if the sound is harsh or heavy-handed, the music will leave the listener cold. By contrast, even the simplest pieces can be played with the most exquisite tone, moving the very soul of the listener and sending chills up the spine. The way to develop this is through the most careful listening.

Articulation (legato versus staccato; that is, smooth versus disconnected), dynamics (loud versus soft), and balance (melody versus harmony) all must be carefully considered to achieve the kind of sound that truly communicates to the listener. To develop smooth, connected playing, have your child close his eyes, play a five-finger pattern (1-2-3-4-5-4-3-2-1) very slowly with his right hand, and listen closely to his playing, focusing on both the sound and the feeling in his fingertips as he plays each key. Tell him to pretend that his fingers form a caterpillar moving from one key to the next, so he needs to match the pressure he puts on each key with that of each previous key. This helps develop the production of a perfectly smooth, connected line. Ultimately, the goal is to imitate the human voice and to produce what is called a "singing line." The student develops this by singing, listening to good singing, and then capturing in his piano playing the breaths and the rise and fall of a phrase that a singer would do.

Another skill that needs to be started early is that of learning to play one hand louder than the other. This is important because piano music generally contains a melody and a harmony, and the melody, which is usually in the right hand, needs to be played louder than the harmony, just as a singer should be heard above the instrumental accompaniment.

This skill can be developed by playing a five-finger pattern with both hands together (C-D-E-F-G-F-E-D-C). Have your child close his eyes while playing this slowly, listening, and again paying attention to the feeling in both hands. Play both hands together loudly, feeling as though the weight of a brick is on each finger. Then play both hands softly, feeling as though each finger is light as a feather. Then play both loudly again. Finally, try to play the right hand loudly (feeling bricks on each finger) while backing the left hand off to the feeling of being light as a feather. Again, this needs to be done with the eyes closed and in that particular order (loud, soft, loud, then loud right hand with soft left hand). The reason is that the full concentration needs to be on the feelings of each finger, and all attention needs to be focused inward.

This exercise is often difficult, as it requires coordinating the hands, and yet separating them in feeling completely at the same time. Don't get frustrated if this exercise has to be repeated many, many times over a long period before it's mastered. The resulting sound will be worth the effort.

Also, practice this exercise in reverse, with the left hand playing louder, as sometimes the melody is in the left hand, which then needs to be the louder one.

The simplest way to put this all together is to take whatever method book you use, identify the new concept for that lesson (it might be a new interval, a new rhythm, or a new scale, for instance), and have the child play it, read it, write it, sing it, listen to it, improvise and compose with it, and find how it's used in the assigned pieces in that lesson. Most method books will cover the playing, reading, and writing of it, but you might have to add the rest. It might seem at first like these extra steps are a waste of time on nonessential activities that just slow down your child's progress through the book. Quite the contrary, however, adding in the singing, listening, improvising, composing, and analysis will not only cement your child's understanding of the language of music, but will also provide such a solid foundation that more advanced concepts will be learned much more quickly and the progress will be hastened.

Further Aspects of a Good Formation

The final two essential components to a solid music education are music history and ensemble playing. As the piano was invented in 1709, we focus on the periods of Western music since then (Baroque, Classical, Romantic, Impressionistic, Contemporary). Your child should learn the names of these periods, and the dates and major composers associated with them, and become familiar with some of the works of each composer, including piano, vocal, and symphonic. There are many fine series for children that include CDs and biographies; all you have to do is work them into a musical timeline.

As early as possible, start playing duets with your child (or find someone who can). Ideally the child should do as many pairings as possible, both with advanced pianists and with pianists on his own level. Take every opportunity to play duets. You can make up the very simplest accompaniments to just about anything, or you can buy a duet book on your child's level. Try to find friends with whom your child can play duets and trios. There are a number of collections of duets written for two players of similar abilities on every level.

Ensemble playing, whether it is with another pianist, a group of instrumentalists, or accompanying a choir, is the icing on the cake for the pianist. There is very little that is more fun or rewarding than being able to share one's music with others by playing together.

Up to now I have written about what *you* should do. While you can certainly teach your child all the basics of piano through at least the first several levels, at some point your child might get serious about the study of music. You'll then want to find a good professional teacher. I stress the word *good* here because there are many "piano teachers" out there whose only qualification is that they took piano lessons for several years. A truly good piano teacher not only plays well, but has been well-schooled in stylistic traditions, peculiar to each composer, that have been passed down from teacher to teacher for the last three hundred years. Unfortunately, a person can't learn these stylistic traditions just from reading about the composers and listening to the CDs. There are differences in pedaling, articulation, strictness of tempo, interpretation, ornamentation, and much more that vary quite widely, depending on the composer, and really need to be demonstrated in person. A nearby university that offers a music degree is a good place to inquire about qualified piano teachers.

Before you get to that point, however, there's no reason you can't teach your child the basics and give him a good solid foundation on your own. If you follow the suggestions here, you'll give him the best possible foundation on which to build. Music is the universal language; start young and teach your child to be fluent in it. You'll never regret it, and your house will be filled with beautiful live music.

Also remember that the young musicians of today might become the church musicians of tomorrow. I run the youth choir at my church, and if my sight-reading skills were weak, it would be impossible to run it well. Because my sight-reading and musicianship skills are strong, however, my practice time is minimal and my choir, whose members' average age is eight, sings in two parts and sounds terrific. I also have written original music for them to sing, including a setting of the Mass. Any well-trained musician can do this. So again, train them well. You might find that your child's calling to ministry is in the music department, and because of the background you'll have provided, he'll be able to add great beauty to the Mass.

"He who sings prays twice."

St. Augustine

Why Latin?

Kevin Conley

The combinations of motivations that make a family decide to homeschool are as numerous as the number of families that homeschool. My wife, along with many others, chose to teach from a "classical" curriculum. This means that our children would learn more Latin, Greek, and theology than they would in most traditional schools. It all sounded good to us and, no doubt, to many, but there was a problem. Neither my wife nor I knew any Latin or Greek at the time!

Of course, it helped that my wife and I are in harmony about homeschooling. We especially agree that one of its benefits is the joy parents rediscover in learning, while proving the adage that if someone really wants to learn something, he should teach it.

This is exactly what my wife began doing several years ago, when our oldest was ready for Greek. She began teaching herself so that she could become an effective tutor. Either by the doctrine of separation of powers, or because I once audited a Latin class while doing graduate studies, I volunteered to be the family's Latin instructor.

My wife and I do have different styles. She's comfortable learning right along with the children, or perhaps a few pages ahead. I, on the other hand, after some stuttering attempts at simultaneous learning, decided it would be better to try to master the material first. I tell myself that in studying to get ahead of the children, I should not underestimate the power of example. When children see their parents' dedication to studying something that's meant to be transmitted to them, surely this is by itself a strong influence on the intellectual habits of the young.

In the meantime, we taught all the children several Latin prayers, which we recite daily, so the pronunciation is down pat. By default, it is a decent start. And I've learned enough to have become a minor zealot, and there's no turning back. I understand what mothers mean when they say that homeschooling is a calling or, to use a Latin-rooted word, a vocation.

I've learned many things during my vocation discernment process, to borrow a phrase, that have strengthened my commitment to provide our children with a solid classical education before they leave our daily care.

Latin is now rarely taught in the United States, although I hear that it's making something of a comeback. Indeed, my wife and I obtained university degrees without ever having attended a school that offered it. It's possible to gain a graduate degree without having studied any foreign language, let alone Latin. The United States is far ahead of the rest of the West in discarding the classics, which is remarkable, considering some of our early history.

The father of our Declaration of Independence and the father of our Constitution were both dedicated classical scholars. Thomas Jefferson was homeschooled in the Classics by his civil-engineer father, Peter; James Madison obtained a degree in Latin as a pre-seminary student at Princeton, where he also studied Greek and Hebrew. In fact, one recent biographer surmises that Madison had read Thomas à Kempis's *Imitation of Christ* at the age of fifteen, in Latin. We'd like to match that feat in our homeschool.

The back of the dollar bill is testimony to the fact that Latin was the foundational study of all the founders of this country, and not just the two mentioned above. *Annuit coeptis* and *Novus ordo seclorum* are the mottoes printed there. *Annuit* and *coeptis* are particularly rare words — words that a typical first- or second-year Latin vocabulary list wouldn't include. Instead, the phrase comes from near the end of Virgil's *Aeneid*. The founders obviously assumed all posterity would understand these mottoes, but today very few do. They mean: "He [God] winks at [i.e., approves of] the [our] undertakings" and "A new order of the ages."

What should motivate a homeschooling family to such an undertaking? A wink from God? Perhaps. Let us consider the opening words of John's Gospel: *In principio erat verbum* — "In the beginning was the Word." A more pregnant theological phrase in all the scriptures would be hard to find. But the phrase is also powerful as a general philosophical proposition: how fundamental language is for the one species of God's creation that uses it.

Whatever subject we end up mastering, from rocket science to sewing, we will have to learn a special vocabulary. There's no way around it. In mathematics there are hypotenuses and hyperbolas; in music, clefs and crescendos; in anatomy, medullas and mitochondria; in geography, longitude and latitude; in chemistry, protons and potassium; and on and on. The point is that the better a person is grounded in language per se, the more prepared he will be to master special vocabularies, and hence, various subjects.

The forces of history and culture have caused more than half of our words to be derived from Latin and quite a few from Greek, with most of the rest being Germanic in origin. The Latinate words come from the fact that the Roman Empire had extended into Britain by the time Christ was born. After the fall of Rome, Germanic tribes invaded Britain, followed some centuries later by Normans, speaking a Latin-derived language called French. The only reason so many Greek-based words appear in English is because Greek was, until recently, a required part of the curriculum of educated persons.

Typically, the simpler words in current English usage, such as *milk*, *cat*, and *swim*, are Germanic in origin. These are the words we learn at our mother's knee. Contrariwise, English words of Latin origin, such as *usually* and *multi-syllabic*, are, well, usually multi-syllabic. Thus, the study of Latin has this benefit: it automatically enriches our appreciation and extends our grasp of English.

The Latin word *gubernator* means the person who operates the rudder on a ship. Who would think of their state's governor in quite the same way after learning that? Other examples: *corporation* comes from *corporis*, meaning "of the body"; *community* from words meaning sharing gifts among one another; and *negotiate*, being the negation of *otious*, meaning "leisure."

Let me offer one more example. In chapters 14 and 15 of St. John's Gospel, Jesus repeatedly uses the word, in the English rendering, *love*, which can have many connotations. However, the Latin Vulgate word used in each of these expressions is a form of the verb *diligere*, from which we get the English word *diligent*. For me, that discovery put a new focus on those commandments.

Not only will the study of Latin enrich and illuminate English words we know and use already, but it will also give students greater confidence in using a more extensive English vocabulary. The typical person hears a word such as *puerile*, looks it up, and forgets the meaning shortly thereafter, just as names of newly introduced people often slip our minds. And, as with names, we might be 85 percent sure of the meaning, but unless we are 100 percent certain, we won't dare use it. The embarrassment of being wrong is simply too great.

The list of English words on the outer boundaries of our usable vocabularies that are derived from basic Latin words is long. Here are some examples: *impecunious* (*pecunia*: "money"); *odious* (*odi*: "hate"); *concatenate* (*catena*: "chain"); *procrastinate* (*cras*: "tomorrow"); *gregarious* (*grex*: "flock"); *puerile* (*puer*: "child"); *incarcerate* (*carcer:* "prison"); *potable* (*potare:* "to drink"). No other language has such leverage to enable your English to leap ahead.

But there's much more to consider in making the decision to learn and teach Latin to the next generation. Latin, it is said, is a dead language. Some say we're better off learning a living language that might one day help us in business or travel.

But the fact that Latin is dead is one of its chief virtues. There will be no temptation to teach mere conversational snippets. Its grammar and vocabulary are fixed and unchanging. The very same regular grammar forms your child will learn will be identical to those learned by Augustine in the fourth century; by Aquinas in the thirteenth; by Shakespeare in the sixteenth; by Madison in the eighteenth; and by John Paul II in the twentieth. The study of Latin or Greek forces the student to pay such attention to every letter of every word that it will help form him for any academic undertaking later in life.

We should consider history, too. It's often observed that we live in an intensely now-focused culture. Last year's war is no longer talked about; what the president said last week is irrelevant; how the team or the Dow did two days ago — no one cares. What's the score *right now?* Live! Latest ticker!

Latin inevitably broadens the student's interests beyond today's concerns to the life and times of Caesar, Cicero, Virgil, and others who happen to be near-contemporaries of Jesus Christ. The vague apprehension many have, that Christianity flourished largely because people back then were so primitive and backward that they would easily fall for any myth, would never be able to take root. An immersion in the life and language of the Roman Empire helps render the temptations of the culture of immediate gratification and "the best is yet to come" and "just do it [now]" much weaker.

Of course, for the Catholic homeschooling family, the reasons to learn Latin, even for the adults, are more manifold. Pope John

XXIII, in the same year Vatican II started, promulgated *Veterum Sapientia*, which includes the following:

> There can be no doubt as to the formative and educational value of . . . the language of the Romans. It is a most effective training for the pliant minds of the young. It exercises, matures, and perfects the principal faculties of mind and spirit. It sharpens the wits and gives keenness of judgment. It helps the young mind to grasp things accurately and develop a true sense of values.

I mentioned before that our family prays in Latin as a prelude for formal instruction. Our *Aves* and *Paters* keep Latin alive in the children even after formal instruction begins. But prayer in Latin should be the point as much as the prelude. Prayers are generally more beautiful in Latin than in English, especially when sung, as anyone who has heard *Panis Angelicus* or Gregorian chant would attest.

Many lovely Latin prayers are unknown to Catholics who came of age after Vatican II (including most homeschooling parents). To achieve greater participation by the laity, that council promulgated greater, *although not exclusive*, use of the vernacular in the Liturgy. The council also made room for more Scripture-reading at Mass by shortening the Liturgy of the Faithful. Lost were many of the priest's prayers surrounding the consecration and Communion. It would be wonderful if some of those could be reborn in the hearts of the laity. One of those prayers I discovered used to be recited by the priest after partaking of the Holy Species:

> *Corpus tuum, Domine, quod sumpsi, et*
> *Sanguis, quem potavi, adhaereat visceribus meis;*
> *et praesta: ut in me non remaneat scelerum macula,*
> *quem pura et sancta refecerunt sacramenta:*
> *qui vivis et regnas in saecula saeculorum.*

"May your body, Lord, which I have eaten, and
your blood, which I have drunk, adhere to my inmost parts,
and be so effective that no stain of sin remains in me,
who has been refreshed by this pure and holy sacrament,
which lives and reigns forever and ever."

I'm ever thankful my wife in her devotion to homeschooling and to a classical curriculum, which foisted on me this duty of teaching Latin. I learned through trial and error that I would have to know Latin better to teach it well. It has truly been a pursuit of happiness (to quote a phrase from those decided Latinists among our country's founders) and the effort has been and ever will be (to quote another phrase, this time the motto of the Jesuits) *Ad Majorem Dei Gloriam.*

"I want a laity who know their creed so well
that they can give an account of it and who know
so much history that they can defend it.
I want an intelligent, well-instructed laity,
[because] in all times the laity have been
the measure of the Catholic spirit."

John Henry Cardinal Newman

Teaching a Foreign Language to Young Children

Mary Glantz

Within each human being is the very essence of communication. God, our Almighty Father, in his infinite wisdom, places within each of us both the need and the capacity to communicate with one another. He who declared, "It is not good that the man should be alone" (Gen. 2:18) plants within our hearts a need to connect with those he has placed in our lives and a way to connect with them.

Think of a newborn infant. He needs his mother to provide milk for his hungry tummy, warmth to regulate his body temperature, and loving arms to comfort and hold him. Although he cannot speak, he communicates through crying and soon learns to express a cry unique to each of his needs. His mother understands what he wants even though no words are expressed.

Similarly, communicating with people who don't speak a common language requires some creative nonverbal mannerisms. Gestures, drawings in the air, and exaggerated facial expressions help to convey a message when words aren't available. Assistance can be provided, greetings can be exchanged, and information can be shared even though conversations are limited by the absence of a common language.

But when a common language is employed in communication, the discourse is more efficient. Each individual is better able to explain, analyze, question, and describe, as well as share thoughts, feelings, ideas, and events with another individual through the element of language. The better the individual is at utilizing language skills — an extensive, descriptive, accurate vocabulary and proper use of grammar — the better the chances for enhanced communication.

In the day-to-day task of home-educating children, communication skills are developed through courses in English grammar, vocabulary, logic and reasoning, reading, and writing, as well as through practice in conversation with family members and others. But developing true language skills means not only preparing children to communicate in English, our mother tongue, but also giving them the skills to connect verbally with those who speak a foreign language.

In the United States, where the majority of the population is literate in the English language and where occasions for encountering people who aren't may be infrequent, it's difficult to imagine a need or practical reason for learning another language. Europeans understand this need better, given their closeness to other countries of foreign tongues. There it's common to begin studying a foreign language — usually English — at the elementary level. Yet, in our own country, students generally don't seriously study a second language until they're in high school. Courses in foreign-language study are often completed only because they're required for entry into schools of higher education.

As home-educating parents, we can prepare our children for a time when facility in a foreign tongue will provide and enhance opportunities for them — in travel, in college studies, in evangelization efforts or missionary work, in assisting immigrants in our own land, and in future careers. Providing our children with communication skills in a foreign language doesn't entail forecasting which language will be of most use to them in their future life. Rather, we must begin their training in the study of a language outside of our mother tongue by exposing them to the sounds (phonics) and words of another language beginning in early childhood. The language we choose to teach isn't as important as the choice to provide this education.

Scientists have found that learning a second language at an early age enables people to learn a third and even fourth language with greater ease. The brain is wired differently than when language is learned later. This provides us, as parents, with the opportunity to teach that language which we consider most attractive for reasons of personal ethnic background, familiarity, interest, or education. If our children later need or want to develop communication skills in a third language, their brains will be organized in such a way as to allow this to occur more rapidly and more efficiently.

When a child learns a second language at an early age, he stores the second language in the area of the brain where the first language is stored. This enables the second language to be spoken with a natural sound, free of any accent introduced by the first language. Thus, those who learn two languages at a young age retain an ability to speak both as if each was their native tongue.

Studying a second language early has other advantages. Young children have fewer inhibitions about speaking with an accent than children in high school who may experience greater self-consciousness. They also easily adopt repetition and memorization as learning methods. This reflects the grammar stage of educational development in a classical education.

Foreign-language study can be of tremendous usefulness to the Mystical Body of Christ. In the early days of the Church, the New Testament was written in Greek. The Septuagint, a Greek version of the Hebrew scriptures, was used for the Old Testament. In the year 382, Pope Damasus wanted to revise the New Testament to reflect the dominant language of the Roman Empire — Latin. So he commissioned Jerome, a young priest fluent in Latin, Greek, and Hebrew, and with a competence in Aramaic and other languages, to translate the Gospels into the common language of his time, thereby making the words of Christ more accessible to all. During the course of his life, St. Jerome also translated all the books of the Hebrew scriptures.

Pope John Paul II represented a contemporary example of putting language skills at the service of the Church. Our Holy Father could converse with people of many nations in their native tongue, as well as use common greetings and deliver prepared speeches in many other languages. He used his multilingual skills to greet, to welcome, to accept, and to touch with the warmth of Christ all the peoples of the world whom our Lord loves.

Tips for Building Foreign-Language Skills in Your Children

Begin early. Most children acquire language skills by hearing sounds and words repeated over and over. In the beginning, Baby makes a sound and Mother repeats the sound, adding to it other sounds to make a recognizable word. Constant repetition of this sequence of sounding, repeating, and expanding helps Baby to develop the sounds of speech.

At the same time, Baby is learning what words mean even if he himself can't repeat those words. Baby can understand simple words and directives even though he can't yet talk.

A child learns a foreign language in much the same way. The spoken word is heard many, many times. The child attempts to repeat the word. Mother or Father repeats the word correctly, and after many repetitions, the word is mastered. At the same time, the child is hearing the second language and begins to understand the content of the conversation. Learning simple words, repeating lists of words (such as numbers, the alphabet, or days of the week), and understanding the spoken word are the initial steps in foreign-language acquisition.

Parents will need to provide many opportunities for the home-educated child to hear the second language. Of course, fluency in another language by one or both parents would be a highly beneficial, but a basic facility in another language by one parent can accomplish great things. The idea is to use what you know, use it at every opportunity, and expand from there.

Whether you or your spouse speak a second language or not, there are a number of resources to help you (see Appendix D). Audiocassettes and CDs are of primary importance because the focus is on the spoken word. Larger bookstores sell many foreign-language books and accompanying audiocassettes. The books include children's picture books, storybooks, and songbooks. Try to find books that include the story in both the foreign language and English, so that you, as the teacher, can see and learn the grammar of the language at the same time as your child.

The Usborne First Thousand Word series of books is wonderful for this purpose. These books have many colorful illustrations of items encountered every day in the life of a child. The accompanying tapes simply repeat the words for every picture that is labeled. Although this may seem like a dry way to learn, you needn't worry about covering the whole book or even all one thousand words. Begin by finding a page of pictures that appeals to you because of the frequency that your family encounters those terms. For example, the rooms in the house, or the animals on the farm, or food at the grocery store might be a good place to start. Learn two new words each time you look at those pages and listen to the tape. Then begin to substitute those terms for their English equivalent in your everyday conversation. "Ann, do you want some *buerre* on your bread?" "Peter, let's go ride *les bicyclettes* today."

If you're studying Latin as a second language, find a local parish that has a Latin Mass and make a commitment to attend once or twice a month. Maybe a local monastery or convent conducts Vespers in Latin and would welcome your family to join them a couple of times a month. The goal is to have children hear the foreign tongue and to understand that the language they're learning is used by others, even if it isn't spoken fluently in the household.

Using the language each and every day is critical to success. Teach your children terms for food, for rooms in the house, for family members, for toys. Then, refer to these items or to people as often as possible in the foreign tongue. Again, Usborne's First Thousand Word books are of great value in this practice.

Another critical success factor is learning key phrases. Such phrases include common greetings, common polite exchanges, and simple directives. These include:

Hello.	Dinner's ready.
How are you?	Good-bye.
Good morning.	Please.
Good night.	Thank you.
I love you.	You're welcome.
Sweet dreams.	See you soon.

Common expressions such as the following can be learned in the second language and incorporated into everyday conversation:

Brush your teeth.	Come to dinner.
Time to get up.	Don't argue.
Set the table.	Merry Christmas!

The key phrases are limited only by your imagination. You might want to consider learning and using one new phrase per week. As the children gain mastery, this exercise becomes almost a game, and they begin challenging parents to teach them their favorite and familiar sayings in the foreign tongue. I also found that as we advance in this exercise, my children try to find more varied responses to my expressions. For example, my expression of thanks to my children produces several responses for "You're welcome," including *je t'en prie, de rien, il n'y a pas de quoi,* and — my favorite — "*A votre service, Maman*" meaning, literally, "At your service, Mom!"

I highly recommend thoroughly learning common greetings, as every person you encounter who speaks the language you're learning will address your children and question them as to their name, their age, their grade, and the number of brothers and sisters they have. Such persons will, of course, expect an answer in the foreign tongue. All levity aside, however, it's a delight for children to practice their new skills with someone who's so obviously pleased that your children are learning the language they speak.

There are a number of options in learning these phrases. If you're studying French, I recommend the book *Speaking French to Your Baby,* by Therese Slevin Pirz. This book includes dozens of pages of common phrases used by mothers and fathers with their children. Even if your children are at the elementary-school level in their overall education, there are a number of phrases you can immediately employ and use for years to come, including "Make your bed," "Tidy your room," and "It's out of the question."

Such books are also available in other languages. Furthermore, there are many books and audiotapes that can guide you in the pronunciation of the language you're studying. These are of great value if you don't speak the language you're teaching your child or if you've gotten a bit rusty since your last high school foreign-language class. Again, you'll need to comb through the foreign-language section of the major book retailers.

If you're fortunate enough to know someone who speaks the language you're studying, ask for his help. Write a list of phrases and plan to meet regularly or telephone regularly for assistance. Ask your family friend or relative to write down and pronounce one phrase for you each time you meet. Each time you ask for the translation of a new phrase, review the most recently learned phrase to ensure that everyone is pronouncing it correctly.

Finally, consider using a tutor for this specific task of translating and supplying phrases. It would be a relatively inexpensive way to hire professional help, considering it would go a long way toward guiding your future progress.

Memorization Exercises

Little children, as well as those in the grammatical stage of education, often develop a fondness for memorizing simple songs, poems, and prayers. Teaching these same songs, poems, and prayers in a foreign language is particularly appealing to the children, because they are already so familiar with the meaning in English.

The "Happy Birthday" song is an example. My children learned this song quickly in a foreign language because of the simplicity of the lyrics. They use every birthday party now to heartily wish the birthday guest of honor a happy birthday in French. Recently, when Grandma turned seventy, my children figured out how to add the second verse to the French "Happy Birthday" song: "How old are you?" (*Quelle âge a tu?*) Although Grandma doesn't speak French, she quickly deduced what my children were singing, and everyone had a good laugh.

For favorite nursery rhymes and songs, there's an assortment of audiocassettes and CDs available at major book retailers, at used book sales, and through other sources (see Appendix D). Most come with picture and lyric books. Curiously, one of my children never liked hearing or reciting nursery rhymes. However, he eagerly learned a humorous French nursery rhyme about *le petit lapin* (the little rabbit) so that he could recite it and translate it for us.

Learning prayers and Scripture verses is another way of expanding your memorization exercises. Instead of saying the Glory Be in English during family prayer time or in each Rosary, say it in your new language. Depending on the age of your children, your goal might be to say one decade of the Rosary in Latin, for example, within six months.

Teach your children simple biblical quotations such as John 14:6: *"Jesus a dit, 'Je suis le chemin, la verité, et la vie.'"* ("Jesus said, 'I am the Way, the Truth, and the Life.'"). This is a great way of blending religion studies with language studies. Ask the major book retailers the best way to purchase a foreign-language Bible or order it online at their website.

Once your second language starts to feel familiar, you'll be ready to expand further. If your child is at the second-grade level in school and is learning math and grammar, there are two easy ways to start. The first, in math, was initiated by my children as a way, perhaps, to relieve the monotony of math flash cards. Rather than responding with the correct answer in English, my children surprised me by mentally performing the operation on the flash card and responding to me *en français*. It was a challenge for all of us — specially when the answers exceed seventy — but quite a bit of fun.

Second, to further enhance the use of Usborne's *First Thousand Words in French*, we picked a verb that correlated well with the group of terms illustrated, and we learned to conjugate that verb. For example, the verb *manger* ("to eat") was studied with the pictures for food. We learned simple verb conjugations that allowed us to express what different people were eating. When we studied the toys in the toy store, we learned the verb *jouer* ("to play") so that we could talk about different people playing with their favorite toys.

Make It a Priority

As with any of the basic courses your child undertakes, the efficacy of the teaching is dependent, in part, on how regularly the subject matter is studied. When we began homeschooling seven years ago, we decided that studying French was as important as studying English grammar, mathematics, and reading. We didn't treat it as an enrichment subject, but as a core subject. This means that we devote time to its study all year round.

The time you devote to teaching each day doesn't have to exceed fifteen or twenty minutes, depending on the child's age. Listening to an audiotape with focus, practicing key phrases, orally conjugating simple verbs, singing a song, or saying prayers in the foreign language can all constitute a day's work. We strive to practice at least four days each week through all seasons, including summer vacation. We often spend twenty minutes three days a week and one half-hour once a week to review all new material, as well as prior lessons. Since my husband and I aren't fluent in French and since our children don't hear the language spoken by others, we find it critical to keep immersing them in the French language through their studies and by incorporating it into our everyday conversation. We believe the benefits — present and future — make this effort well worth it.

"In the beginning was the Word,
and the Word was with God,
and the Word was God."

John 1:1

Learning Geography Through the Missions

Laurie Navar Gill

"Go out into the whole world and preach the Gospel," our Lord told His disciples before he ascended to heaven. Since that time, the missionary effort has been at the heart of the Christian endeavor, as Christ's followers took his message from the Middle East, to North Africa and the continent of Europe, to Asia, to the New World, and to the remotest ends of the earth. That effort continues, with much of the world yet to embrace the gospel. In other parts of the world where Christianity was once the pillar of civilization, other creeds dominate to the point where the Church is actively persecuted.

There is much to do if we are to obey our Lord's missionary command. Therefore, geography is a natural study in the Catholic homeschool. It prepares our children for mission work, whether they grow up to be priests, religious, or laypersons, at home or abroad. All Catholics are obliged to be a part of the missionary effort of the Church. Through our prayers, our material support, and our obedience, and especially if we're actually called to go out to mission work, every Catholic must take responsibility for seeing that the gospel is preached everywhere.

This mission endeavor is the starting point for geography study in my homeschool, but it isn't the ending point. I have other learning objectives in geography as well. I want my children to have an easy familiarity with maps. I want them to have a general idea of the locations of nations, cities, and natural features they encounter in literature, history, and on the news. I want them to understand differences and similarities in cultures and to be able to make the connection between the geographical features of a place and the events that happen there. With Christ's command and these goals, we've built a geography course that is virtually limitless in its scope and is truly multicultural.

Our family has greatly enjoyed studying geography in a co-op. Initially, my motivation for co-oping had much less to do with taking on a particular subject than with providing a group learning experience for my children. I wanted them to participate in a structured class where they could learn give-and-take with other students, how to sit still and raise their hands, and all those other skills so important in life but not essential to homeschooling. As I considered what we would study in a co-op, it didn't take long for me to realize how geography could also help us to lead our children to a deeper appreciation of their duties as Christians in the world.

At the time we started, my family had recently moved from a diverse urban neighborhood to the affluent, homogenous outer suburbs. In no time at all, my children observed that we were "poor" because, for example, they were the only children on the street who didn't drive battery-operated toy cars. In a situation like this, I think it's very important to be able to put things in perspective!

We structured our mission/geography co-op to support several objectives:

• To participate in the missionary work of evangelizing the world through prayer, sacrifice, and raising financial support.

• To promote sensitivity to the needs of less fortunate people in our community and understanding of our personal responsibility for social justice.

• To teach the countries, capitals, and major physical features of the world.

• To provide practice for study, research, project planning, writing, and presenting.

• To teach class preparation and personal responsibility for assignments and deadlines.

• To provide fun and to glorify God through respectful interaction and giving our best effort.

The format of our club is very simple. It can be easily implemented with any group of children. Our participants have ranged from first grade to high school. We meet nine times a year, with an introductory meeting, a class devoted to each of the continents, and a final party to close the year. The monthly meetings begin with a Rosary, in which we pray for the needs of the entire world. After the Rosary, we collect dues. The children are encouraged to work to raise money to support a child we sponsor through a Catholic social-service agency. After that, the students take a quiz.

The quiz is based on a set of worksheets I provide for the children at the beginning of the year. I've used a number of resources for this purpose. In recent years, we've been attacking the very thorough book *Geographic Literacy,* by Pat Rischar Haroz (published by Walch). In past years, we've worked from *The Continents: Puzzles for Learning World Geography,* by Jeanne and Arnold Cheyney (GoodYear Books) and *U.S. and World Map Skills* (Instructional Fair). Each of these resources provides a different take on the study of the continents, so even children who come back from year to year learn something new each time.

At the beginning of the year, the children are asked to solicit pledges for their quiz grades. This is one way of raising money. I, as their teacher, have sponsored all the children for a penny a point, so when they receive 100 percent, I contribute a dollar to our sponsored child. Extra credit is always offered to students who name saints hailing from the particular continent we're studying. As you can imagine, I give lots of extra credit when we study Europe or the Middle East! (So far, no one has managed to come up with a saint from the continent of Antarctica.)

After the quiz, each child makes a five-minute presentation on some aspect of the continent we're studying. The work ranges from maps and models to costumed readings and country reports. Since geography encompasses culture, language, and history as well as place, we always have a very wide range of interesting presentations, usually accompanied by projects.

The monthly co-op meetings are but a small part of the work that the children actually put in. Between meetings, they have to study their maps, do enough reading on the continent under study to choose a topic for their presentation, and then research and prepare their talk. To participate fully, the children will need to study geography almost daily.

One very important aspect of successful co-oping in Catholic homeschool groups is to have meaningful experiences for younger siblings. Geography makes very good subject matter for preschoolers, I've found. Babies and toddlers are usually looked after by a couple of mothers, but all those old enough to work together, but too young to sit in on the class, have been invited to join an international cooking class. They chop fruits, shell nuts, knead bread, and always turn out a delightful treat that their older brothers and sisters gratefully sample at the end of class. It has been a delicious format.

Our first club has grown to six active groups meeting in the St. Louis area. I believe this format, which begins with prayer, gives concrete assistance to the poor, and studies the world that our Lord has charged us with evangelizing, can be of great value to any Catholic homeschooling effort.

☞

Here are addresses for two mission organizations. CFCA does child sponsorship, and CWM is the Legion of Christ's missionary and relief apostolate.

Christian Foundation for Children and Aging
One Elmwood Ave.
Kansas City, KS 66103
(800) 875-6564

Catholic World Mission
33 Rossotto Dr.
Hamden, CT 06514

"Religion must not be taught to youth only during certain hours, but the entire system of education must be permeated with the sense of Christian piety. If this is lacking, if this holy spirit does not penetrate and inflame the souls of teacher and pupil, small benefits will be derived from any other sort of education; instead damage will be done."

Pope Leo XIII, *Militantis Ecclesiae*

Teaching Civic Duty

Maureen Wittmann

Because we have the ability to take the real world and make it our classroom, we homeschoolers have the unique opportunity to teach our children about the political process firsthand. We should not hesitate to give credit for such nontraditional coursework. One Carnegie unit or credit consists of 150 hours of class time. By keeping track of volunteer hours, we can give our children credit for civics or government when working on a pro-life initiative or a political campaign.

Teens who are developing their worldview need to learn to discern the issues and their proponents. Getting to know a candidate personally by working on his campaign will give the teen incredible insight into what motivates that candidate, which issues are most important to him, what sacrifices he has made in order to run for office, and more. If working on a ballot initiative, the student has the opportunity to see how such an initiative is brought to the people, the petition drive to get the initiative on the ballot in the first place, the organization required to get the issue recognized in the media, and the marketing savvy required to influence voters.

A thesis paper can be assigned to address these topics at the end of the campaign.

Even small children can benefit from being involved in the political process. Young children can fold flyers, lick stamps, and sort mailings. They can be pulled in a wagon to put flyers in neighbors' doors and ride in the family minivan to deliver yard signs. These activities will prompt wonderful discussions. Children will see firsthand how important it is not only to vote, but to be educated on the issues. They will be able to see so clearly the importance of having leadership that is moral and virtuous.

I've found that people are more open to a candidate's message when you're pulling a wagon full of children. I'd like to think this is because my children are so beautiful, but I have to admit that it's true universally. In fact, I've found that people will often base their voting decision on the visitation of a candidate or their volunteers.

Once, while canvassing a neighborhood, I noticed that someone had my candidate's yard sign right next to another candidate (in a different race) of a completely opposing viewpoint. I asked the homeowner about this, and she said that both candidates had visited her door and both were "so very nice." She based her voting decision on the personality of the candidate visiting her door. As sad as this is, it's reality and must be recognized when campaigning. Go out, meet your neighbors, ask them to put up a yard sign, ask for their vote, and, most important, be personable.

We live in a country where we're free to take part in the political process, a freedom that people all over the world have died to attain. For this reason, my children are absolutely fascinated by China. This began when we were sending homemade rosaries to Chinese missionaries, and it grew when we studied Ancient China in our homeschool. Learning of the political and religious struggles in China has inspired my children to become more involved in the political process here in our own country.

Look for occasions to talk about our country and government. Dinnertime can provide many opportunities to discuss political topics. One thing I insist upon in my home is that everyone be on time for dinner, especially my husband. It's incredible how much my children learn from dinnertime banter. I was reminded of this once while attending a Confirmation party for the two daughters of a dear friend. This friend's sister was a big proponent of President Clinton and asked my children, "Don't you love President Clinton?" (This was before the Monica Lewinsky scandal.) My son, six at the time, put his hands on his hips, looked her square in the eye, and exclaimed, "Don't you know he's selling us out to China?!" I didn't teach that to my son; he picked it up from the political debates that occasionally take place at our dinner table between my husband and me.

I know of one family that keeps a globe and dictionary close to the dining room. Through their example, I've taken the initiative to get up from the table and look up a definition in the dictionary or find a location on the globe when discussing world events at the dinner table.

I don't allow my little ones to read the newspaper, as I'm not ready for them to be *that* worldly. However, they do see me reading the paper, and I tell them of important news, local as well as national and worldwide. I also write letters to the editor on occasion and make sure to point out my letters when published. It's my hope that this example will make them comfortable in expressing their political and religious views in the public square as they grow into adults.

Volunteering on a campaign provides a multitude of lessons. Even the simple task of folding and stuffing flyers has educational benefits. Volunteers may be instructed to fold flyers in such a way that the candidate's face is seen upon the opening of the envelope — a lesson in marketing. Stuffing hundreds of flyers in envelopes is a lesson in patience and work ethic. Sorting the stuffed flyers by zip code so that the candidate can receive a pre-sorted postal rate is a lesson in thrift. Just witnessing all the details that a campaign entails teaches our children that the important issues of life are not easily tackled. The most important lesson of all is that of knowing that we as individuals can indeed make a difference in our world.

"Freedom is a fragile thing and is never more than one generation away from extinction. It is not ours by inheritance; it must be fought for and defended constantly by each generation, for it comes only once to a people. Those who have known freedom, and then lost it, have never known it again."

Ronald Reagan

Chapter 3

High School

"There's appearing on the horizon of education a dim but very definite and most promising light. The light is coming from the homes of families that have placed their staff in the soil and given notice: This far and no farther.

"Home education is the clearest indication that the new day is coming in America and a new age of wonder in God's creation is opening before us in the third millennium."

Francis Crotty
Implementation of Ignation Education in the Home

High School Literary Analysis Made Easy

Carol Maxwell

Any parent can guide his child through literary analysis, even if he never has read — and likely never will read — the book in question. With a bachelor's degree in English, and as a production editor for Harcourt Brace Jovanovich Publishers, I might be considered qualified to teach literary analysis. Yet, any other parent can do it just as well as I do, if not better.

Knowing how to analyze a work of fiction prepares a student well for liberal-arts colleges that use the Great Books as, or as part of, their curriculum, such as Thomas Aquinas College (TAC) in California. My son has a goal to finish high school one year early and attend TAC. Thus, I knew that he'd need to start practicing how to pick a book apart in order to grasp its underlying meaning. Each time a student does this, he becomes more adept at determining the author's purpose in writing the literary work. I usually assign my son one book analysis per month.

Let's start with the prerequisites for your high-schooler. He should have a basic knowledge of English grammar: parts of speech, sentence structure, and punctuation. Second, he should be able to read and understand high-school-level novels and must have completed either creative writing or research or some other kind of nonfiction writing in past years. That's it. Now you're ready to go.

Next you need to find classic books. There are great lists of high school literature in Laura M. Berquist's *Designing Your Own Classical Curriculum* (Third Edition, Ignatius Press) and on Seton Home Study's web site (www.setonhome.org). For my son's ninth grade, I chose an easy English version of *Beowulf* (Bethlehem Books), *The Red Badge of Courage*, *Twenty Thousand Leagues Under the Sea*, and a variety of Shakespeare plays, to name a few.

Now it's time to decide the assigned topic for the book that your student will be reading. It's important to inform him of the topic before he reads the book. If you do, he'll be able to mark certain passages as he's reading that will serve to support the theory he develops about the book, making it much easier to write when the time comes. Even though I'm somewhat familiar with most of the books, I still rely heavily on reference material to determine which topics will be appropriate for a book analysis. (There are some study guides available for selected titles, but the ones I've seen are cumbersome and not conducive to helping your student come up with original ideas to support his paper.)

My favorite resource, and the most convenient one, is the Internet. I look up the title of the book on a search engine, and then glean topics for an analysis by reading about the book on the websites. Most times, many ideas for analyses are specifically spelled out, so all I have to do is print out the page and let my son choose what his topic will be. It's best to offer at least two themes from which your high-schooler may choose. If he's undecided, he may choose more than one and make his final decision after he has read the book. Good websites for research are www.novelguide.com, www.ipl.org, www.gradesaver.com (click on "Classic Notes"), and www.sparknotes.com (click on "Study Guides").

Novelguide.com contains literary analyses for most of the classic novels and Shakespearian plays. Its library ranges from Chaucer to Ernest Hemingway and offers novel summaries (real handy for the busy homeschool mom), character profiles (which I like to give my student before he reads the book), metaphor analyses, top ten quotations, and author biographies. The other two sites are similar in content.

I know that many homeschooling families, however, have quite intentionally chosen not to have access to the Internet. (My husband and I insist upon a server with strong parental controls.) Your local library and used-book stores are fantastic resources. It might sound funny, but the best information on classics may be gleaned from Cliffs Notes. This series was banned in my college English courses because it contains chapter summaries and analyses for most books. However, it's perfect for Mom to read and use to create assignments. Also, if your student has trouble understanding a writer's style, you might present the Cliffs Notes, or resources such as Norton Critical Editions, to him at your discretion.

Almost every classic work of fiction has been analyzed in some published book. Your public or college library should contain at least one of these books, written by different authors, for most of the literature that you assign. Just search the title of the novel on the library's database, and resources should start to appear. It takes only a few minutes to skim parts of these books to get a feel for the plot of the novel and what you might assign as a choice of topics.

After your student finishes the book, and before he begins the literary analysis, it might be helpful to discuss the book with him. You might ask questions based on what you've read in your reference material. It helps to ensure that you know he's capable of stringing his ideas together to form an intelligible argument to support his topic. He should quote some of the passages that he marked in the book, noting the page numbers, to show that the text supports his opinion. The process is very subjective, and one passage might be used for a variety of themes. However, if the quotation makes sense in your child's paper, and you can follow his logic, he's well on his way to becoming analytical in his approach. Tell him that he should just write a draft for you to review. Thus, if you and he decide that changes are necessary, he won't be crushed because some of his hard work has to be redone.

My son's first high school paper was to analyze the religious symbolism in *Beowulf*. He wrote about three-quarters of a type-written page that tied in various Christian symbols from the book, and it was quite good. However, I had neglected to ask him to weave the plot into his paper. By this I do not mean synopsizing the story in a "book report" but including enough information to let someone unfamiliar with the book follow the analysis. Thus, you want to stress that within the analysis itself, your child should weave the plot, characterization, and setting in a concise, yet comprehensive, manner. He can accomplish the weaving by adding clauses after the name of characters introduced in the paper.

When the first draft is complete, read it thoroughly before you discuss it. You needn't be familiar with the book in reference to the topic; the paper should be self-explanatory. If the analysis seems to have gaps, or is otherwise confusing or unsupported, that fact will be clear as you read the paper. You'll then have the opportunity to ask your student questions about the book and his chosen theme, especially if you don't know the answers. He should be able to see, through his discussion with you, how his intended audience might not understand his theories as well as he does. In that case, he might want to go back and use more text references to substantiate his topic, or write better transitional sentences, or add a simple explanation of something he has presented. He might need to dig a little deeper to find a meaning for the words and symbols that the author uses. His ideas should come across clearly by the time his final draft is handed in.

If you have a reluctant writer, don't fret. Remember that your objective isn't to have your student read and expertly analyze every work of classic literature in his high school years. Your goal should be to teach him how to become analytical in general. If you're able to convey this skill, through conversations about books or by any other means, he'll be able to analyze any work of literature when the time comes. If you need to hold his hand through the first six months or so by directing him through every book analysis step by step, you'll be teaching him a valuable tool. All you need is a little information about the book. You accomplish the rest by asking him questions and having him find the answers within the assigned work.

It comes in very handy at this point if you've taught your child obedience in the past. Some of the work is frustrating, but for the most part, you'll see lights come on in your student's eyes when he finally realizes, "Oh, that's what the author meant to say!"

"Whatever your task, work heartily,
as serving the Lord and not men."
Colossians 3:23

Apologetics:
Sacraments, Service, and Study

Alicia Van Hecke

It doesn't generally cause much of a reaction when I tell people that I'm homeschooling my children. American society is becoming accustomed to the idea of homeschooling, perhaps even accepting of it. As the discussion progresses, however (particularly if people start inquiring into my "qualifications" to homeschool), I usually manage to garner a bit of surprise when I explain that I was homeschooled myself for all of my high school years. Although the concept of homeschooling has become quite familiar, many people haven't considered the long-term result of homeschooling; that is, homeschooled children growing up and entering the adult world. Throwing out this tidbit is always a little fun, because I can almost see the conclusions forming in their heads, especially if they've known me for a while. "Wow, she's pretty normal. I would not have expected that she was homeschooled." It would be fun to answer, "Yes, we homeschoolers do go on to lead completely normal lives!"

Humor aside, Catholic homeschooled teens have the chance to develop — physically, academically, and spiritually — without the crushing pressures most teens face today. Although this prolonged preservation of innocence during the early years is positive and healthy, eventually the focus changes to developing maturity and preparing to meet the challenges of the real world. Some of the greatest tasks for which homeschooled teens must be prepared are keeping their faith in a society that will challenge it in a multitude of ways, learning to work with others well enough to have a positive impact, and having a solid foundation from which to draw on answers and arguments to question those who might be persuaded to the truth. There are three key parts to building this foundation.

The Sacraments

The primary ingredient in providing a solid formation is God's grace. The font of his grace is found in the sacraments. Allow the sacraments to be very accessible to your teen, and provide a good example yourself, particularly in frequent reception of the Holy Eucharist. The sacrament of Confirmation is the sacrament of apologetics. The gifts of the Holy Spirit (wisdom, understanding, counsel, fortitude, knowledge, piety, and fear of the Lord) are the exact tools needed to share the Faith with others successfully. Ideally, this sacrament should be received before the high school years. According to official Church teaching, if the child is sufficiently prepared, the sacrament cannot be refused him, even if he is not of the standard age as dictated by the particular diocese (see Chapter 9, "Homeschooling, Canon Law, and the Right to Receive the Sacraments," by Pete Vere).

Service

Next to prayer and the sacraments, I highly recommend providing ample opportunities for volunteer work, particularly in Catholic or pro-life settings. Service projects help build up self-esteem during the sensitive teen years, allow teens to begin understanding the reality of problems in the "real world" while being part of the solution, and provide valuable opportunities for interacting with and learning to understand others. Although it's healthy for teens to have a little experience in a broad range of activities, allowing them to begin specializing and focusing on certain areas of interest can blossom into long-term vocation or career choices. Be sure that competent and reliable adults supervise activities.

My own high school/homeschool years provided time and flexibility for many interesting and beneficial works of service that wouldn't have otherwise been possible. I was involved with the Junior Legion of Mary at our parish, distributed literature for pro-life political candidates, sang in several church choirs, coached children's soccer, and was active in our church youth group. While not directly relating to apologetics, some of these activities afforded some interesting conversations with those who were unsure of Church teaching on issues such as contraception and women priests. Others allowed me to work side by side with faithful Catholic adults who became mentors.

One especially interesting project I enjoyed during my high school years was running a Catholic BBS (the equivalent of a modern-day website). It was a branch of Catholic Information Network, founded by my sister before my senior year of high school. It allowed me to try some simple apologetics in a safe and non-threatening environment. It also kept my age from being an issue to those with whom I was conversing.

Other service project ideas and volunteer opportunities for teens include candy-striping at a local hospital, volunteering at a pregnancy help center or a St. Vincent de Paul store, assisting in a preschool or CCD class, visiting convalescent homes, tutoring, serving at church dinners or soup kitchens, and assisting an elderly neighbor or relative with housework. My mother met most of her contacts for these sorts of activities while on pro-life marches.

Basic Catechetics
I can't overemphasize the importance of reading the Holy Bible, especially the Gospels. What more important story could we

study and reflect upon than what God did and said when he became man upon the earth? Next, the lives of the saints provide living, breathing examples of imperfect people who struggled against temptation and their fallen nature, cooperated with the grace of God, and lived the gospel in their own lives. I can think of no better heroes for our children to admire.

Basic knowledge of Church teachings is essential. I highly recommend the *Catechism of the Catholic Church* (CCC), which is reasonably accessible to homeschooled Catholic teens and parents working side by side. There will be quite a bit of unfamiliar vocabulary, so I recommend the revised edition, which includes a helpful glossary, as well as the finalized translation. Although the CCC wasn't around when I was in high school, I've used it successfully in leading a study group for mothers, and impressing upon them, some of whom had taught in parish religious programs, what the Church really teaches and why it makes sense. A solid background in the study of history and religion will also acquaint teens with the most common myths and misunderstandings that others have about the Catholic Church, and provide plenty of ammunition to correct these errors.

Recommended Books

The Holy Bible, especially the Gospels

The Catechism of the Catholic Church

The Catholic Encyclopedia of 1910: www.newadvent.org

On the Incarnation, by St. Athanasius

The Autobiography of St. Thérèse of Lisieux (Image)

The Curé d'Ars: St. Jean-Marie-Baptiste Vianney, by Abbé Francis Trochu (TAN)

A Place to Hide: True Stories of Holocaust Rescues, by Jayne Pettit (Scholastic)

Stories of the Saints, Volumes 3 and 4, by Elaine Woodfield (Catholic Heritage Curricula)

A Treasury of Catholic Wisdom, by Fr. John Hardon, S.J. (Ignatius)

How the Reformation Happened and other works by Hilaire Belloc (TAN)

Surprised by Truth 2 and *3*, by Patrick Madrid, ed. (Sophia Institute Press)

Faith and Reason, by Schmidt and Perkins (Sophia Institute Press)

Rome Sweet Home, by Scott and Kimberly Hahn (Ignatius Press)

Websites

Biblical Evidence for Catholicism: www.biblicalcatholic.com

Catholic Information Network: www.cin.org

Catholic Answers: www.catholic.com

Catholic Educator's Resource Center: www.catholiceducation.org

Nazareth Resource Library: www.cin.org/users/james

High School Catechisms

Fr. John Laux's High School Religion Series (TAN)

Our Quest for Happiness (Lepanto Press)

Catholicism and Reason Series (C. R. Publications)

Didache High School Textbook Series (Midwest Theological Forum)

History and Literature

Aside from basic religious studies, history and literature should be a high priority for general formation and developing maturity. History is the ultimate story of the battle between good and evil, of the consequences of sin, and of the influence of God and those who love him upon the world. We gain valuable experience and perspective from the safety of our own homes by learning from those who have gone before us. The student learns to understand many specific errors, from the foolishness of Napoleon's invasion of Russia to the temptation to think that we can really be more Catholic than the Pope.

Until I had an exceptional history teacher in the seventh grade in a Catholic school, I found history as boring as most people find it today. During my homeschool years, I was introduced to excellent texts and stories that made history come alive and that began to give me a greater sense of what the Catholic Church really is. I was able to slow down and delve deeper into topics of particular interest.

Like history, literature allows us to consider the consequences of good and evil, and reflect on the big questions that challenge our lives. It also lets us look at something from a different perspective — by "walking in someone else's shoes" for a while. This is particularly important for apologetics. Most people won't become interested in the Faith just because someone gives them a few good books to read. We have to understand and perhaps even sympathize with their present situation to help them remove their impediments to the Faith and gradually progress in the right direction.

By the high school years, the value of literature goes well beyond the "moral of the story." Although stories that provide an occasion of sin, especially during the sensitive teen years, should be avoided, books that cover serious topics should be read. Even books that don't directly provide all the right answers should be considered, since these can lead students to find answers to tough questions by looking to Catholic teaching. Reading imperfect books also develops the ability to think critically and discern truth from fiction in what we read, particularly what comes to us from the media.

Recommended Books

Literature

Father Brown Mysteries and other books by G. K. Chesterton (Penguin)

The House of the Seven Gables and other books by Nathaniel Hawthorne

Kristen Lavransdatter, by Sigrid Undset (parental guidance recommended)

The Lord of the Rings and other books by J.R.R. Tolkien

Maria Chapdelaine, by Louis Hemon (Lepanto)

Pride and Prejudice and other books by Jane Austen

The Shadow of the Bear and other books by Regina Doman (Bethlehem)

The Space Trilogy, *The Screwtape Letters*, and other books by C. S. Lewis

A Tale of Two Cities and other books by Charles Dickens

To Kill a Mockingbird, by Harper Lee

The Works of Shakespeare

History and Biography

Cheaper by the Dozen and *Belles on Their Toes*, by the Gilbraiths

1917: Red Banners, White Mantle and other books by Anne and Warren Carroll (TAN/Christendom Press)

The Quiet Light, by Louis de Wohl

Death Comes for the Archbishop, by Willa Cather

The Ides of April and other books by Mary Ray (Bethlehem)

Joan of Arc (Ignatius) and other books by Mark Twain

Karen and *With Love from Karen*, by Marie Killeleia

My Heart Lies South, by Elizabeth Borton de Trevino
   (Bethlehem)

Our Lady of Fatima (Image) and other books by William
   Thomas Walsh

The Scarlet Pimpernel, by Baroness Orczy

The Shadow of His Wings, by Fr. Gereon Goldman (Ignatius)

The Song at the Scaffold, by Gertrude von le Fort (Sophia)

The Story of the Trapp Family Singers, by Maria Augusta Trapp

Uncle Tom's Cabin, by Harriet Beecher Stowe

Witness to Hope, by George Weigel (Cliff Street Books)

Marriage and Life Issues

Most of the questions that Catholics face from the outside world concern Church teachings on marriage and life issues. "Why can't Catholics divorce someone if they really don't love each other anymore?" "Can't a woman use contraception if another pregnancy would be life threatening?" "Why can't we let terminally ill patients choose physician-assisted suicide?" It would be valuable for young adults to be familiar with the stages of development of an unborn baby, the natural reasons for avoiding artificial contraception, the success rates and basic workings of Natural Family Planning, and so on. I'm not talking about *sex education* here. The focus needn't be on the details of the marital act, but on the dignity and beauty of God's gift of human life. Your children might save many lives and souls through simple conversations on these topics if they're duly prepared.

Recommended Resources

Faithful for Life, by Fr. Paul Marx (Human Life International)

Familiaris Consortio, Pope John Paul II

Humanae Vitae, by Pope Paul VI

Love and Family, by Mercedes Arzu Wilson

Our Character, Our Future, by Alan Keyes (Zondervan Publishing)

Pope Paul VI Institute: www.popepaulvi.com

Naturally, a strong academic foundation is a vital prerequisite for the studies mentioned in this essay. Particularly helpful are mathematics, diagramming, intellectual discussions, extensive reading, foreign-language study (especially Latin), and even playing chess. These develop analytical thinking skills, which are critical for grasping complex arguments, for making important distinctions, and for general discernment. These skills can be further enhanced in the high school years through the study of logic and philosophy.

Staying Faithful in Tough Times

Modern times have seen a great deal of confusion arise among Catholics, many of whom have left the Church for Protestant denominations, schismatic or dissident groups, atheism, the New Age movement, and so on. Recent scandals in the Church have only fanned the flames. The Devil wants to attack the Church from all sides and uses whatever tactics it takes to draw people away from the true Church. Historical perspective shows us that the Church has survived many great crises in the past and provides us with heroes to emulate, allowing us to struggle through the difficulties of our own day with more courage and confidence. A strong faith and foundational preparation will help our children remain faithful through the challenges ahead.

Overall, we want our children to be aware of the evils of the world, while understanding that the Catholic Church provides reasonable solutions. We don't want to overwhelm them so that they lose their youthful optimism. Rather, we want them to develop a healthy sense of skepticism and caution as useful tools in a rough world. Homeschooling can provide an excellent foundation.

"There's little point in keeping children out of Hell
if you don't afford them the means of getting into Heaven.
So give them solid catechetics, strong preaching, good example,
healthful exercise, supervision in a general and determinant
way but not in each particular and, by all means, permitting
them the freedom of the good, dangerous books as well as
the dangerous games such as football or mountain climbing.
Given the state of man, some will break their necks and sin;
but in good Catholic families with common sense, the falls
should be few and the bodies and souls recoverable."

John Senior, *The Restoration of Christian Culture*

From High School to College

Barbara Little

Five years ago, our oldest son was busy filling out applications and writing essays for various colleges, with the hope of being accepted into the schools of his choice. The process was time-consuming, but relatively painless because we had benefitted from the experience of other homeschool families. They had taught us how to lay the groundwork for a smooth transition to college. I hope that the information here will provide the same guidance for you.

Many people who wouldn't hesitate to homeschool their younger children are understandably hesitant about teaching their high school children. They're afraid that they can't provide their teenage children with a strong foundation for their future. They're afraid that their children won't be accepted into college if they don't have an official diploma and transcript, or that their children might not be able to land a decent job without a certified high school diploma. Although these concerns are valid, they certainly can be overcome.

First, the parent and student must look at what direction the student's future will take. The following questions need to be asked:

- What career interests does he have?

- Is he interested in higher education or the military, or is he eager to join the job market right out of high school?

• If college is in his future, what type of college is he interested in?

• Is admittance into an Ivy League school important to the family?

• Does it matter whether the college is private or public, Catholic or secular, large or small?

• Is a community college an acceptable choice?

It's important to help your student set goals for his future. Not only short-term goals such as, "Which college do I want to attend?" but also "What vocation and profession do I want to pursue?" "Do I see marriage or a call to the religious life in my future?" It's important to explore all these issues with him while he's still under your roof and accessible to your guidance.

A first question frequently on parents' minds is whether to have the student obtain his GED (Graduation Equivalency Diploma). Generally the answer is no. The various branches of the military frown on the GED because they assume it means the student was unable to graduate from high school, and colleges seldom ask for a GED. Generally, the only time it makes sense to obtain a GED is when the student intends to go directly into the job market.

If your high school student is college-bound and you're wondering whether he, as a homeschooled student, will have a chance of being accepted at a good college, the answer is a resounding yes. Most college admissions departments have procedures specifically designed for homeschooled students. Many even have an admissions counselor assigned to homeschooled applicants. At a recent Senior Visit Day, the head of the admissions department at a prominent Catholic university was heard remarking to a homeschool parent that some colleges actually prefer homeschooled scholars because they excel in all areas: academically, socially, and morally.

If your student is enrolled in an accredited homeschool program or a satellite program, the college admissions process will be much the same as for a student graduating from a public or private high school. For those who choose a less conventional method of educating their children, the procedure can run smoothly if a few details are attended to. The most helpful resources we have found are published by Family Academy: *Homeschooling the High Schooler* and the corresponding workbook, *High School Your Way*, by Diana McAlister and Candice Oneschak.

To apply to a college or university, three things are necessary: a diploma, a transcript, and standardized test scores. By keeping records throughout your child's high school years, these documents will be easy to produce.

A diploma is simply a certificate that states that the student has satisfactorily met all the state requirements for graduation. This certificate may be obtained from a stationery supply store, or it may be designed on your home computer. But the piece of paper isn't so important; the records that support it are essential. Prior to the high school years, the homeschooling parent should contact the state Superintendent of Public Instruction to find out which subjects and credits are required for graduation. These are the minimum courses mandated by the state.

Many colleges have additional requirements for acceptance. For example, your state might require only two years of science for graduation, yet a college of engineering will surely require four years. Therefore, be sure to keep the state requirements and specific career-oriented requirements in mind as you plan your student's coursework for high school. Before the freshman year, draft an outline of which courses will be studied for each of the next four years to fulfill the necessary requirements for graduation, as well as to challenge your student's interests.

In addition to specific classes required, a certain number of credits will also be required by the state for graduation. Again, an individual college may require more than the state minimums. It isn't uncommon for the state to require only twenty credits for graduation, while many colleges require in excess of twenty-four. Each course will be assigned a certain number of credits based on the amount of time spent in the classroom. The most common credit measurement is the Carnegie unit. One Carnegie unit is 180 classroom hours, or 150 clock hours. It's simplest for a home-school to measure the hours with clock hours. For our purposes, then, one credit is equal to 150 hours of study.

Alternatively, a credit can be awarded when a certain quantity of work is completed. This is especially useful in mathematics, where a textbook is generally used. When the textbook has been satisfactorily completed, the credit is awarded. Of course, if 150 hours are completed, yet the student has not completed nearly what would be required in a classroom, it would be inappropriate to award the full credit. In this instance, a half-credit could be awarded.

It's important that we, as homeschooling parents, abide by the highest standards when issuing credits and grades, so that our in-tegrity as a group will never be questioned. If we arbitrarily award credits for incomplete coursework, the post-secondary community will eventually question the validity of our diplomas and make the admissions procedure more difficult.

As the high school years progress, your student should keep track of the coursework studied, the resources used, and the number of hours engaged in that study. Beginning in the eighth grade, you can have children practice tracking their hours and coursework, so that the habit is well established before they enter the critical high school years. The homeschooling parent should grade work as it's completed and keep a portfolio of some of the most significant work. This record will supply all the information needed to fill out the diploma and the transcript, and for figuring the grade point average (GPA). Keeping a sampling of work is also advisable, because some colleges will ask to see a portfolio of work by a homeschooled child.

Pre-college test scores are the single most important factor in the student's being accepted at the college of his choice. Every college determines which test or tests it will require and what the cut-off scores will be for admission. Begin no later than the freshman year to acclimate your student to the classroom environment for test-taking. Sign up for testing through your homeschool group or a local high school. The PLAN is preparation for the ACT (American College Testing), while the PSAT (Preliminary Scholastic Aptitude Test) is preparatory for the SAT. Either the PSAT or the PLAN can usually be taken in the fall of the sophomore year at a local high school. Each high school chooses which test or tests it will offer. The PSAT is commonly taken at the beginning of the junior year in preparation for the SAT in the spring of the junior year. The ACT can also be taken during the junior year, but more schools require the SAT for entrance. Therefore it's advisable to check with the colleges of your choice to determine which tests your child must take. Although many schools don't require the ACT or SATII, these can be helpful in proving a student's strength in a particular subject. Consequently they are recommended for those who apply to Ivy League schools or when proof of expertise in a certain subject is necessary.

Each college has a minimum standard for SAT or ACT scores. If the student's score falls below that level, he'll automatically be disqualified. To discover the cut-off point for various colleges, check a college guide, such as *Lovejoy's College Guide*. These guides can be found in the reference section of your local public library. They include other valuable information about college size, courses and majors offered, location, and quality of education as well.

After the junior-year coursework is completed, assemble a temporary transcript with your child. This will include a list of all the courses taken so far and courses the student plans to take in his senior year. For each course, list the year it was taken: freshman, sophomore, junior, or senior; the number of credits earned or to be earned; the grade received for those classes that have been completed; and the GPA. If a course hasn't yet been taken, you can write TBC (to be completed) in the column with the year and leave the grade column blank.

It's advisable, although not necessary, to include course descriptions. These are especially helpful in giving the college admissions department a sense of the quality of education your student received. Include in this description a listing of resources used in the class, and note outstanding projects completed, such as term papers.

In addition to the necessary ingredients for college acceptance, we found some additional skills that were helpful for our son to be successful in the college environment. Essay-writing, speed-reading, time management, and note-taking were prime among them. An excellent place to start is *Teaching Writing: Structure and Style*, by the Institute for Excellence in Writing (see Appendix A). Any speed-reading course from the library or local bookstore would be helpful. Have your child practice time management at home, and consider checking into resources produced for the business world. By using these materials, the student might also build his enthusiasm for goal-setting, which can optimize his time-management skills.

Note-taking can best be practiced by attending a community college or church lectures, or listening to teachings on audio-cassettes. Have your student practice recording the content of the lectures until he can choose easily between the important and unimportant details and can take notes quickly, concisely, and accurately. Taking a class at a local community college can also help the student build skills and confidence before embarking on a full-scale college career. Be aware, however, that any such course will be counted in the student's permanent college record. Therefore, the grade he receives is of utmost importance.

Alongside all the skills you're helping your child to develop, an understanding of the worldly distractions offered on a college campus will be necessary for certain students who are not worldly-wise. More college freshmen fail because of unmonitored drinking at college than because of any other single factor. We must make our students aware of the pitfalls, so they won't fall prey to the temptations.

When you have all the ingredients necessary for graduation, it will be time to apply to the colleges of your student's choice. Applications can be sent early in the senior year, and in some cases, the earlier the application is sent, the better chance the student has to gain acceptance and to secure substantial scholarship money.

Of course, no discussion on college is complete until the issue of finances is discussed. The cost of a post-secondary education can be staggering. Although the local community college might cost only $3,000 per year and a state university in the neighborhood of $6,000, a private institution could cost $25,000 to $40,000, or more, per year. Once you understand the game, these figures aren't quite as insurmountable as they seem at first. There's a lot of scholarship money and financial aid available. In fact, the cost of a particular school should never be an initial reason for not applying to a school. In the case of our second son, it cost virtually the same for him to go to a private university nearby, known to have an excellent engineering school, as it would have cost to go to the local community college, because of the generous offer of scholarship money from the university. There are also private scholarships available for unusual situations, from students with asthma or disabilities to minorities to athletes to journalists.

Therefore, don't automatically assume that your student can't afford his first choice. Check out *How to Go to College Almost for*

Free, by Ben Kaplan. Also, make friends with your local high school guidance counselor, who can be an excellent source of information on scholarships. Most high schools have a scholarship bulletin board and a file cabinet with extensive information on opportunities. If your student is enthusiastic and presents himself well, the guidance counselor might even become your ally in gaining scholarship money. Our local counselor actually called and asked if she could recommend our son for a state scholarship. We couldn't refuse!

Not only are scholarships readily available, but there's also a lot of federal financial assistance for lower- and middle-income families. These monies come in the form of grants that don't need to be repaid and loans that do. The loans will either be the type that accrues interest during the college years or the type that doesn't, based on the need that the family demonstrates. The official form for applying for financial aid is called the Free Application for Federal Student Aid, or FAFSA. It should be filled out and sent out as early as possible after January 1 of the student's senior year. All colleges use this form in determining the financial-aid packet for your child.

Just as in filling out the IRS 1040 form, on which most figures for the FAFSA are based, some strategic moves can be implemented. To maximize the aid you receive, think ahead and plan. You might wish to defer a cash payout on an investment until after January 1, or you might want to take a loss before the end of the filing year. Ideally, your child should make some money, but not more than $1,600, as beyond this point financial aid is decreased (check for current dollar figure). If you and your child hold mutual assets, such as education bonds, these may be better placed in your name (check with your tax preparer). Parents are expected to have assets, while assets in the student's name will decrease the amount of financial aid granted to the child. Of course, all of these strategies must be within the law and within the realm of right conscience.

Following the path set forth by our friends, our second son was also accepted into a fine university. Once again, the process was time-consuming, but painless. Our oldest daughter is now looking toward her college future. If we do this a few more times, we might even come to enjoy the college-application process.

EDITORS' NOTE: For a college-prep timetable and samples of a transcript and record sheets, please send a large manila SASE with $0.83 postage to Wooly Lamb Publishing, P.O. Box 411, Dickinson, ND 58602.

"Could I climb to the highest place in Athens,
I would lift my voice and proclaim,
'Fellow citizens, why do you turn and scrape
every stone to gather wealth,
and take so little care of your children,
to whom one day you must relinquish it all?'"

Socrates

Job-Search Skills
for Teens and Graduates

Maureen Wittmann

As Catholic homeschoolers, we know that our children's education goes beyond "job training." We're raising our children to be
saints and scholars, not just future members of the workforce.
With that said, it's also important to teach our children how to
find and attain a job. For it isn't enough to have the appropriate
qualifications; a person must be able to convince an employer that
he's the best person for the job. I've seen wonderfully talented people struggle in job searches because they couldn't properly market
themselves.

Some will not need job-search skills as much as others, since
they might be called to the life of a religious, or perhaps to be a
stay-at-home mother. However, they're still good skills to learn,
even for those individuals who might need to work a summer job
while in college or run an at-home business someday.

The following is taken from a seminar that I give for homeschooled teenagers. Before embarking on my current career of
homeschooling mother, I spent more than ten years in human resource and in payroll management. It's based on this experience
that I offer the following advice, addressed to teens and recent
graduates.

Finding Your Vocation

Before embarking on a job search, you must first prayerfully ask for God's guidance in your career decision. Open your mind and heart to his call. Lead a virtuous life so that your mind and heart will be clear enough to hear the call. If your soul is muddled with sin, God's voice will also be muddled.

I suggest that you read *Life Work: Finding God's Purpose for Your Life,* by Rick Sarkisian (Ignatius Press), which is also available on video.

Preparing for Your Vocation

Once you've determined your vocation, you need to take the appropriate steps to attain that goal. You need to be prepared to make the sacrifices necessary to get the education that your future vocation requires.

Search out apprenticeships and co-op programs. These give you the opportunity to learn on the job while you attend college or trade school. Many such programs offer tuition assistance.

If your chosen vocation requires a college degree, consider taking a part-time job while in school. With work experience under your belt, you'll have an easier time finding a position after you graduate. If you're working toward a degree in accounting, search for a position as a data-entry clerk in an accounting department. If human resources is your goal, answer that want ad for a file clerk in the personnel department. If engineering is your future, ask your neighbor if there are any entry-level positions available at his engineering firm.

Mentors are very important. They can provide you with insights that you can't find in books or in school. They can share their enthusiasm for the job and why they continue in their particular profession. They can also lead you to resources you might not otherwise find, such as co-op programs, the best companies to work for, and the best schools for training.

If you don't have a mentor in mind, search one out. For example, if you're studying to be a civil engineer, be bold and call an engineering company and ask to speak to the person in charge. Tell him that you aspire to work in his chosen field and you'd like to take him out to lunch. Once you have a lunch date, spend your time together listening. You won't learn anything if you do all the talking. Instead, ask questions, and let the interviewer do all of the talking. Once lunch is over, pick up the tab, and, if all went well, set up another date.

The most important tool in preparing for your vocation is prayer. Take time every day to ask the Lord to guide you and direct you in your vocation. Ask him to provide you with the resources necessary to follow his will in your life. Most important, ask him to help you spread the joy of being a Catholic Christian within your chosen vocation.

Resume-Writing

Find the most recent book on resume-writing in the library to help you develop your resume style. The most important thing is to keep it neat and simple, holding it to one page. The average human-resource manager spends less than a minute scanning a resume. Use bullets and *action* words at the beginning of each sentence to grab the attention of the reader — words such as *facilitated*, *managed*, and *directed*. Keep the sentences short. You can discuss details in an interview. Leave off salary and references. "References Available Upon Request" should be typed at the bottom of your resume. If a want ad requests salary history, you can put that information in your cover letter. Prepare a separate sheet with references to have available in case the request is made during an interview.

When you mail a resume, it should always be accompanied by a cover letter. Keep the letter short, neat, and simple. Triple-check spelling and grammar. When I was in the position of hiring personnel, I'd cringe when I saw cover letters with statements such as "I am detail-*orientated*."

Use matching stationery. Your cover letters, resume, and envelopes should all be made up of the same paper and use the same font.

Treat your resume as a living document. Even if you're in a job that fulfills your every dream, keep your resume up to date. You never know what life will throw at you, and you should be prepared. Many years ago, I worked for a company that I loved, and I planned to work there forever. Unfortunately, I came into the office one day to find that this company was taken over by a conglomerate located out of town, and suddenly I was out of work. Treating my resume as a living document saved me an enormous amount of time in my immediate job search.

Making a Job Search

There are three ways to find job openings.

• The first and least effective is *cold-calling:* mailing a resume even though there are no indications of a current job opening. This is done when you wish to target a certain company — whether for its great pay and benefits, or for its reputation for hiring the best of the best, or for whatever reason — and there's no immediate need for a new job.

Research is fundamental if you're cold-calling. Find out all you can about that company. Find out the names of the human-resource manager and the head of the department you wish to work in. Find out what type of experience and education they look for in their personnel. Perhaps find a mentor in that company.

Follow-up is essential. A resume received cold will likely be filed away and promptly forgotten. Call and ask if your resume was received. Ask whether the company regularly hires individuals with your experience. Ask if they have any openings that fit your experience or if they expect any openings in the future. Ask if there's anything you can do to improve your desirability as a job candidate.

• *Want ads* are the next way to find job openings. Sunday is the day to search the want ads in your newspaper. Ads that ask for a reply by letter should be answered immediately. Prepare your cover letter and resume so that they can be mailed on Monday.

Monday is also the day to answer ads by telephone. If you wait until Tuesday, you might very well lose the opportunity to interview for the position. Before making your phone calls, dress as you would if you were calling on the prospective employer in person. Years of experience has taught me that this is vital in giving you an edge over your competition. If you're dressed in your robe and slippers, it will come through in your voice that you're casual about this opportunity. Dress professionally, and your voice will reflect your professionalism to the person on the other end of the line.

Keep records of the ads you answer. A simple notebook will do for this task. Tape the answered want-ad to a page, then write in the date, your action (mailed resume or called), any response, and your follow-up. This is important for several reasons. If the same want ad runs for several weeks or in more than one newspaper, you'll have a record showing that you already answered that ad.

Follow-up is another reason to keep a record of ads answered. If you don't hear from a perspective employer in a week, make a follow-up call. Ask if the position has been filled and if they're still scheduling interviews.

• *Personal contacts* are the most effective technique in acquiring a new job. Once you embark on a job search, contact everyone you know. Although your Uncle Bill works as an architect, and you're looking for a warehouse position, your uncle might know someone who works in a warehouse, or he might have seen a job posting on the bulletin board at his office for warehouse help.

Working with a job-search agency can be put into this category of personal contacts. An agency works on your behalf. Never pay for their services! There are many good reputable agencies that don't charge job candidates. If an agency tells you that you don't have enough qualifications and that they can locate a job for you only if you pay for their services, walk away and don't look back. I also advise working with only one agency. These agencies often deal with the same client companies and being presented to an employer by more than one agency can actually work against you.

Again, as with cold calling and answering want-ads, always follow up.

Completing the Application

When asked to complete an application, make sure that you come prepared. Bring your job history, references, and resume with you. Bring two pens of the same color, preferably black. If one pen runs out of ink, you don't want your application to be completed in two colors. And don't depend on the receptionist to provide you with a pen, or you might end up completing your application in red or with a dull pencil.

Make sure to fill out the application completely. If something doesn't apply to you, simply write "N/A" or "Not Applicable." It's okay to include your resume with the application, but never write, "See resume" when asked specific questions about job history or experience. Employers are just as interested in seeing how you fill out the application as they are in seeing your qualifications. They want to see your attention to detail, your ability to write neatly, and your ability to think on your feet. When the application asks for the salary you desire, write, "Open" or "Negotiable."

Make sure to follow instructions explicitly. I often had job candidates who completed both the front and back of an application, even though the bottom of the front had written in bold letters "Stop here and return to the receptionist." The back of the application stated clearly, "To be completed by office personnel only." Once a candidate completed the back of the application, including a section that asked for the candidate's top three attributes. This candidate listed her number one attribute as "Attention to detail." She was never asked back for a second interview.

The Interview

Once an interview has been scheduled, be sure to prepare yourself well. Go to the library or search the Internet to find out as much as you can about a company. If you're knowledgeable about the company's type of business, its prospect in its particular market, its philanthropic tendencies, and so forth, you'll have an edge over other interviewees.

Review these questions most often asked by human-resource managers:

- What salary are you expecting?
- Where do you see yourself in five years? Ten years? Twenty?
- Why do you want to work here?
- Why did your leave your last job?
- What are your best skills?
- What is your major weakness?
- What are your hobbies?
- What were your favorite subjects in school?
- What qualifications do you have that relate to this position?
- What is your greatest accomplishment?
- How will this job fit into your career plans?
- What did you like the most/least about your last job?
- Do you plan to continue your education?
- What have I forgotten to ask?
- Do you have any questions for me?

It's a good idea to write down your answers to these questions when launching a job search and then review them the night before an interview. Some people have very visual memories. If you become nervous during the interview and begin to stumble through the question-and-answer segment, you can close your eyes and visualize your answers. This will help you tremendously. Make sure to keep your answers as positive as possible, and never speak poorly of a former employer — or *anyone*, for that matter.

You should also have a few questions prepared to ask the interviewer. These are all good questions to keep in mind:

- Will you please tell me how your career developed at XYZ Company?
- If I work hard and prove my value, where might I be in five years?
- Describe a typical workday/week for this position.
- What is the length and structure of the training program?
- To whom does this position report?
- What characteristics best describe individuals who are successful in this position?
- Which other positions/departments would I interact with the most?
- Does your company encourage employees to pursue additional education?
- What makes your company different from its competitors?

Here are some questions that you should *never* ask on an interview. These are actual questions I've been asked by job candidates:

- So, how much do you pay?
- How much do you make?
- What does your company do anyway?
- Does the benefit package include psychiatric coverage?

- Are you married?
- Do I really have to be here at 7 a.m.? I like
    to sleep late.
- Can you guarantee that I'll still have a job in a year?
- Why do you want to know how much I made at my
    last job? It's none of your business!
- Will I get to keep all of my frequent-flyer miles
    when I travel on company business?

I have one last homework assignment for you in preparing for your job interview. Take a piece of plain white paper, and draw a line down the center. On the left side write down your ten best features. If you have a hard time coming up with ten, ask your mom or dad. Your parents know all of your great attributes. On the right side write down how those features benefit an employer.

This will be your feature/benefit list, and it's a very important tool. If you're asked why you'd be an asset to the company, you shouldn't just tell them your best features. You need to tell them the benefits of those features. The employer is more likely to get excited about hiring you if you say, "I'm a quick study. That means you'll spend less time in my training and your company will save money in training expenses" than if you just say, "I learn fast." Companies always like to hear how you can save them money.

There's one question that I left out in the first list. That question is "Tell me about yourself." There are human-resource managers out there whose whole interview is that single question. Their goal is not to learn about your life, but to see how you react under pressure. This is the perfect opportunity to use your feature/benefit list and ace your interview.

On the day of your interview:

- *Dress as if you were the boss.* Your clothing and appearance should be conservative and neat. No faddish clothes or jewelry. Ladies should wear only light makeup, go easy on the perfume, and never wear pants. This probably goes without saying, but remember that you shouldn't smoke or chew gum.

• *Bring resume, references, and letters of referral* (originals and copies) in a portfolio, or at least a nice neat manila folder.

• *Be on time* — not too early and definitely not late. Make sure to call ahead for directions. If the interview is in a neighborhood with which you're unfamiliar, you might want to make the extra effort to drive to the location the day before. Getting lost on interview day will not impress your prospective employer.

• *Make a final check in the mirror.* Make sure you don't have spinach stuck in between your teeth and that your appearance is neat. Give yourself a little pep talk in the mirror as well, and ask the Holy Spirit to guide your words and actions.

• *Once the interview begins, keep a positive attitude.* Do this even if it becomes apparent that you don't want this job. Human-resource managers talk to other human-resource managers, and they might know someone who would be interested in an individual of your caliber. It's also possible that they might have another position that better fits your qualifications. The best employee who ever worked for me was hired this way. She applied for an entry-level clerical position that was obviously below her skills. Even though this became apparent right at the beginning of the interview, she remained upbeat. This paid off weeks later when I needed to hire a human-resource assistant. I remembered her and called her to offer the job, without even placing a want ad for other applicants.

• *Above all, remember that emotions are contagious.* If you are excited about the employer, the employer will be excited about you. This is short and simple, but vital.

• *Do not bring up salary.* The employer will do this.

• *If you're offered the job on the spot, be prepared to say yes or no.* You should have thought this possibility through before the interview. Never keep them waiting more than twenty-four hours for an answer. That would not only be rude, but the employer will no longer be hot about you. The longer that you wait, the colder the employer will become, and they might even pull the offer.

• *Always send a thank-you letter.* Whether your note is typed or handwritten is a judgment call. I prefer a neatly typed letter, on stationary that matches your resume. Prepare the letter immediately following the interview and put it promptly into the mailbox. You may even hand deliver it the following day. There were times in my human-resource career when I had trouble deciding between two or three candidates. If one candidate sent a thank-you letter and the others did not, guess who got the job.

In case of a luncheon interview, there are a few tips to follow (keep these tips in mind for future business luncheons). Keep your order inexpensive. Stay away from sloppy food, such as spaghetti. Season food after tasting it; you don't want your prospective employer to think that you make hasty decisions. Of course, use proper etiquette, and mind your table manners. Most important, keep conversation on business; don't get personal.

Now that You Have the Job
Once you are hired, you still need to be mindful of several things.

- Always be a professional.
- Never gossip or get involved in office politics.
- Always do more than is expected of you.
- Don't be afraid to volunteer for those tasks
  that everyone else hates, such as filing.
- Keep a positive attitude.
- Dress as if you were the boss; when it comes time
  for a promotion, it's more likely that you'll
  be offered the boss's job.
- Keep good hygiene. Employees who don't care for
  their appearance aren't likely to be considered
  for promotions or raises.
- Keep skills and education up to date. The job market
  in the twenty-first century is ever changing, so
  don't allow your skills to become outdated.
- Join professional organizations, if possible, to keep
  up to date on the future of your chosen vocation.
- Remember your feature/benefit list. This will come
  in quite handy at review time. Don't be afraid
  to let your employer know why he should give
  you a raise.
- Finally, if you leave your job, ask for a letter of
  reference for future use, and make sure to
  leave on good terms.

Most important, be open to God's will in your vocation and strive to be a beacon of his light in the workplace.

"When they become adults, children have the right and duty to choose their profession and state of life. They should assume their responsibilities within a trusting relationship with their parents, willingly asking and receiving their advice and counsel."
Catechism of the Catholic Church, par. 2230

Chapter Four

Homeschooling Styles and Strategies

"The mediocre teacher tells.
The good teacher explains.
The superior teacher demonstrates.
The great teacher inspires."

William Arthur Ward

Character-Building and Academic Readiness: The Early Years

Cynthia Blum

One of the things I enjoy most about homeschooling is being able to experience daily and firsthand all the little things about my children as they grow up. For example, I knew that one of our twins, who was four at the time, could apply learned concepts about the workings of a VCR to new situations, when, after having been put in time-out for a while, he called out rather plaintively, "Mommy, I'm done rewinding!" He was ready to press "Play."

That was one of those irreplaceable moments that showed me how blessed I've been to be not only mother, but also primary educator from infancy for each of my children. Certainly the early years are particularly special ones, filled with fun, innocence, trust, and unlimited expectations and horizons. These are unequaled opportunity years for laying solid foundations in knowledge of the faith, intellectual preparation, and the beginnings of a truly noble character. As our family has grown, we've become more creative, out of necessity, in finding times during which we provide for the academic and spiritual needs of the youngest, while continuing to meet the ever-more-demanding needs of the older children.

The attainment of heaven with the greatest possible sanctity is our ultimate goal for each of our children. That has been the fundamental, guiding principle in the education of our children. We measure and choose everything — every book, every activity, every opportunity — with that end in mind. After that, we'd like to see our children lead happy, productive adult lives, lives that in some way contribute to the building of a Christian culture. Confident that God has a plan beyond comparison for each of our children, we make every possible effort, fueled with much prayer, to provide enriching opportunities for forming gentle, humble hearts; disciplined wills; selfless, trusting attitudes; and enlightened minds. Whatever their chosen vocation might be, we hope that when they're called, their hearts will be ready.

The essential first place to begin, both in character formation and academic readiness, is with the will. This is best reached through the heart in an atmosphere of trust and unconditional love. It is by the will that all choices are made, and a will trained through the heart by a loving parent will give rise to a disciplined will at the child's command at maturity later.

The single most important factor in training the will in a small child is *consistency*. Train the child to obey the first time and every time the command is given. There are a number of excellent parenting manuals available, including Fr. Lovasik's *The Catholic Family Handbook* (Sophia Institute Press), Gregory and Lisa Popcak's *Parenting with Grace* (Our Sunday Visitor), James Stenson's *Lifeline* (Scepter), Dr. James Dobson's *The Strong-Willed Child* (Tyndale), and Dr. Ross Campbell's *How to Really Love Your Child* (Chariot Victor). Each of these resources provides parenting suggestions that can be used along with the sacramental grace inherent within our vocations.

It's so important to expect and reward prompt, cheerful obedience in the early years while the child's natural desire to please is in place.

Of course, we have to temper our expectations of perfect obedience with a healthy dose of reality. This fact was again made apparent to us by a recent "eureka moment" from our three-year-old. He woke me up with a happy, "Mommy, *you* be the boss today, and I'll be your *hero!*" Clearly we must expect the male leadership trait — as planned by the Creator from the beginning — to surface occasionally.

When it comes to building character, modeling age-appropriate character traits is the best method. Children truly do learn from example. A two-year-old is certainly ready to learn orderliness. Remember the adage "A place for everything and everything in its place." It's also important at this age to stress sincerity as truth rather than fantasy, as well as gentleness, diligence, patience, generosity, and cheerfulness. Good habits are formed by continual repetition of a good act. There are several good story resources for illustrating what constitutes good character, such as William Bennett's *The Children's Book of Virtues* and *The Children's Book of Heroes*. Pick out the shortest stories for the three- to five-year-old crowd. Also highly recommended are the Treasure Box series (TAN Books) for twos and up, and the four-volume set of *Catholic Stories for Boys and Girls* (Neumann Press) for all ages. Another excellent resource for stories and activities can be found in Books I and II of Ron and Rebekah Coriell's *A Child's Book of Character Building: Growing Up in God's World — At Home, at School, at Play* (Fleming H. Revell Co.).

Nothing can compare with the heroic example of virtue in the saints. Two of the best collections of saint stories that we've found for reading to children five and up, as well as to the more precocious younger children, are Ethel Pochocki's *Once Upon a Time Saints* (Bethlehem Books) and *Saints for Young Readers for Every Day* (Pauline Books and Media). For illustrating the incontestable reality of good versus evil that every child already knows, read from a solid collection of non-politically correct fairy tales and fables, such as can be found in *The Baby's Story Book,* by Kay Chorao.

Usually somewhere between eighteen months and two and a half, children reach a milestone impossible for a first-time mother to anticipate, when all the fancy plastic toys and the chunky board books just aren't enough anymore. Suddenly the explosion of connections in the brain begins to take off, and the child is ready for more, a lot more. Puzzles, pegboards, shape sorters, and nesting toys are excellent, natural teachers of fit and form — the beginnings of analytical thinking.

Now is also the time to start on the alphabet, for future ease in transition to phonetic reading. Teaching the alphabet is really an uncomplicated process if you think of it as first telling the child the names of all those funny little squiggles. Teaching the names of both upper and lower cases together is best. It makes talking about and recognizing the letters in reading and letter-formation lessons later much easier. Start with the alphabet song. Make it a cozy lap-time activity with an alphabet book. Surround the child with alphabet puzzles, games, blocks, and books.

Somewhere around three years old, begin to work on one letter per week. Simply read aloud a good alphabet book emphasizing both the letter's name and phonetic sounds one at a time and have the child repeat the names and sound of each letter after you. Teach letter formation with big gross-motor movements in the air. Describe each stroke as you make it (e.g., slant left, slide right), and have the child stand behind you watching as you form jumbo size letters on a chalkboard or paper taped to the wall while imitating your movements. Reinforce that week's letter with a page each day from different alphabet coloring books to discuss, color, and think about.

After covering all the letters, relate and stretch by forming three-letter short-vowel words with a manipulative, such as magnetic letters on the refrigerator. Make the sound of each letter as you put it up. Build the child's name, emphasizing letter sounds. Run your finger under the lines as you read to the child.

For building vocabulary and a storehouse of knowledge, nothing beats a regular story time for children ages two and up. The more integrated and thematic in subject the picture books, the better. Choose a theme — ducks, playgrounds, cars — and check out carefully selected picture books from the library to illustrate the theme. Screen the books for wholesomeness and educational value. Read slowly, enunciate carefully, and point to the appropriate pictured object. Answer every question. After asking about the main events in the story, help the child verbalize the overall story. Have a special collection of heirloom-quality picture books, including nursery rhymes, to read and reread in your own library at home.

The goal is to expose the child to the true, the good, and the beautiful in order to form the standard by which he'll make sound judgments later. Read the very best, expose the child to classical and sacred music at meal times and in the car, and fill the child's visual environment with masterpieces from the great artists.

Every educational experience is formative for preschoolers and will pave the way for future learning. Little ones thoroughly enjoy, and certainly learn well by, being actively involved in the learning process. The more integrated all of the activities you're doing with the child at a given time, the more the child will gain. There are a number of resources available for hands-on, interactive language, art, math, and science activities. Natural experimenting, critical thinking, counting, sorting, sequencing, and narrating experiences in the early years will definitely lead to clearer understanding, confidence, and success as formal schooling begins. All of the educational experiences the little ones receive will be of significant value and will continue to bear abundant fruit for years to come. Your children will spend the rest of their lives building upon the foundation you'll have given them in their early years.

Clearly the single most far-reaching, important activity we parent educators can do is to guide the pure, simple, little hearts temporarily entrusted to our care to the One who is Love. He is the Source from which springs a noble character and all wisdom. Isn't it true and comforting that all God asks of us is to do our best, and to trust that he will do the rest? The grace is always there to accomplish what he has asked of us. I'm learning to trust the One who gave us his only Son to bless our every effort in forming our children for him: "For I, the Lord your God, hold your right hand; it is I who say to you, 'Fear not, I will help you' " (Isa. 41:13).

"You cannot be half a saint.
You must be a whole saint
or no saint at all."
St. Thérèse of Lisieux

Raising Children with Integrity

Mary Jo Thayer

Besides a love for God and the Church, I think the most important thing we can give our children is the gift of integrity. Writing
about this subject brings to mind my mother's words of wisdom:
"Remember to keep your own front door clean" and "Trust your
children as far as you can see them." This might sound like advice
from a hundred years ago, and it is. It's advice given to my mother
by hers, and it most likely is advice that was given to my grandmother by her mother. In fact, it could go back centuries. As Catholics, we know that truth never changes, and neither does good
advice.

Most of us Catholic homeschoolers might be inclined to think
we don't need such advice. We already work hard to raise children
with integrity. After all, we homeschool our children to help get
them to heaven. Of course, we are too busy to criticize how someone else is running *her* household, and of course, *our* children can
be trusted. I really think we have to be careful, though, not to rest
too much on our homeschooling laurels.

What my mother was warning me about were the pitfalls faced
by many a mother who prides herself too much in the accomplish-
ments she has enjoyed as a mother. It's so easy to look down our
noses at other parents who don't appear to have all the kinks

worked out yet. It's so easy to raise someone else's children from our perspectives. "If only they would do things our way," we say to ourselves.

It's also quite easy to be so enamored with our own children that we can't see their faults or even admit that they have faults. Many parents really think that their children would never lie to them. They really think their children can be trusted to act with integrity all the time. This is a philosophy begging for trouble. Children, above all, want to look good to their parents. They come with a built-in instinct for that. Lest we forget, they also come with another built-in instinct — to sin. How can we really expect our children, no matter how wonderfully gifted by our Creator, to act with integrity all the time? They don't have all the tools, yet.

So, how do parents give the gift of integrity to their children? I believe the answer lies in big things, such as the cardinal virtues of prudence, justice, fortitude, and temperance, as well as in little things — nuances almost. Often a lesson in integrity is almost imperceptible.

Following are some ways I've tried to build integrity in my children, and some ways I've observed others doing it for their children. To help make a point, I've categorized the list into four groups, each representing a cardinal virtue. Arguably, most of these integrity-builders could float back and forth from one virtue to the next, but it's always good to have a starting point.

Prudence: "The virtue that disposes practical reason to discern our true good in every circumstance and to choose the right means of achieving it. . . . It guides the other virtues by setting rule and measure" (CCC, 1806).

• Never blame someone else for your problems.
• Know that the end never justifies the means.

• Expect your children to act the same way
  when they're out as they do at home.
• If you don't like the way your children act,
  it's time to change something.
• Live all the teachings of the Church out
  of obedience and love for Christ.
• Remember that everyone is made in the
  image and likeness of God.
• Be on time and well prepared for events,
  engagements, and so on.

Justice: "The virtue that consists in the constant and firm will
to give their due to God and neighbor" (CCC, 1807).

• Never speak ill of clergy, especially in
  front of children.
• Give people the benefit of the doubt.
• Apologize to your children and your spouse
  if you've wronged them.
• Don't talk about private family business in a group.
• Before a party at your house begins, tell your
  children to include everyone. Then make
  sure that they follow through.
• Keep a tidy house out of respect to God for
  giving it to you, and also to show respect
  to the provider of your household.
• Keep a date with a friend even if a better offer
  comes up. Have your children do the same.
• Take care of your things so that they won't
  get lost or wrecked, and teach your
  children to do the same.
• Make your children pick up toys at
  other people's houses.

- Teach your children that family always
  comes before friends.
- Remember that God made everything
  to get us to him.
- Tell your children to pray for those
  who wrong them.

Fortitude: "The virtue that ensures firmness in difficulties and constancy in the pursuit of good. It strengthens the resolve to resist temptations and to overcome obstacles in the moral life" (CCC, 1808).

- If you commit to doing something, make
  sure it gets done.
- Punish your children less severely if they come
  to you and admit their wrongdoing.
- Insist on quiet, still behavior at Mass. Be sure your
  children kneel at the Consecration and fold
  their hands respectfully at Communion time.
- Make your children sit still and listen if you take
  them on a field trip.
- Teach your children to ask for a snack before
  they prepare it.
- Pay for items at a store before you allow your
  children to open, eat, or play with them.

Temperance: "The virtue that moderates the attraction of pleasures and provides balance in the use of created goods. It ensures the will's mastery over instincts and keeps desires within the limits of what is honorable" (CCC, 1809).

- Write the thank-you note before you use the gift.
- Confess the sin before you commit it again.

• Put a limit on how many cookies your
    children can take at a function.
• Hold your children accountable for debts
    and promises.
• Have your children pay for some of their things
    even if you can afford to pay for everything.
• Be fussy about your appearance and that of
    your children, remembering that cleanliness
    is next to godliness.
• Eat the dinner prepared — no special foods.
    No dessert without finishing.
• Teach your children to eat at the table and
    over their plates.

As Catholic homeschoolers, we must always be on our best behavior. Be sure to keep constant vigil. Children forget, and parents get lazy. We can't afford that. We should never rest on our laurels.

We must know that our vocation is to raise pure and holy souls, rich in integrity, for the Lord. We must also make sure that our children are clear about their vocations. Right now, they're being called by God to be the best students and children they can be. They must learn to heed the words of Jesus, "If you love me, obey me," and "Come follow me." What kind of parents are we, to expect our children to follow us? Do we have the kind of integrity we want our children to have?

We must remind ourselves daily that our children are the Lord's. We must remember daily that we're all created to know, love, and serve the Lord with integrity in this life so that we can be happy with him forever.

———————

*"Blessed are those who have
not seen and yet believe."*
John 20:29

Education in the Out of Doors

MacBeth Derham

"It's like the giant's bridge in *The Silver Chair*!"

"Yeah, but these jagged rocks on the sides are dragon's teeth! We must be in the mouth of an evil dragon!"

"This *is* the way to the Enchanted Castle!"

Elizabeth (10), Trip (9), Annika (7), and Paul (5) are crossing an old stone bridge in the middle of a winter wood. The bridge is our landmark; covered with snow, it looks like the stuff of which fairytales are made. We cross the bridge and head to a new trail. It's marked by evergreens, and many of the trees have nest boxes for birds mounted high on the trunks. There's even a bat box. We see troop numbers written on the boxes, and we know the boy scouts have been here.

Eagerly the four children inspect the bases of the trees, looking for owl pellets. A squeal of delight brings us all running to one big pine. Underneath this tree, they've found not an owl's leavings, but a fox's, a decomposed pile of fur and tiny bones in a long, thick bunch. We try to identify the remains: probably a white-footed mouse and an unfortunate chipmunk. This is an interesting find and is the highlight of our hike. We leave the scat under the pine and head back along the trail. Back home, the children write or draw a narration of our hike. These narrations are added to their nature notebooks and are a lasting record of our school that day. This isn't a special field trip, but part of our typical school day. Our lessons are short, and afternoons are spent outside in nature study, either in our yard or on vigorous nature hikes.

One hundred years ago, a British educator named Charlotte Mason knew that all children, rich or poor, thrived in nature. Finding her works, six hefty volumes of educational theory (The Original Homeschooling Series), has been wonderful for us, and her ideas have defined our homeschool. Before I married and had children, I worked as an outdoor educator, a field naturalist who took children out of their classrooms and set their feet on paths and trails beyond their schools. Charlotte Mason was an early proponent of outdoor education for children. Her philosophy is mine: "The outdoor life for children." Miss Mason suggests that young children should be outside for four to six hours a day, including meals, in most weather; and older children should spend at least one afternoon a week out of doors.

When I was a professional educator, I often wondered whether outdoor education had much effect on my students. As a homeschooling mother, educating my own children in this method, I can easily see the effect it has on their lives. Their education is a joyous thing. Each day in the outdoors is different; there's no typical day, except for the short lessons in the morning. We don't use textbooks or workbooks; instead we use *living books*. When real books and primary sources are combined with nature study, they provide us with a real education, full of the connections and relations of which Charlotte Mason was so fond, that the child will keep with him all his life.

On another day, we begin with basic lessons: phonics for the youngest and silent reading for the older children. Elizabeth is reading *Wolves of Willoughby Chase*, and Trip is reading *Prince Caspian*. Everyone enjoys a short math lesson and a Bible reading. Copy work, a combination of handwriting practice, grammar, and language arts, with passages chosen from a favorite book, takes another fifteen minutes. I read aloud, and it's soon time for lunch. The children choose sandwiches, eat, clean up, and put on their hiking clothes. We check our backpacks. Do we have our equipment? Flashlights working? Snacks? Notebooks and pencils? When everything is ready, we hop in the car for a drive to our hike. In the car, we listen to an audiotape: Jay O'Callahan's *The Herring Shed*. Time spent in the car, long or short, is never wasted.

We rarely travel for more than twenty minutes, but today we decide to drive to a state park about an hour away. Like many of the preserves on the north shore of Long Island, this park is a former estate, now very different from the Gatsby days, when it was built. We like this park for its lush, wide-open fields, old trees, abandoned cow barns and outbuildings, ninety-acre salt marsh, seashore, and pond — and relative isolation. It isn't easy to find uncrowded spaces on Long Island.

Today there are close to thirty people hiking the 1500-acre preserve. We find a quiet trail through some secondary forest and hike into it, well-sheltered from the strong northwesterly wind that's suddenly blowing off the Long Island Sound. The children have never hiked this trail. They're delighted by the big open field at the end of the half-mile path, and there's a beech tree in the clearing.

Or is it several beech trees? When we come under its sweeping branches, we see that there are three trunks blending into one glorious tree. The smooth bark of the old beeches is carved with hearts and initials. Some are quite old; others are quite high up in the branches. We take a break for a snack in the sheltering leeward side of the trees. Trip notices a hole in the trunk, and remembering Pippi Longstocking's advice, he reaches his hand into the dark hole to see what treasure he might find inside. Lo and behold! On this day, in this hole, in this tree, he finds a beautiful black polished stone. We all marvel at his fortune and pack our things to hike out of the park.

On the way, we see a small moth fluttering in the sunlight, despite the dropping temperatures typical of a late February afternoon. Where will it spend the night? Will it die? We don't know the answers. We hike on, wondering and speculating. We pass young woods, which, in a month, will be full of daffodils. I make a mental note to return then and show these signs of spring to the children.

Our visit today includes the history of the park, as well. I narrate a brief history to the children as we pass areas of interest. Marshall Field III owned the estate, which he modeled after an English manor. There were nearly forty buildings when he lived here. Today only a few are left. He had guesthouses, because his guests would stay for months. He had prizewinning dairy cows and a champion bull named Dynamo. We imagine what it would have been like to have lived here in those days. Then I point out that Field hired only English and Scottish workers, and didn't care for the Irish; he wouldn't have hired our family to work on his land. That discussion leads to talk of Ireland, the Manor system, and the hedge schools, where Catholic children were secretly educated in the Faith. We pass a hedgerow, and hide behind it, unnoticed for a moment as other hikers pass. History comes to life.

Back home, the children narrate, or retell, the history of the Field estate, and add their work to our *Book of the Centuries*. This book, kept in a three-ring binder, is a chronological collection of our history narrations. It helps us keep history in perspective, although we often study it in a random order. They file their narrations of the history of the park under "Early Twentieth Century." On another day, when we talk about earlier inhabitants of the park, there will be entries under "Seventeenth Century," and "Prehistory," as we learn that the Native Americans were living on this land for many years before the settlers came.

It's too cold to take our evening meal out of doors, so we settle for supper at the kitchen table. My husband, Don, comes home from work and gets plenty of spontaneous narration of our day from the children. After the table is cleared, the children take out their instruments and play their pieces for us. Elizabeth plays violin, cello, and piano. Trip plays the cello. Annika and Paul play violin. Tonight they play some Irish country tunes: *The Rakes of Mallow* and *Delaware*. The younger children get ready for bed as the older two finish by playing Bach and Elgar.

As I sum up the school day in my notebook, I recognize how great ideas are rarely isolated; rather they flow gently from one subject to another. Everything is connected; there are no truly separate subjects. Literature, nature, history, and faith all relate to one another. Charlotte Mason knew that real learning could easily take place beyond the traditional classroom. "The outdoor life for children" is full of possibilities, connections, and education.

⌒

A Charlotte Mason Reading List
- *Real Learning: Education in the Heart of the Home*, by Elizabeth Foss (By Way of the Family)
- *A Charlotte Mason Companion: Personal Reflections on the Gentle Art of Learning,* by Karen Andreola (Charlotte Mason Research and Supply Co.)
- *For the Children's Sake*, by Susan S. MacAulay (Good News Pub.)
- The Original Homeschooling Series, by Charlotte Mason (Charlotte Mason Research and Supply Co.)

*"Education is an atmosphere,
a discipline, and a life."*
Charlotte Mason

Integrated Learning or Unit Studies?
Design-Your-Own or Ready-Made?

Pattie Kelley-Huff

There are so many different styles to facilitate learning that it's pretty easy to get confused about your options. One term you've probably heard is *unit study*. You can use a unit study by itself or as a supplement to other studies. Simply stated, a unit study focuses on one particular topic, and the course of study is designed by using this topic as a theme across the curriculum. There are many advantages to using a unit study, including the ability to teach at several grade levels and to use your children's interests to foster learning. The best feature is the flexibility it affords. Some people take a thematic unit study as the foundation of learning for the entire school year. Just as easily, you could add a unit study or even a mini-unit study as a supplement to your existing curriculum. The possibilities are endless.

If this idea of a unit study intrigues you, and you need help designing your own, or want to find a ready-made unit study with a Catholic flavor and perspective, let me offer you a primer of sorts.

Designing Your Own Unit Study

Have you found a topic or a few attractive materials you'd like to build a unit study around? Or are you a brave soul who really likes to roll up your sleeves and plan every detail of your curriculum? In either case, I have some suggestions. Here's a checklist you can use to make sure that you don't forget some important or fun detail:

• *Choose your topic of study carefully.* A topic that interests you and your children obviously has a big advantage. Be sure to give some thought to limiting your study — and its scope and purpose — so you won't get bogged down in a project that's too large to manage.

• *Decide how much time you want to spend, and write it down.* The time limit will help you decide how much material you can cover and will help you stay within your limitations.

• *Gather your own resources, and then head to the library to see what resources it has on hand.* Check everywhere for available books, tapes, videos, websites, other computer resources, music, art, puppets, posters, games, field-trip opportunities, plays, museums, and so on. Remember to look for a wide range of resources relevant to religion, literature, composition and writing, vocabulary, foreign language, art, science, geography, history (including historical fiction), math, social studies, crafts, cooking, music, and physical education.

• *Plan your schedule, and allow plenty of time for meaningful diversions.* Consider building in extra time as your child's interests are heightened.

• *Keep some basic resources on hand for quick references;* for example, maps, atlases, a globe, a timeline, a history encyclopedia, a dictionary, a thesaurus, notebooks, and pencils. There's nothing worse than getting involved in something, only to be frustrated because you can't find a tool that would be helpful.

• *Consider having your children keep a notebook or journal,* and have them record important and interesting things they learn. Encourage lots of writing and artwork.

• *Wrap up the unit with something exciting and fun,* such as a field trip, a special meal, or a presentation.

NOTE: Don't overlook the possibility of another unit emerging from your studies, particularly if your child's interest has been keen.

Ready-Made Unit Studies:
Some Really Good Stuff Already Exists!

Let's say you aren't quite ready to jump in and design your own study. Maybe you simply don't have the time, or you'd like to get the feel of a ready-made unit study. There are wonderful unit studies out there, with a distinctly Catholic perspective from which you can choose.

Heart and Mind is an independent Catholic homeschooling magazine and has a pullout unit study in every issue. (To subscribe or purchase back issues, see Appendix A. Some of the units are available at their website, www.heart-and-mind.com.)

A sampling of the pullout unit studies include:

• *John Paul the Great,* by Nancy Carpentier Brown, Cay Gibson, and Maureen Wittmann (Vol. 2, No. 2, Summer 2005). Written to honor Pope John Paul II upon his death, this unit concentrates on his beloved Poland and his papacy. A wide variety of resources are provided.

• *Traveling the USA with Paul Bunyan and Babe the Blue Ox,* by Cay Gibson (Vol. 1, No. 3, Fall 2004). A fun geography unit for the younger student.

• *Niels Stensen: Scientist and Saint*, by Lesley Payne (Vol. 1, No. 2, Summer 2004). Designed for the older student, middle to high school. Ties together anatomy, geography, geology, history, philosophy, and religion.

• *Lepanto, by G. K. Chesterton*, by Nancy Carpentier Brown (Vol. 1, No. 1, Spring 2004). *Lepanto* is one of Chesterton's best-known poems and tells the story of the famous battle at Lepanto in 1571. This interesting unit brings together poetry, history, geography, and more.

Catholic Home Educator is the former quarterly publication of the National Association of Catholic Home Educators (NACHE; see Appendix A). Back issues are available for purchase, and older issues may be found at www.nache.org. This publication usually included original unit studies among many other wonderful reviews and articles. Here are a few examples (the first two written by yours truly):

• *DNA, Genes, Chromosomes, and Cloning Experiments* (Vol. 7, No. 4, Michaelmas 2000). This is for the scientifically challenged and offers great resources geared toward children, including a link that explains how to extract DNA from an onion in a way anyone can follow. There is a section that discusses the ethics of it all from a Catholic perspective.

• *A Funny Thing Happened on the Way to the Ballot Box: Elections Unit* (Vol. 7, No. 4, Michaelmas 2000). This unit covers the basics of elections, voting rights, history and responsibility, and offers a Catholic approach to informed voting as a moral obligation.

• *Martyrs of Ancient Rome*, by Maureen Wittmann (Vol. 8, No. 1, Advent 2000). Maureen offers a great way to incorporate our Roman roots into our children's studies. Learn about the early saints, who can be most inspiring. Martyrs were considered spiritual athletes of their times; they're great examples of a strong faith and loving our neighbors, even those who persecute us. You don't want to miss the great stories of our saints.

• *Black History Month*, by Lesley Payne (Vol. 8, No. 2, Lent 2001). Lesley provides a nice framework in which to study black history in the United States, particularly where the Church plays a role. She includes a long list of resources. This unit will be fascinating for your children.

Homeschooling Today is published six times a year. At one time the publisher was Catholic, and it wasn't unusual to find Catholic articles, unit studies, and other help in this magazine. Check your library or the Internet (www.homeschooltoday.com) for back issues. Here are a few examples of the unit studies that have been offered (not all are Catholic, but many are Christian):

• J'aime Ryskind had a regular art feature that focused on understanding and appreciating art, as well as on art techniques.

• *Children of the Lord: Noah's Ark* is a unit for preschoolers by Marti Pieper (Vol. 9, Issue 4, July/August 2000).

• *Religious Persecutions* (adapted from the Family Research Council; Vol. 9, Issue 4, July/August 2000) is a great unit study for teens on the current persecutions in the world.

• Maureen Wittmann has written several unit studies for *Homeschooling Today*; find these at www.catholictreasury.com:

The Donkey, by G. K. Chesterton: Living Literature for the Upper Grades. This is a very short, manageable unit that incorporates Mortimer Adler's concepts from his *How To Read a Book*. Maureen helps students tackle the writings of an author usually considered difficult to grasp. His short delightful poem has tons of potential for exploration, and the unit offers an abundance of wonderful activities.

Missionary Primer. This unit begins with Leo Politi's Caldecott Medal–winning book *Song of the Swallows* to explore the San Juan Mission and other California missions. It comprises language arts (including Spanish), Bible study, health, history, social studies, the arts, and science, all as you learn about a Franciscan priest named Fr. Junipero Serra. He was responsible for bringing the Catholic Faith to huge portions of the United States.

The Hunting of the Snark, by Lewis Carroll: Living Literature for the Lower and Middle Grades. Carroll's nonsense poem *The Hunting of the Snark* provides the opportunity to combine lessons in math, logic, poetry, and language.

The Burning Babe, by Robert Southwell: Living Literature for the Upper Grades. Robert Southwell was a Jesuit priest and martyr in Elizabethan England. This unit centers on Southwell's Christmas poem *The Burning Babe*, encompassing lessons in poetry, history, and religion.

Lesley Payne, editor for *Heart and Mind*, along with Philip Healy, wrote one of the first Catholic unit studies. *The Robert Southwell Unit Study* is a high-school-level program and integrates the life and martyrdom of St. Robert Southwell with a study of the English Reformation, poetry, the Catholic Faith, and more. It can be adapted for any teaching style and is available from Emmanuel Books (see Appendix A).

Unit studies can also be found at many homeschooling and Catholic education sites on the Internet.

Alicia Van Hecke has a wonderful Catholic website that caters to Catholic homeschoolers: www.love2learn.net. Here's a small sample of what you will find in the vast goldmine she offers:

• *Reading Your Way Through History:* www.readingyour waythroughhistory.com. This page is quite extensive. The suggested books are listed by century and have been checked to ensure that they don't contain anti-Catholic bias.

• Chronicles of Narnia Discussion Guides: www.love2 learn.net/literature/studyquestions/narnia.htm. This series of books is a favorite of my children, particularly *The Lion, The Witch and The Wardrobe*, which is an allegory written to illustrate Jesus' life, death, and resurrection. You can't go wrong with a discussion on C. S. Lewis and his books.

History Links

Barb Little and Jennifer Alles, two homeschooling mothers, offer what are, in my opinion, the best Catholic unit studies on the market, called History Links. At this time, there are nine units available, with new units continually added. These wonderful, in-expensive books are published by Wooly Lamb (see Appendix A).

I wish History Links had a name that indicated their broader focus. For a long time, I thought they were strictly history materials. But history is only the beginning of a flexible program that provides as much structure as you'd like. I understand that they're being remarketed with an emphasis on their integrated, across-the-curriculum focus. The first unit, General Studies, is a perfect alternative to some more expensive, less flexible boxed-curriculum offerings.

The units are family-friendly and easy to use. They incorporate encyclicals and documents of the Church, writings of the saints and early Church Fathers, and reading from Sacred Scripture. The foundation of these programs is critical-thinking skills. They incorporate all subjects and use fun resources such as timelines, living books, historical fiction, and lots of hands-on learning.

Another really neat feature of these unit studies is a set of symbols used in the margins to indicate the level of difficulty, the subjects covered, and the supplies necessary to complete each activity. The authors also have cross-referenced the *Catechism of the Catholic Church*.

I simply can't say enough good things about these unit studies. Here's a summary of what is currently available:

• *General Studies*. The unit includes a mini-unit to introduce the Links program and history to children. It can be used with any age, can be adapted for several children, and could be used to plan your yearly curriculum for as long as you have children to homeschool.

• *Creation*. A balanced teaching of the Church on this subject. Younger children follow the six days of Creation with a shadow box while the older children analyze the dating of archeological artifacts and finds.

• *Mesopotamia*. Learn about the patriarchs, Abraham, Isaac, Jacob, and Joseph, their land, and culture. Gain an understanding of why Abraham left to go to Canaan.

• *Ancient Egypt*. The Egyptians practiced advanced mathematical and engineering skills and had complex concepts of religion. The unit has lots of things to do; for example, contrast the Egyptians' worship of many gods with our devotion to saints; mummify a carrot; or follow the path of the Israelis into and back out of Egypt.

• *Ancient Israel.* Catholicism is rooted in the traditions of the Hebrew people; Jesus was Jewish. Explore your Jewish roots and the peoples of the Middle East. The unit is a great way to reinforce your knowledge and understanding of the Old Testament.

• *Ancient Greece.* Explore the culture of Greece, a major contributor to modern civilization, through its government, art, architecture, literature, science, and so on.

The last three volumes are dedicated to the Roman culture, our roots as Roman Catholics. They can be used by themselves or as a series on Ancient Rome:

• *The Roman Republic* focuses on the lifestyle, literature, military, and government of ancient Rome.

• *The Pax Romana* concentrates on the life of Christ.

• *The Roman Empire* studies the development of the empire and its demise and traces the development of the early Church, its people, and its sacraments.

I've had the privilege to edit the new Medieval and Renaissance units, which are equally wonderful. They should be available soon, if not now.

Whether you design your own or find a prepared unit, explore the possibility using integrated studies in your homeschool. You can structure your entire homeschool around unit studies or just use them during down times, such as summer or holiday breaks. Either way, they offer a fun way to accomplish learning in your home.

"The man who does not read good books has no advantage over the man who cannot read them."

Mark Twain

Baptizing the Imagination:
Using Fantasy Stories to
Develop a Sense of Wonder

Monica Sohler

"I propose to speak about fairy-stories, though I am aware that this is a rash adventure," wrote J.R.R. Tolkien, in his wonderful essay "On Fairy-Stories." I propose also to speak about fairy-stories, and myths, and fantasy literature, and their use in our homeschool. This also might very well be a rash adventure, as many home-schoolers seem to have a distrust of fantasy in this neopagan world in which we live.

But I will speak up for fantasy and its importance in develop-ing a holy imagination in our children. Fantasy has as its core a search for truth, beauty, and goodness, figuratively explained. And whether in clearly Christian works, or ancient myths, children can find this core and greatly benefit from the adventure.

When I was growing up, my mother read good books to us, es-pecially poetry and fantasy literature that conveyed truth in a non-literal way. These fairy tales and fantastic works of fiction can convey truth by captivating a young mind and engaging the heart in a way expository writing couldn't. We see our hero struggle with and overcome temptation. We see dark lords and how they turn to evil. We see pride causing a fall. We see little folk showing great courage and doing great things, where kings and queens have failed.

Do you see the gospel truths here? Fantasy literature can be a vehicle to teach these truths to our children, and ourselves.

As C. S. Lewis wrote in his allegory A *Pilgrim's Regress*, "Child, if you will, it is Mythology. It is but truth, not fact; an image, not the very real. . . . For this end I made your senses, and for this your imagination, that you might see my face and live."

Fantasy literature also develops a sense of wonder. Flying horses, unicorns, doorways into other worlds: all develop the imagination. I believe this is important, for we are created in the image of God, and he has a great imagination. He is, in fact, The Imagination. What he imagines comes to pass. Our imaginings are part of who we are: beings in his image. Tolkien called us "sub-creators," driven by our natures to create. "Fantasy," he said, "remains a human right: we make in our measure and in our derivative mode, because we are made: and not only made, but made in the image and likeness of a Maker."

The sense of wonder is a pathway to the Reality of our faith. It might sound contradictory to say that fantasy can lead to reality. But when children have their hearts lifted by the thought of something imaginary, and then find out that the Reality of our faith contains things akin to these, but far greater and more good and real, their wonder and worshipful appreciation of our God is all the stronger.

If I hadn't had my heart lifted by fantasy tales as a youngster, my great awe and wonder at the reality of the Mass might not be the same. I tell my children, "You like hearing about these fairy tales, but look what we have: the real thing. It's even better. At Mass the Sacrifice of Calvary is made present to us, now. Talk about the mystery of time. Wow! And that host that looks like bread is not bread, but Jesus himself. And you know what? He is God made man. Wow!"

The imagination is the playground where our minds and our hearts develop, so that we can grow up and experience the greater reality, which is far greater and more wonderful than all our imaginings.

Of course, I don't advocate a work simply because it's fantasy. As in any genre, there is good fantasy and bad. Some is bad because it's poorly written, boring, poor storytelling.

There's also the problem, in today's neopagan world, of works that promote a distorted worldview. But this isn't a problem particular to fantasy. It's a problem in every genre. In fact, I'd say it's a more common problem in lifelike fiction than in fantasy. In most children's fantasy, although not all, we at least find noble ideals mixed in with a fallen worldview. A child who has been raised to see the Truth and Beauty of God all around will pick up on these things.

The young child can understand and love fantasy tales as "pretend stories." We needn't fear that they'll lead our children to fashion their own druidic circle in the backyard and sacrifice the neighbor's cat (although some might not consider that all bad, depending on how they feel about the cat). Children understand "pretend." They blur it in play with "real," but we need to give them credit. I tell my children that old myths are stories that people invented when they didn't know about the real God and they tried to explain the world. I tell them that because we're made in God's image, we also like to invent "worlds," and this is what people did when they made these stories.

My kids sometimes ask, "Might some of these worlds and creatures be true?" I tell them what my mother always told me: that God is so creative, he could have made anything. So surely he *might* have made other worlds somewhere. This satisfies them and doesn't over-explain for a younger child.

It also helps further develop their sense of awe toward God. If human beings can make such an interesting story, God certainly can do it even better! These pagan works, made by men whose minds, although still in darkness, were grasping for God, have been baptized, and now help our children to fix their eyes on the real God.

And here we come to the second part of "baptizing" the imagination: raising our human and limited minds into the realm of wonder. This was another great gift my mother gave us, partly by her reading of myth and fantasy. She did what Christians have done for centuries. She baptized the secular. She baptized the pagan. She transformed the world around her children so that all we saw was through a Christian lens. She focused on the good in the world, not on the evil. She praised and amplified the good in books, and as a result, the bad parts lost their power over us. We were too busy looking at the good to notice the bad.

This is how we got Christmas on December 25. Long ago that day was the time of a great pagan holiday. Instead of shouting, "Cut out this horrid pagan nonsense!" the Church wisely countered with a huge Christian celebration: the feast of the Birth of our Lord. The pagan was not eliminated but *transformed*. To do otherwise would allow evil to define the world around us. But we Christians baptize the world around us. We elevate and transform; we do not cut off.

Think about this when you look at your Christmas tree or at the holly and ivy decorating your door. Many Christian symbols were once pagan symbols, but we gave them a new and higher meaning.

Whatever kind of book you read to your children or let them read, whether it's based in old pagan myth, modern children's fantasy, or the clearly Christian fantasy of C. S. Lewis or J.R.R. Tolkien, be sure to define in it what is good and noble: courage, fidelity, truth, and honor. This will enable your children to baptize the secular, the non-Christian, and see it all in a Christian light. Their imaginations will be developed and raised up by wonder, and they'll learn to discern and find the things of God in the works of his imaginative creatures.

"Authentic Catholic education relies on and includes
all that is true, good, and beautiful — in short, everything
that points the way to God, the source of all truth, goodness,
and beauty. . . . Our own faith, the Catholic atmosphere
we create in our homes, the specific resources we use to teach
the Faith, and our ability to weave the Faith into the fabric of our
children's lives are really what ensure a Catholic curriculum."

Kimberly Hahn and Mary Hasson
Catholic Education: Homeward Bound

Establishing a Cooperative: Guidelines and a Checklist

Maureen O'Brien

What could possibly go wrong when a group of well-intentioned homeschool mothers decide to form a learning cooperative? Answer: nothing, anything, and everything.

A co-op is a group of individuals who pool their resources for the greater good of the group. In theory, everyone contributes and everyone gains. Benefits might include group discounts, a broader experience-base and talent-base from which to draw, a source of encouragement, and a vehicle for accountability. A co-op requires a commitment of time and talent from its members.

The difference between a successful co-op and a failure often depends on how well expectations are articulated, so as to fulfill the needs of the greatest number of participants. Successful co-ops result in memorable, enriching experiences. To set up a successful co-op, first establish a common vision, agree upon learning goals, define ground rules, and expect the unexpected.

Although this process might sound rather cumbersome and bureaucratic, the homeschooling mothers in my co-op did this in less than three hours during a summer picnic lunch in the park. All of us knew at least one other family, but we didn't all know each other. We shared the common belief and prayer that the Holy

Spirit would guide us in our planning. Cooperating with the Holy Spirit was our first step toward a successful cooperative learning experience.

Often a co-op is the brainchild of one or two mothers, and word spreads until a group is born. Although each family has equal say in all matters concerning the group, one person needs to step forward as the facilitator. This person is essentially responsible for assuring that everyone receives group communications, including schedules, vote tallies, cancellation notices, and so on. With email, this task is easily accomplished. Without this leadership/facilitator role, details become lost in the shuffle, leading to a variety of confusions and hurt feelings. Only the Trinity works in perfect unity; the rest of us need a point person to keep us all headed in the same direction!

The facilitator also leads the initial organizational meeting(s), posing the basic questions for a successful cooperative learning experience. Who? What? How? When? An organizational meeting is best held at least one month before the start of regular meetings. This is the time for everyone to share their expectations and learning objectives honestly, and to decide whether participation in a co-op can meet each individual's learning goals. The facilitator summarizes participant feedback and solicits consensus on proposals made to the group. But you can't stop there.

The next step is to establish ground rules as a group. Our heavenly Father gave the Ten Commandments to Moses. In his infinite wisdom, God knew that people needed ground rules in order to function more happily together. This biblical model teaches us how to use specific rules to help any group of people, including faith-filled home educators, work together effectively.

Ground rules can cover the mundane, from absences and timelines to the agreed-upon consequences of student misbehavior. The group should brainstorm all possible problems or issues that might arise, and decide how the group will choose to handle them.

Anticipatory planning for the unexpected is the best method of prevention. All group decisions need to be orally summarized by the facilitator and distributed in writing to the group for future reference.

Let's examine some of these precepts in two sample cooperative learning groups, the Alpha and the Omega:

Alpha Co-op	Omega Co-op
Members want to work together and form a co-op.	Members have a written purpose statement.
Members want a variety of learning opportunities to meet their individual learning goals.	Members have agreed upon some shared learning goals.
Members agree that all children will act appropriately and families will come to meetings as their schedule allows.	Members have decided on the required level of participation for each family and have written a statement about student conduct.
Educational methods to employ weren't specifically considered.	Members agreed to include field trips, didactic and hands-on experiences in combination.

Although well-intentioned, the Alpha group is so loosely defined that they've set themselves up for potential failure. In contrast, the Omega co-op is more apt to succeed, having invested the time up front in careful planning.

Guidelines

The following planning guidelines and checklist are included here to help you work through the process of starting your own cooperative learning group:

1. Create a written mission/purpose statement, agreed upon by all members.

   Example: The Prairie Primer Co-op will study westward expansion of America utilizing the *Little House on the Prairie* book series during the 2004-2005 academic year.

   ❑ Clearly state a general purpose.
   ❑ Include a time frame.
   ❑ If the group is ongoing, plan to re-evaluate your purpose annually.
   ❑ Obtain consensus.

2. Evaluate individual learning goals and decide which goals can be met through the cooperative learning experience. Some goals will likely remain individual, and met within the family.

   Examples: Fulfill academic history and science requirements. Improve writing and public-speaking skills. Learn library skills.

   ❑ Solicit all desired outcomes.
   ❑ Evaluate which goals the co-op will focus upon together.
   ❑ Obtain consensus.

3. Agree upon governing principles and ground rules for effective group function. Include anticipatory planning for potential problem areas.

   Examples: Meet every Friday afternoon from 2 to 4 p.m. Start and end on time. Rotate teaching responsibility equally. Co-op limit: twenty students. Student will be remanded to parent for disrespectful behavior.

   ❑ Define expectations for both the parent and student:
      Attendance
      Meeting schedule

Participation
Teaching
Expenses incurred
Behavior
Communication
Transportation

❑ Obtain consensus.

4. Evaluate and employ agreed-upon educational methods.

Examples: Guest speakers, projects, writers' workshop, demonstrations, field trips, outside reading, research, games.

❑ List all available educational methods available to the co-op.
❑ Obtain consensus on those most suitable for desired outcomes.

Successful cooperative learning can be an abundantly rewarding and fun-filled experience for students and parents alike. Or it can feel like an obligatory drudgery that slowly dies when morale declines and fervor wanes. Diligent pre-planning with input from all members is essential for a fruitful adventure. Start with a vision, and purposely commit to written guidelines for your co-op, and you'll be on your way to a successful outcome. Having had a successful experience hasn't made me an expert, but it has made me an enthusiastic supporter and promoter of cooperative learning endeavors.

"We can do no great things;
only small things with great love."
Bl. Teresa of Calcutta

Virtual School

Annie Kitching

How can anyone not have, at best, a love/hate relationship with computers? It's extraordinary to think how significantly they've changed our lives in just the past few years. Unless a family has taken a strong stand against all modern technology, it's almost impossible to have completely escaped the computer's influence. Yet, however much we wrestle with it as a family, the computer's influence continues to be a tangled mass of good and evil, the many strands difficult to distinguish and to separate.

Our family really couldn't escape from the computer. I've had the unique opportunity of schooling my children at work. As the religious-education director of a large suburban parish, there's no way I can avoid the computer in my office, which is also my children's schoolroom. As a matter of fact, in this traditional, but forward-thinking parish, the parish leadership made an early decision to employ technology of all kinds in our education and evangelization efforts.

I was on the lookout for ways in which technology could enhance not only our parish program, but also my own children's education.

Our first discovery was computer games. It wasn't long ago that my son was thrilled to have worked his way through the various levels of a game we picked up at the Christian bookstore, identifying Bible passages and identifying the tinkling tunes of Protestant hymns. In those days, the simple game was novel and intriguing. After religious-education classes, I'd often see a huddle of children gathered around the computer, offering suggestions and advice as one child served as spokesman and managed the mouse. How wholesome it was.

Then came the web. I will never forget my son's first research paper. I let him select his own topic, which turned out to be the FBI. I suggested that he use the Internet for at least one source. Imagine my horror when I sat down at my computer one afternoon after he had been working, hit the "Back" key, and the screen suddenly displayed in shocking clarity a nude woman swinging her anatomy in my face, and blaring some crude statement that began with the letters "F B I." I pushed so many keys in my desperation to get her off the screen that I froze the computer, causing the woman to leer out at me that much longer. Finally, my white-faced son ran over and turned the power off.

Eventually, I stopped yelling. Maybe I overreacted, but at that time I was fool enough to believe that no one could access such a site by accident. Shortly thereafter, my own search for "Victorian Party Games" resulted in suggestions so lewd that I could no longer doubt my son's protestations that it was all "by accident." Fortunately, the parish soon installed a blocking mechanism that has done an exemplary job of preventing any repeats of that sort of incident. Now I'm extraordinarily grateful for the many excellent Catholic websites I use every day that offer me instant access to Church documents, a Scripture concordance, the writings of the saints, and more.

I hadn't yet discovered the resource that was to change how we homeschooled. One day, while idly surfing around, I stumbled on a treasure, Regina Coeli Academy (RCA; www.reginacoeli.org). RCA is an online college preparatory program for Catholics and operates under the auspices of the Society for the Study of the Magisterial Teaching of the Church. In addition to a full high school program, RCA offers a junior program in which students ages ten to thirteen can study a number of subjects. Because my eighth-grade son was so drawn to the computer, I signed him up for a summer writing course. He attended the pre-class tutorial to familiarize himself with the technology. Although to this day I remain ignorant of how it all works, neither of my children has had any trouble connecting to the school and participating fully.

The option of Regina Coeli classes has been a blessing for me as a working mother. Now, although my son has gone on to a site-based high school, my daughter takes a number of classes from Regina Coeli.

Regina Coeli classes are real-time; that is, a teacher is sitting at a computer somewhere in the world while simultaneously his students sit down at theirs. It's quite extraordinary how virtual this learning environment really is. Apart from the necessity of the universal rule to "Keep hands and feet to yourself," the Regina Coeli classroom is very much like any classroom. Students can joke around (and frequently do), ask questions, and interact with one another and with the teacher. The teacher can quiz the students, lecture, and give assignments. Classes always start with prayer. Like a regular classroom, students even hang out in the "hallway," and "pass" notes. The social aspects of the school, and the fact that the students answer to another adult in addition to their parents, has helped me over some of the strain of home-schooling my children during their early adolescence.

The Junior Academy works very much in cooperation with parents, who are recognized as their children's primary educators. Classes generally meet once or twice a week, and homework is given, but parents are expected to follow through by making sure that homework is completed. Other assignments are provided, if needed, to ensure that lessons are learned. Just like a site-based school, the personalities of the teachers and students are evident. Some teachers are quite rigorous, both in academic expectations and in their insistence on classroom rules. Others expend a little less energy keeping control of their classrooms, but make up for it in their enthusiasm and loving support of each student.

Whatever the personality and style of the teacher, parents are an intimate part of the process. Each teacher has a website for the class, where parents can access logs of each session. This arrangement allows parents to follow what is being taught and to check on their child's participation. The websites also list homework, reading assignments, and other resources, so parents are never in the dark about what's expected. The Regina Coeli staff is available by email and promptly responds to any query or suggestion.

An unexpected benefit of RCA has been the surprising sense of community among the school's families. Although they live throughout the United States, it isn't uncommon for students to visit one another, go to camp together, or find other ways to connect more fully than online. Students organize youth group meetings and study sessions. Once I stumbled onto a group of Latin students who had gotten together to put on a play, choosing characters and improvising scenes, all online.

Although science and math classes are part of the Regina Coeli Preparatory School curriculum, presently there are no math or science classes offered for the younger students during the regular school year. Since the computer was working so well for my daughter, we explored another computer-centered option. Alpha Omega offers Switched-on Schoolhouse (www.aop.com), a full homeschooling curriculum on CD-ROM. The program is described as featuring a "dynamic mix of state-of-the-art text, multimedia clips, and animation," and that's exactly what it is. I found both the math and the science to be fun. (My own lack of enthusiasm for these subjects is one reason I thought it might be a good idea to bring in reinforcements.)

Parents have a great deal of control over how students progress through the lessons. For example, the parent can set the program either to allow the student to proceed regardless of errors, or to require mastery of all questions. Some activities require grading by the parent. The science program suggests a wide variety of learning activities, including papers, experiments, graphing, and so forth. Parents always have the choice of having their child participate in an activity or not.

There aren't as many downsides to all of this computer-centered instruction as you might imagine. My daughter is constantly on call around the parish to run errands, provide childcare, and serve as general office help. She also participates in parish activities and is a serious dancer, so I didn't have to be concerned that her school day was too sedentary. Parents in a more typical homeschool situation might need to make sure their child has opportunities for physical activity. Both Regina Coeli and the Switched-on Schoolhouse programs offer a lot of guidance, but also a significant amount of self-direction that will prepare a student either for more intensive home study as a high-schooler, or for a site-based school experience.

The only concern I have is my children's obsession with emailing and instant-messaging their friends. Since all of their friends, homeschooled, Catholic-schooled, and public-schooled, seem to share this fascination, I can't lay blame for it at the door of the computerized instruction. I might call to task the technology itself, except that the whole phenomenon is so reminiscent of my own generation's obsession with the telephone. Nevertheless, the temptation to email friends comes with having a computer available, and it requires parental vigilance.

Regina Coeli Academy and Switched-on Schoolhouse are only two of many computer-centered home-education options, and new resources become available every day. We found that these resources suited our needs, and are particularly grateful for the deep, orthodox Catholicism of Regina Coeli, but undoubtedly there are other programs and options that might work better for other families or students.

Although there are many scary things about this computer age, once you recognize them and meet them head-on, you can move forward to discover many blessings as well.

---

*"Learning unsupported by grace may get
into our ears; it never reaches the heart.
But when God's grace touches our innermost
minds to bring understanding, his word
which has been received by the ear
sinks deep into the heart."*

St. Isidore of Seville

Chapter Five

Children with Special Needs

"Do not free a camel of his hump;
you may be freeing him from being a camel."

G. K. Chesterton

You Can Teach Your
Dyslexic Child at Home

Janine Cerino Seadler

There's so much confusion about what dyslexia is, that a definition is in order: "Dyslexia is a specific learning disability that is neurological in origin. It is characterized by difficulties with accurate and/or fluent word recognition and poor spelling and decoding abilities. . . . Secondary consequences may include problems in reading comprehension and reduced reading experience that can impede growth in vocabulary and background knowledge" (National Institute of Child Health and Human Development, 2002).

Despite the challenges this condition presents, homeschooling parents *can* teach their dyslexic child at home with proper diagnosis, training, and outside support. The specific approach that has proven to be most effective is called the Orton-Gillingham technique. Although it has been used for over seventy years, it's still not commonly known or used in site-based schools. The core of the Orton-Gillingham technique is sequential, multisensory instruction, which improves phonemic awareness. That is, the teaching of symbol relationships must be done in a step-by-step fashion through the eyes, the ears, and the hands. If you think the reality of teaching your dyslexic child can be a daunting task, keep in mind that the success rates in traditional school settings are low only because the Orton-Gillingham techniques are not commonly used. With external support and training, you can have an excellent program for your dyslexic child at home.

Before embarking on an extensive program, it's necessary to have a proper diagnosis. A licensed child psychologist or psychiatrist should do screening and formal testing. This is often expensive, but if you have medical insurance or a generous family member, it would be my recommended first course of action. Another valid, yet less expensive course of action would be an informal evaluation, such as the WADE (Wilson Assessment of Decoding and Encoding), given by a trained reading specialist or tutor. This type of assessment will give an indication of phonemic strengths and weaknesses in decoding (reading) and encoding (spelling). (Parents often underestimate the importance of the spelling component of their child's language skills. They say to me, "He can just learn to use the spell check." This is true, but not nearly sufficient. We measure our success in this world by our ability to communicate in it, and that communication needs to be both oral and written.)

Once the diagnostic phase is complete, you can begin to plan your child's homeschool program. The two key components that will make homeschooling a dyslexic child a successful reality are parental training and outside support. Fortunately, there are several reputable programs available that provide training sessions across the United States and Canada. Wilson Language Company and Lindamood Bell are companies that offer training sessions to parents with college degrees. For those who can't reach a training session, videotapes are also available. Recently, distance-learning experiences were made available to persons who have participated in the two-day workshop of Wilson Training.

Training is paramount because the methodology and curriculum that works for dyslexic children — that is, the Orton-Gillingham approach — isn't the type of reading instruction most of us received in school. It isn't the "vocabulary, story, question" method of teaching reading. It's more highly structured and phonologically based.

There are several essential elements to Orton-Gillingham instruction. It must be *multisensory*, *phonetic*, and *synthetic* — that is, the student must be taught how sounds blend together into words. Using all of his senses, the child learns initial consonants and short vowels. The child is taught to identify digraphs (ch, ck, sh, th, wh) as being different from blends, at a very early stage in the instruction. Because the instruction is highly structured and repetitive, it's often tedious, and the need for outside support to maintain the program is paramount. The last two elements are that the instruction is *cumulative* — every new concept is taught while reinforcing the previous concepts — and *cognitive*, so that the student understands the logic behind the word patterns.

Initially the language and style of Orton-Gillingham instruction may actually seem like a foreign language, as you learn digraphs, syllable patterns, and the value of fluency. However, as time passes, diligent parents will become comfortable with phonemic awareness, the nuances of the language, and the ability to teach spelling, handwriting, and reading together as a cohesive unit. Most programs are written for third-graders, but if the child is under the age of seven, courses in emerging literacy and *Sound Beginnings*, by Julia Fogassy (www.ourfathershouse.biz) are appropriate.

With the aid of a trained tutor, you can learn to teach your dyslexic child at home. A trained tutor can be the "cheerleader" for the child, a person who isn't as emotionally invested as the parent, but definitely cares about his success. Tutors can also support parents and encourage them to be trained. A dyslexic child has very specific strengths that must be developed as his weaknesses are improved. Teaching a dyslexic child is a study in inconsistency; one day he can read the word *and*, and the next day he can't, or small words like *saw* and *was* stump him, but *butterfly* is no problem. A child's awareness of his difficulties can lead to depression and despair if the road to remediation isn't paved early and steadily with the right material.

In the work I do at the Learning Home, I often write the plans for the child to complete independently during the week. I encourage all of my parents to attend training. This way, I know that the program is being completed in a systematic and thorough fashion. Orton-Gillingham tutoring needs to occur three or four times a week, year-round. This method actually encourages the brain to read differently and more efficiently than before.

There are some Orton-Gillingham-type programs in manual form for homeschoolers. Although these may be excellent in theory, they're difficult to implement without training. I use the *Wilson Language Program* because it's user-friendly. After a two-day workshop, parents can continue the work with a trained tutor by assisting with sound cards and workbook pages. In my experience with tutoring dyslexic children and adults over the past seven years, I've found the Wilson card system, along with the sequential readers and workbooks, easy for parents to use at home. It's both a reading and a spelling program. By adding comprehension development through the use of high-interest, low-readability texts such the *High Interest Classics*, a total reading program can be put into place for your elementary-school-age child.

I know firsthand the difficulty of balancing a family and a special-needs child. A practical program that's clear and easy to follow is your very best bet. For more intensive Orton-Gillingham programs, try The Outreach Center at Jemicy School in Owings Mills, Maryland, or at The Lab School in Washington, D.C. They both have an extensive set of workshops in language programs, study skills, and Project Read. The Jemicy Parent Outreach is developing training workshops for homeschoolers.

Many times I hear of homeschooling parents tutoring children of other homeschoolers. The tutoring parent might have been a teacher or a reading specialist before homeschooling. Although this willingness to help is both noble and charitable, in the case of the dyslexic child if the instruction is traditional — not multi-sensory and progressive — the results will not equal what a trained Orton-Gillingham professional can provide. I often see the negative results as a frustrated young child grows into an angry, frustrated, or depressed teen who can't read or spell fluently. Don't let this happen to your child. If you suspect a severe reading difficulty, do everything in your power to unlock the puzzle and seek to solve the problem immediately. Early intervention is the best money-saver there is to correcting reading difficulties.

Teaching a dyslexic child requires a thorough understanding of the child, including his strengths and weaknesses. A multisensory program that's sequential and progressive in its presentation will unlock the code of the English language. The Orton-Gillingham philosophy of instruction incorporates the methods needed to teach dyslexic children how to read, write, and spell successfully. Help is available to parents through outreach centers and language book publishing companies. Tutoring provides the support that most parents need to make the intensive program work in a homeschooling environment.

Dyslexic children can be taught successfully at home. Be the one in your child's life to whom he can later look and say, "My parents made sure I learned how to read!"

EDITORS' NOTE: To find the resources mentioned here, please see Appendix C.

"See to it that no one makes a prey of you by philosophy and empty deceit, according to the human tradition, according to the elemental spirits of the universe, and not according to Christ."

Colossians 2:8

Teaching a Child with Attention Deficit

Carol Maxwell

My frustration was beyond belief. I couldn't understand why my second child, who was in second grade at the time, wasn't completing his assignments. I would teach his lessons carefully. He would explain them back, and I could tell that he completely understood the concepts. As a matter of fact, I thought his intelligence level was quite high. However, I wondered why he would sit in our home-school room for *three hours* straight and not write a single character. Outside of school, he could never seem to follow my requests. For example, when I'd ask him to clean his room, he needed constant reminding. He took days to complete the task.

He was excellent in math, but wouldn't write the answers in his MCP Math book. He could read and write somewhat, yet refused to write a word for fear that he wouldn't be able to spell it, even though I told him not to worry about the spelling. My husband and I were in a quandary. After much prayer and consternation, my husband asked me to look into placing him back in school. (My son attended a public school for kindergarten.) My frustration over the situation was upsetting the entire household, and all I could do was yell at my son. He didn't want to go to a site-based school, but he also couldn't bring himself to complete any of his work at home.

Before I had a chance to contact the local elementary school, my husband happened to be discussing our situation with a psychologist he knew. The psychologist said that my son's symptoms were classic Attention Deficit Disorder (ADD). I knew that he must be wrong because it never occurred to me that my son fit the criteria. With my husband's insistence, I did my research and checked out every book on ADD in the library. To my shock, every resource described my son precisely. I checked off each behavior that my son exhibited, which was the entire list. Some of these characteristics included being easily distracted, being hypersensitive to noise and touch, not remembering directions, having difficulty waiting to take a turn, having a short attention span, shifting from one uncompleted task to another, and engaging in physically dangerous activities without thinking about the consequences.

I wondered how this could be and how I could not have seen it. Even more questionable was why his kindergarten teacher didn't give me a heads up on ADD. Although he was her favorite student, and the work that he did was impeccable, she constantly badgered him in front of the class for not completing his assignments. Her pet name for him was "Pokey Little Puppy," which hurt his feelings. She also noted his lack of assignment completion on his report cards and in the parent/teacher conferences. Because it caused him great anxiety, I told her in person and in writing that she was not to discuss his incomplete work with him or in front of the class. She was to send it home with a note about what was to be completed, and I would ensure that it was done by the next day. After all, I explained to her, people work at different paces, and I didn't want to inflict an arbitrary standard upon my little five-year-old. With me sitting at his side every night, he did the assignments, and I could see that he understood all of the subjects.

With the psychologist's suggestion, it was all beginning to make sense. But I needed some kind of confirmation so that I'd know what to do in our home studies. We decided to have him tested at our local school. I wasn't looking for a reason to point my finger and blame him for all my troubles. I *needed* to know so that I'd be able to revise my teaching strategies to fit his way of learning. I just wanted to help him love the daily acts of gaining knowledge, and, at that time, I didn't know how to do it.

My son was tested over several days. The first test assessed his knowledge. Sure enough, he was average to above average. The second test screened his language and speech abilities, which were good. The third was an attention screening, in which he rated low. Then I filled out a very lengthy questionnaire. In between, about seven representatives from the school, including the principal and teachers, met with me as a group to discuss our issues. I never told my son that he would be tested for ADD. I just informed him that I was trying to find ways of teaching him better, which was the absolute truth.

Inevitably, I was told that, although the school psychologists weren't allowed to issue official diagnoses, my son exhibited all of the classic ADD symptoms. I was even informed that, by my description of him, he had what is known as ADHD, or Attention Deficit Hyperactivity Disorder. The representatives from the school met with me again and gave me information and resources on how to improve my teaching methods to fit my son's way of learning. Basically, his brain processes information differently than others, even though the outcome is the same. I was able to focus on this when watching him learn a new concept or listening to him explain something to me or even observing him write. Now it all made sense. I told the school representatives that I didn't want a file started on my son. Since he wasn't a student at the school, they readily agreed that they had nowhere to place his file anyway. So I took home all of the paperwork and documentation that had accumulated during this process.

Now I was ready to help my son work to his potential. His level of distraction was very high, so I had to change things in order to keep his interest. First, I no longer required him to do all of the rote arithmetic equations in the MCP book. If I was sure that he understood the concept, I scratched off all of the problems except five. Then for the next year, I ordered Saxon Math 3 for him, and he did well with all of the different hands-on activities and sensory exercises. Sometimes I would use a timer and that would motivate him to focus and finish his math problems. However, he began to experience some stress over having to race the clock, so it didn't always work.

Next, I allowed him ten-minute breaks for about every ten minutes of work. This schedule was very time-consuming, but was more productive than having him become distracted by his pencil lead for three hours in an empty room and not completing anything. I also picked curricula that I knew would capture his interest.

For science, instead of ordering textbooks that never seemed to captivate his attention, I bought small paperback books filled with experiments using everyday items. My son had a great time performing the challenging work involved in completing each task. Best of all, he remembered the concept behind the experiments. He also loved to take things apart, so I would scour garage sales looking for old items that he could dismantle and explore. He never tired of doing so.

Writing was still a challenge for him because he felt that he couldn't do it perfectly. We've been diligently working on it for over five years now, and I've noticed great improvement. By the end of second grade, I could get him to write one line with much coaxing on my part and tears on his part. Also, he would think of ideas and I'd write them down for him so that he'd feel some sense of accomplishment without the pressure. By the end of third grade, he would write a two-line story or book report. In fourth grade, he could write one paragraph, only with much guidance from me. In fifth grade, I taught a writing class for him and four of his peers. He was eager to complete the assignments and read his work to the class at the end of each month and accomplished one page of writing. By the end of seventh grade, he could easily write a simple two-page paper, as long as its parts were assigned over a one- to two-week period.

To this day, my son has no idea that he was diagnosed with ADD. My husband and I know, though, and it has given us great insight into our son and much appreciation for his unique way of thinking and doing. Today, he loves to read and learn about many things. We don't have to accommodate him as often, but we still have to work around his way of learning. He's truly a blessing, and I'm so glad that I didn't give up on him or let him down by sending him back to a system where I might have never figured out his struggles or been able to help him through them.

"I have fought the good fight, I have finished the race, I have kept the faith. Henceforth there is laid up for me the crown of righteousness, which the Lord, the righteous judge, will award to me on that day, and not only to me but also to all who have loved his appearing."

2 Timothy 4:7-8

Homeschooling on the Autism Spectrum

Melissa Ramirez Naasko

In college I read a book about post-reconstruction black Americans and how they would sometimes pray for the ability to "pass"; that is to say, the ability to be mistaken for white. I used to pray for this ability for my son, Joseph, that others might not catch a glimpse of what makes him different. It isn't as obvious as the color of his skin, but subtlety has its own drawbacks. My son has Asperger Syndrome, a pervasive personality disorder (PPD) that's found on the autism spectrum. Although academically advanced, he suffers behavioral setbacks and processes information differently. He has difficulty interpreting non-verbal cues and at times behaves in a manner off-putting to other children.

In the safety of the family and the home, Joseph can learn his faith and academics as well as important social skills without the fear of teasing, harassment, or the threat of being ostracized. Joseph's nature admittedly makes homeschooling a challenge, but it also makes it ideal for his needs.

The mere suggestion of homeschooling a special-needs child can bring about a myriad of responses from well-meaning friends and relatives. When we decided to homeschool, my grandmother's cousin was overjoyed. She told me she thought it was wonderful to keep my children around me. Others were reticent, to say the least, suggesting Joseph would wind up socially inept. Many wanted me to consider what "a child like Joseph" needs in terms of social interaction. I answered that, although it's true that a person must be exposed to others to gain familiarity and comfort with customs, these skills aren't always learned in the classroom.

Joseph started in the local school and performed well in kindergarten, thanks, in no small part, to a wonderful Catholic teacher with whom I had attended elementary school. However, this was not the case for first grade, where poor Joseph endured ridicule and more for his cultural and behavioral challenges. My heart was breaking for my child, and for a while I tried to change Joseph to adapt to the educational system. Thankfully, the Lord placed people in our path who questioned my husband and me and helped us to see that it was not for us to change Joseph, but for his educational environment to change.

Curricula

Just as it is not only ludicrous but also insensitive to demand a left-handed child to use scissors, desks, a computer mouse, or any other item designed for a right-handed person, I don't ask that my son use materials inappropriate to him. I must tailor his curriculum to meet his specific needs. Children who are concrete learners have difficulty with many mathematics workbooks because these often teach abstractly through a series of directives. My son has difficulty with such a process and needs to see clearly the reasons and applications for such work. Teaching using manipulatives and word-problems can aid their understanding. While this method requires more parental input than assigning a workbook page, it consumes much less time and effort than calming a crying, angry, or frustrated child and coaxing him to work. My personal suggestion for mathematics is the Math-U-See program, by Steven Demme. This program uses manipulatives in an inventive and surprising, but easily understood, way to teach elementary arithmetic through advanced trigonometry. Because no brief description can fully explain the program, I recommend that you obtain the demonstration video: www.mathusee.com; (888) 854-MATH.

Science can be another awkward subject because of the theoretical approach of many books. There are many fine books of experiments that enable parents to demonstrate concepts in a meaningful way to their children. Consider the different approaches between reading a few paragraphs on velocity, lift, and airfoils before answering a few brief questions and building an airfoil and using a hair dryer to provide the wind while discussing how and why this results in lift. The latter is not only a more interesting and practical manner of learning but also concrete for the hands-on learner.

The physical act of writing is also a stumbling block for my child and, as I understand it, for other children of similar nature as well. I use the Charlotte Mason approach of "narration" (after being read a story, the child retells the story) to develop sufficient comprehension of reading materials and employ much memorization and verbal work. This isn't to say that I don't require writing. I require much more than my child would choose for himself, but I do try to find the delicate balance between challenging and overwhelming. This is a fine line, but I watch my child carefully and look for signs that he's becoming overly frustrated before he becomes angry. Painting and drawing increase his fine-motor control and his ability to sit still without seeming like busy work. He's slowly increasing the amount of time he can spend writing through his artwork and studied dictation.

Magnetic Poetry, magnetic word pieces that you find at bookstores (to make your own, see www.catholictreasury.com and click on "Thrifty Homeschooler"), are great for grammar work. I put them on a magnetic white board, and Joseph puts together sentences and then diagrams them. The diagramming books from Ye Hedgeschool (see Appendix A) are good primers.

I've relied a great deal on Seton Home Study School, which takes a lot of work off of me. They plan it. They grade it. I just teach it differently. They truly want parents to present information in the way the child needs to learn it. Their slogan "Adjust the program to fit the child, not the child to fit the program" is no mere axiom. They say it; they mean it. They have a learning-disability counselor who assists parents like me. I just call them, and they're available for help.

Scheduling

This is perhaps one of the most difficult aspects of home-schooling my child. He needs structure, but *forgiving* structure. He works in brief increments, and I change the subject matter every fifteen minutes whether he has accomplished something or not. This method seems frightening to other homeschooling mothers, but it's really not so cumbersome. Joseph divides his work into morning- and afternoon-session activities, and I have a clearly written lesson plan for him. He copies his tasks onto a laminated to-do list, and he's responsible for completing his session work before moving on. The to-do lists are remarkably effective because Joseph sees these as authority and will complete the work better if he has the opportunity to cross items off his list. Frequent breaks are essential, and we use these as incentive. Outside play is in order if work is completed with a satisfactory attitude; otherwise, we stretch and play Simon Says. The physical outlet is critical and can serve to vent frustration and hostilities before these become problematic.

Also, we find that scheduling the first day of the week as an abbreviated day with only art, music, and Spanish eases us into the week.

Monitoring your child's mood fluctuations and determining when he or she is most amiable and cooperative and what contributes to good moods are just as important as discerning which subjects are particularly vexing. In this way, you can introduce popular, well-liked subjects to induce a willingness to work, and find ways to temper the frustrations of more challenging subjects. In our case, we save spelling for the last subject because introducing it at any other time can stall our day. By Joseph's choice, we start our day with religion, followed by reading, so that we always start with favorite subjects. He readily begins these, and this makes my job as a teaching mother much easier.

In scheduling, I cannot underestimate the value of preparing my child for the day ahead by providing him with a written agenda and frequent reminders of what is to come. In this way, I can smooth the transition between activities and this helps keep the cool.

I have an interesting activity I use during transition. First, we put away materials not in use and take out new materials, then we "change our heads" by pretending to take off our heads and place on new ones. I'm quite willing to tolerate great silliness in this, so long as order is resumed once our new heads are on and our books are opened. Making verbal reminders of expectations before the need arises can prevent some disagreements and misbehavior.

Compromise and Discipline

Flexibility and willingness to compromise, where possible and appropriate, are necessary in working with children, and special-needs children in particular. I permit Joseph to work standing up, lying down, or wearing peculiar hats or clothes. So long as he's attentive and working consistently, he makes his own choices; however, he can choose to give me the decision-making power by failing to make appropriate choices. When reading aloud, or listening to music, or watching educational films, a child with surplus energy can be focused by "illustrating" what he or she sees and hears. I've found this extraordinarily effective in keeping him attentive during music appreciation or family reading time.

Joseph has a special name badge he wears for school to help remind him to behave, and he earns computer time and alone playtime for excellent behavior. I work diligently to notice positive behavior and to comment on it immediately. Positive feedback is essential if criticism is going to function as a deterrent, because why would he care about criticism if it didn't mean the retraction of appreciation? Catechism is extremely beneficial in the instruction of expected behavior, because it outlines all that I demand of him. He's asked to remind himself and other family members to obey the teachings of the Church. This capitalizes on children's natural tendency to police others and encourages him to follow these same regulations, lest he be policed in return.

Brag-tags, or small adhesive labels, can also act as a reward. I write praise, not mindless praise but *well-earned* praise, on these so that when my husband comes home from work, the children can greet him and show them their brag-tags. The children also love showing people at the post office, grocery store, and daily Mass. They enjoy the compliments they receive.

Joseph loses particular toys and a favorite bed comforter for poor behavior. I also use time-out as a place for Joseph to think and calm down and to separate him from whatever is causing the problem behavior. He has a special place to go to calm down, and he's supposed to imagine a rocket preparing for takeoff; he loads in his "bad works and thoughts" and sends them off in the rocket after a dramatic countdown. I also use an unusual tactic of requiring silent time. Beginning with one-minute increments, I require absolute silence from Joseph, although he's able to stay in the room and even sit with his father or me. When he begins to speak or complain, I increase the amount of time by an additional minute. This is useful for disciplining a *screamer* or a *stomper* and is less violent than spanking.

For help in dealing with the emotional volatility of Asperger children, and any child with behavior or emotional issues for that matter, there is a fantastic book: *Asperger Syndrome and Difficult Moments: Practical Solutions for Tantrums, Rage and Meltdowns*, by Brenda Smith Myles and Jack Southwick (Autism Asperger Publishing Company; see Appendix C). There's a specific section for public-school teachers, but the methodology is applicable to home-schoolers as well. This is a critical book to have, as dealing with the emotions of such a child is often the most difficult part. The academics, in contrast, are not usually too hard. Asperger children often develop into the stereotypical brilliant but socially inept genius.

Disaster Management

The best-laid plans can fall to ruin, and this is certainly the case with homeschooling a special-needs child. Developing techniques for salvaging a day or even a whole week is essential. I've developed several tricks to teach my child. First, the previously mentioned curricula, scheduling, compromise, and discipline areas should be fully implemented; thereafter I can focus on "fire-fighting," as I call it. We walk to daily Mass and to the library and anyplace else within a reasonable distance, because I find the exercise helps my children vent their physical frustrations. As parents, we need to remember that we can act on the things that cause us discomfort, whereas our children are unable to communicate these needs to us or to act on these needs without our assistance. At times, we need to anticipate these things, so that we can best serve our children.

Also, I can't over-represent the grace of God obtained through prayer. We start each day with a reading about the saint of the day, followed by a brief discussion on how to embody this model of behavior, and a prayer to God. We pray for the baby to sit quietly with me, for the toddler to be happy to work with us or to play by himself until the break, for Joseph to be a docile and obedient student, and for me to be a patient and understanding teacher. Daily

Mass also serves to keep us focused on those things that should center our lives: frequent reception of the Eucharist and Mass attendance. If we miss one or more days, I find all of the children less agreeable and cooperative.

During the day, if all else fails and the day seems to be unraveling in my grip, we stop and pray the Rosary. This calms us all, and we're usually ready to return to schoolwork afterward; otherwise, we take a brief walk to the park for a break and have been known to finish schoolwork there. Sometimes we end academics for the day and practice math skills by doubling or tripling a cookie recipe.

Final Reflections

Homeschooling clearly benefits my son. His behavior and general attitude have greatly improved since returning home to me. But he isn't the only one who is changing. I see the blessings in homeschooling in me as well. I have developed patience, ingenuity, and sources of strength I didn't know I had. While it's true to say that I was originally intimidated by the thought of homeschooling, I'm no longer afraid that I won't be able to give my son as much as a teacher with a specialized advanced degree. I know that I can offer so much more because, more than any teacher, I know him, I love him, and I can constantly reinforce taught skills — because he's with me not for only a few hours of the day or a few days of the week, but for his entire childhood.

Also, I no longer wish to *change* my son; I wish to love him and guide him. I've accepted him for who and what he is and will spend several years fully preparing him for the world rather than prematurely forcing him out. I no longer wish to "pass" him off as someone else because I've learned to truly appreciate his vitality. My house isn't quiet or immaculately clean, and Joseph is decidedly different from some of the more calm and mild-mannered homeschoolers in our Catholic group, but there's no reason why he should be just like them. My son is a blessing from God, and he has a unique purpose in this world, and I can do no better than to help him find his calling. As his mother, I will aid him in maturing so that when it's time, he'll meet the world with his sense of justice and invigorating personality and take it by storm.

In the mornings, when the neighbors hear us laughing as we dance to our favorite Latin music CDs before we start school, I hope they hear the noise and see the wildness and know that I love this life and my children.

"Education is simply the soul of a society
as it passes from one generation to the next."

G. K. Chesterton

Count It All Joy

Kim Fry

Recently my family hosted a homeschool support-group meeting at our home with the topic "Highs and Lows of Homeschooling." I hadn't chosen this topic; rather, it seemed in some ways that it had chosen me. In the weeks preceding the meeting, I had thought over our homeschool journey. Certainly there had been countless peak experiences, but reflection revealed that they were meaningful primarily in relation to those other times that have come and gone over the years. Those other times, times of struggle, fear, illness, and uncertainty, in fact, paved the way for the peak experiences along the journey. That journey began not when my son reached kindergarten age, but the night he was born to two very young, very hopeful people: my husband and me.

We had met in high school and married during our first year of college, when tuition money was running out. He elected to enter the Air Force rather than accrue more debt. We were shipped to Germany shortly after his basic training, eighteen and nineteen at the time, totally unaware of the adventure we were embarking upon.

Our first son, Colin, was born the following year, after a troubled pregnancy and whirlwind birth. We had expected this to be the first "peak" experience. Indeed, in many ways it was, although it didn't play out as expected. Shortly after Colin was delivered, they whisked him out of the delivery room, later explaining he had a meningomylocele, the medical term for spina bifida, and would need to be flown to another hospital in southern Germany for immediate surgery. It was the first of what would be a long string of medical procedures this child would have to endure. While we knew the situation was grave and spelled lifelong complication, in our youthful optimism all we could think was that he surely was the most beautiful baby ever born. The same determination that had seen us through the challenges of a young marriage most certainly would see our new family through whatever else might be in store.

After Colin was stabilized, we were transferred back to the United States. Two more sons and many surgeries, therapies, and medical appointments followed in rapid succession. My husband had reentered college, attending evening classes after work. It was during this time we were introduced to homeschooling. It was an intriguing, if completely foreign, idea to us. I began by teaching my sons preschool after realizing that tuition at the local Montessori school was beyond our reach. When it came time to enroll Colin in kindergarten, he was far more advanced than his peers, already reading fluently and doing basic math. Despite his remarkable academic progress, the local private school was uncomfortable enrolling him with his medical situation. Homeschooling seemed the perfect, albeit incredibly unconventional, solution. It seemed perfect to me at any rate; my husband wasn't so sure at first.

We had a wonderful first school year at home. Colin sailed through Calvert School's first grade. We were blessed to find a group of devout Catholic homeschoolers, despite years of being away from our faith. We returned to the Church and discovered our rich and fascinating heritage as Catholics. In many ways, this was a time of unprecedented blessing, although not without its challenges. The birth of our third son had exacerbated long-standing health problems for me. By the time he was a year old, I was experiencing periods of nearly incapacitating illness. There were times we weren't sure whether I'd even be able to *care* for the children, much less teach them.

We pressed on, seeking out alternative therapies and embarking on a rigorous nutritional program. In time, a good deal of time, the illness became more manageable, and we looked forward to enlarging our family again. The good news came just as my husband earned his degree and was accepted to the four-month-long Officer Training School. He returned in my seventh month and moved us to his next base across the country, where our first daughter would be born.

In the years that followed, he was deployed on numerous missions totaling more than a year away. As fate would have it, Colin's surgeries almost without fail landed during those times. More than one of those procedures involved his brain or spinal cord; several required months in body casts and more months of rehabilitation. Our second son developed significant behavior problems that eventually became so severe that we sought outside intervention. Another daughter and son were born, our marriage was tested, and we questioned my husband's career choice more than once. It all sounds so innocuous on paper, but there were moments when I questioned my ability to move forward.

If you had asked me during that time why I was homeschooling, and people did, the answer would have been the same as the day we began. Indeed, it remains the same today: simply because we love it. Through the years, it has been the glue that kept us together and enabled us to stay the course. For us, it wasn't just an educational option; it was a lifestyle. It allowed continuity for the children through our eleven moves, enabling us to travel with Dad on his trips when possible, as well as accommodating medical needs. Regardless of where we were or what else was happening, the children and I had each other, all day. There is very little you can't face under those circumstances.

We never felt victimized and always considered ourselves very fortunate to have each other and to live the homeschooling lifestyle, despite the frequent trials. Knowing that God is all-good and all-powerful in our lives helped me refrain from asking God "Why?" and instead asking, "What?" *What would you have me do or learn here, Lord? What are you showing and teaching us through this circumstance?* Instead of viewing all of life's unexpected challenges as crises, we felt that they could, in fact, be opportunities. God consistently answered our prayers through these very challenges, even if it wasn't always clear at the time.

One area in which God's will wasn't always crystal clear was curriculum selection. A perceived shortcoming, my utter inability to stick to a syllabus, plagued me for years. To remedy it, I began a fervent — no, desperate — search for better directions. I so longed for a neat and tidy label, to fit into a clear-cut homeschooling niche. We invested hundreds of dollars in correspondence courses, lesson plans, and miscellaneous curricula that went largely unused. As the mountain of discarded programs grew, so did my guilt. What was wrong with me? Did I lack the organizational skills and wherewithal to follow through responsibly in this homeschooling venture?

These questions, however, only led to the real questions: which program available could tell me how to teach my child while he was in a body cast, or while his father was off serving in Cuba, or while I was on bed rest with a difficult pregnancy? What curriculum addressed the needs of a distractible child, a nursing baby, a sick mother, or a family making a cross-country move?

And even if such a plan existed, would it allow for serendipity? Would it take into account unexpected surprises, such as life lessons drawn from a children's storybook, or a sickbed, or a mountain sunset happened upon by chance? Likely, it would not. If we were to not only survive but also to thrive in this adventure that we had set ourselves upon, particularly under the unusual circumstances of our lives, we had to let learning find us and be open to these discoveries in whichever times and places they turned up.

One thing that prodigious stack of how-to manuals did was to teach me how to teach. After reviewing dozens of scope and sequences, I understood what was taught at each level in the core subjects and unearthed many useful techniques and ideas. I culled the best from each, taking what we needed and leaving the rest. While the manuals themselves went unused, the ideas they contained were assimilated into our little schoolroom.

Most important, I learned to "make hay when the sun shone," making use of the spare minutes of each day to sneak in moments of learning, cleaning, talking, and praying. There are seasons to this life, cycles of moving, pregnancies, babies, surgeries, illnesses, behavioral challenges, alternating with more mundane, routine periods and times of sheer bliss. Each has its own gifts and lessons, and requires different methods of adaptation.

My life leaves few, if any, large windows of time for any of those activities, but by making the most of isolated moments here and there, I get much more done than would seem possible. I don't function very well with a to-do list. I make them, to be sure, but I often forget to check them or I lose them altogether. A wise friend suggested making *done lists* instead, and few things have helped my morale more. To-do lists generally turned out to be little more than speculation and rarely came to pass as they were laid out. Done lists, in contrast, record all the many things we do manage to accomplish, sometimes things completely different from we what had planned.

To keep us on track, I create a chart on which I post the resources and activities I hope to use for each subject. (Frankly, without this chart, I tend to forget what we own.) Using the chart and recording our daily activities has been a workable arrangement. I can see our big picture but retain enough flexibility to accommodate our varying schedule.

The children keep notebooks for each subject. As in anything, the success of this system relies upon consistency. Most assignments are done on loose-leaf paper or typed and placed in my to-be-checked file folder. After reviewing them (ideally that day, but more often later), I put them into appropriate binders. Like seeing the done lists, watching a collection of history summaries or compositions grow is deeply satisfying. It's a boost for those days when I ask myself, "Are we getting anywhere?" Such days do happen.

All the children study a basic topic from which we derive lessons in various subject areas. These topics are generally taken from historical eras, but at other times will center upon a place we're traveling through or a science topic. In a given week, the children typically read, or listen to me read, historical fiction or biography. They then research the people and events using our encyclopedia and the Internet, complete outlines and essays, make maps of the areas covered, and enter the most noteworthy data on a timeline they keep in their binder. The older boys are required to analyze every topic they study in relation to their faith. Each month they read about a new artist and composer, again from the era they're studying, and write a short summary in the notebooks. They color reproductions of the artists' work and file those as well. Literature usually includes, but isn't limited to, a novel from this same time or topic.

High school students cover science by using a text. Our elementary students study similar topics from age-appropriate library and reference books. We pull out information from that mountain of texts for the younger levels from time to time, rather than moving through the books as they're laid out. We try to do illustrative experiments weekly, although there are times when this isn't feasible. The key is to do as much as possible during the slow times so I don't feel guilty when it gets hectic and we have to let some work go.

We have streamlined religion and Bible study also. The chapters of the *Baltimore Catechism* 1 and 2 are similar, and can be taught to all elementary students at once. Bible study is taken from the Sunday readings. Using the *Bread of Life* scripture study and the *Daily Word* mailings from the Internet, we take a different reading from Sunday and study it each weekday. We often tie in a very simple liturgical craft for the littlest ones. My high-schooler, additionally, has his own religion texts, and we enjoy sharing religious and apologetics articles and books with each other.

We also try to make good use of all the real-life opportunities each new community brings us by way of theater, classes, sightseeing, and fellowship. That sometimes necessitates finding innovative ways to complete lessons. If this means less regularity, it also keeps things fresh and helps us keep out of a rut.

During our more regular times of homeschooling, we keep fairly normal study hours. The older children alternate helping with the baby and preschooler while I work with others or make meals. We've had to work out different arrangements during different seasons of our lives. When my oldest was beginning school, we had a baby and a three-year old. Our days were filled with Colin's medical appointments, physical therapy, and childcare. We covered most of his seatwork after dinner while my husband bathed and read to the younger boys. It was a quiet, special time for my son and me, as well as for my husband and the babies.

Now our days are fuller yet, with my husband returning to school in the evening and four full-time students in our homeschool. Our sixth baby is learning to walk and explore, and nap time has long since been spoken for. Colin is now fourteen, and is a wheelchair athlete in very good health, but he still has many appointments each month. He must meet half a dozen specialists who follow him, and replace or repair durable medical equipment. To this we add basic healthcare appointments for the other siblings and myself, membership in an active homeschool support group, and service to our parish. Additionally the children are active in sports. We have limited outside activities to one or two per child, but when you do the math, that still amounts to many practices and games. The adventure continues.

In all, it has been wildly successful. We can't imagine our lives any other way. The children are excelling, academically and otherwise, and I have the confidence I once lacked. I've learned to trust in the Lord's leading and trust my children to learn, knowing it doesn't all depend upon me. In fact, the need to step back and simply let the children interact with the wonderful resources and opportunities that have come our way is continually driven home to me. The focus now is less on being Supermom and more on just being Mom and enjoying the family. I don't always have the answers, but I realize now that I don't always need to. To be honest, it has taken some time to make peace with that fact.

In retrospect, I realize that each challenge ran its respective course. I worried more over some than over others. At times I was thoroughly demoralized and certain we couldn't go on. Each time we were forced to walk by faith and not by sight, because there was no visible assurance that a solution to the current trial was forthcoming. I prayed to love it all, and each prayer was answered in abundance. As paradoxical as it sounds, I'm not sure that I would have comprehended the apostle's words to "count it all joy" (James 1:2) had we not been visited by such sadness, fear, and doubt. I can testify that God has heard our call and provided abundantly. All those well-laid plans we collected presumed to improve upon his providence, and always fell short of the great good God had in store for us.

While we may have let go of our attempts to plot exactly what we would learn and when, we do have a plan. We plan to learn, explore, research, and experiment diligently. We plan to pull together to do the work that must be done in a mobile, growing family. We plan the regular family prayer, the morning offering, the Scripture reading, the Angelus, and the Rosary. From this we derive the regularity and order that seemed to elude us before.

Essentially, home comes first in our homeschool, and school is a natural outgrowth of our trials and adventures, our work and play. Time is showing us that homeschooling is also forming my husband and me at least as much as the children. We have been forced to lean on the Lord more than on our own limited understanding, and to be more patient and flexible. We look forward hopefully, and backward thankfully. Even with its bumps and turns, it has been a marvelous ride.

"Let nothing disturb you
Let nothing frighten you
All things are passing
God never changes
Patience attains all things
He who has God lacks nothing
God alone suffices."

St. Teresa of Avila

Chapter Six

Homeschooling in
Unique Circumstances

*"Of what use to me is all I learn
in school if I do not become holy?"*

St. Francis de Sales

School Is Where the Army Sends Us

Stacey Johnson

There are so many great reasons to educate your children at home.
For our family, the ability to pass on our Catholic Faith is, by far,
the most important. However, it seems that I can think of yet another reason nearly every day. Many of the reasons are shared by
most other homeschoolers, and some are unique to our family —
connected with the fact that my husband is in the Army. A military career brings its own special challenges to the homeschooler,
but it also means that there are additional benefits to this proposition. Furthermore, some of the benefits that other homeschooling
families report are magnified for the military family.

One of the biggest benefits that home education offers a military family is stability. Our family is in its sixth year of homeschooling. Since my husband is in the Army, you might imagine
that it's quite likely that we have moved during this time, and
have we ever! We began this adventure while we were living in
California, continued it overseas in Austria, returned to our native soil to find ourselves in Kansas, and are currently located in
Georgia. Yes, that worked out to a completely different location
every year for the first four years.

Although that has meant educating ourselves about the homeschool regulations in a number of places, timing our school year to

be finished in time to pack up and move, and worrying about misplacing records, supplies, and catalogs, homeschooling has also meant that our children have had additional stability throughout all of our relocations. We haven't had to worry about starting out at yet another new school. We haven't had to worry that we don't know anything about the teachers or the facilities. For that matter, we haven't had to wonder which neighborhood we should live in so that our children can attend a particular school. Instead, our children have the benefit of a school with which they are intimately familiar and a teacher who knows them like no other ever could.

Now, these last two are benefits that any homeschooling family can appreciate, but I happen to think that they're especially important to children who have moved as many times ours have. Additionally, I think that homeschooled children tend to be closer to their siblings, for obvious reasons, and this has proven to be an additional benefit when we've moved. While the children work out new friendships with neighbor children, they always have each other to fall back on.

Our family would homeschool our children regardless of the availability of good local Catholic schools, but I know of many others for whom this isn't the case. For those families, homeschooling provides an alternative when the military inevitably sends them to a place where there's no Catholic school.

Moving a lot has been wonderful for providing us with new material for field trips. My children have been to some pretty amazing places, from Rome to Fatima, from the Monterey Bay Aquarium to the U.S.S. North Carolina, and have had some interesting experiences, from hearing President George W. Bush speak to seeing a presentation by a local naturalist at the Tybee Island Marine Science Center. One year, we took an extended field trip via a Space Available military flight to Hawaii. The flight cost us $10.50 each way for all of us, and that was only because we ordered food!

As far as challenges go, we've found ways to work with them. In some cases, we've even turned a challenge into a benefit, as when we were preparing to move overseas to Austria. The local public school wouldn't be finished with its school year by the time we were scheduled to depart, but we were able to start our year and time our vacations so that we had completed our required number of days with time to spare. That meant that I didn't have to worry about packing and schooling at the same time, and the children had some down time before the move.

We've also been able to work learning about our next location into our curriculum. We deal with the worries about packers misplacing our important documents by hand-carrying the most important ones, including my latest copies of homeschool supply catalogs tucked into my tote bag. Besides eliminating the worry over whether those catalogs will be lost and whether I'll be able to remember the name of the catalog that had that new art program I had been meaning to try, I really enjoy poring through the catalogs while we're driving to our next location.

As with many military families, my husband is frequently gone. He has been all over the globe during the course of his career, and I have no reason to expect that to change anytime soon. Even when he's home, he often works long hours. With the wonderful flexibility of home education, we can take time off as a family when he can take time off without having to worry about the children missing school.

One fall, he was able to take a week off at the end of September, a time when most children are in school. We went to North Carolina to visit my folks. We brought some schoolwork with us (the essentials, such as math and reading) and went on three wonderful field trips during our one-week stay. If we hadn't brought any work along, though, that would have been fine, too. We wouldn't have had make-up work hanging over our heads the whole time. We can just schedule the work at other times. While we've been in Georgia, my husband has been deployed numerous times, and I'm so thankful that we can work around his schedule, as we will often not see him again for a number of months.

One challenge that I still struggle with, which is probably exacerbated by my husband's career choice, is availability of support groups. I'm currently involved with a support group, in fact, for the very first time. I find that there are plenty of military home educators, but compared with home educators at large, a significantly small percentage of them are Catholic.

The number of non-Catholics isn't necessarily a problem, but sometimes a homeschool support group will have a statement of faith that members are required to sign. Many times, that statement will be problematic for a Catholic. The group may call itself nondenominational Christian, but what that usually means is nondenominational Protestant. There could be references to the Bible as the sole source of faith (*sola scriptura*) or to salvation by faith alone (*sola fide*), or both. In the first instance, a Catholic would be denying the role of Tradition in our faith. In the second instance, while it often seems as if many Catholics and Protestants are saying the same things when we talk about salvation, what we mean by what we say can oftentimes differ, and a Catholic will usually not have the same understanding of how one "works out" his salvation as an Evangelical Protestant does.

Additionally, much of the available homeschool curriculum has a very strong Protestant bias, so these groups, although usually well-intentioned, are often quite misinformed about Catholicism.

For the past two years here in Georgia, however, I've been blessed to connect with a number of other Catholic homeschooling families, all military, and we've formed our own small support group.

Moving so often has meant that it has been more difficult for me to meet other homeschoolers who are Catholic, and there have been times when I would have liked the additional support of a homeschooler who shares my worldview. I have, however, found a reasonable substitute: online support groups. I've been involved with a number of email groups for homeschoolers. The one I've been with the longest is for military homeschoolers, and there are a few Catholics in this very small group of wonderful ladies. Another is for homeschoolers of children with autism and related disorders (see Appendix C), and there are a few Catholics there, too. One of these women even picked out that my husband and I use Natural Family Planning based on something I had said in an email, and sent me a note of support and encouragement.

Overall, I have to say that homeschooling has been wonderful for us as a military family. It has made all the moving easier, and it has given us the ability to take advantage of all the really neat places that the Army has sent us to. Most especially, it has brought us closer as a family — something that I think is extremely important for a military family stressed by deployments and relocations — and it has allowed us the privilege of imparting our Catholic Faith to our children, wherever we are.

_____

"I can do all things in him who strengthens me."
Philippians 4:13

Surviving the Real-Life Drama
of a Family Business or Apostolate

Joan Stromberg

You know, I will never, ever, get one of those video cameras for my computer or my telephone. Are you kidding? The scene behind the phone call at my house would go something like this:

Mom, picking up ringing phone while nursing Baby: "Ecce Homo Press," she says cheerily.

"Hello, I'd like to place an order." *Great,* Mom thinks, *maybe I will be able to pay the printer after all.*

"Sure, just a moment, please," Mom tries to get off the couch, phone at her ear, without disturbing Baby. Awkwardly, she steps over the puppets lying on the floor. She notices someone has pulled the head off the king and the puppet of Mother Seton doesn't have any hair. The twelve-year-old is sitting at the computer playing solitaire. *She always gets her schoolwork done first,* Mom muses.

"I need that," Mom mouths to her daughter, her hand over the phone receiver and pointing to the computer. Mom sits down in the now-vacant chair and opens the database program. It's painfully slow to open. Meanwhile, Baby, still at breast, but now disturbed, is curious about the keyboard. Baby starts reaching behind her to play with the keys. Mom, unable to sprout any more hands, drops the phone.

"I'm sorry," she says as she retrieves it. "Have you ordered from us before?"

"No, this is my first time," comes the reply.

As Mom begins to take the information, an eight-year-old girl presents a phonics book in Mom's face.

"Not now," Mom mouths silently. Girl drops the book and walks away.

Mom glances at the computer screen, horrified. The information fields she has been filling in are blank. Panicked, she asks the caller to hold a moment while she tries to figure out the problem. She vaguely remembers this happened before, when son number one was playing a game on the computer and changed a setting. *Oh, what was it? The number lock key — he turned off the number lock.* She finds the key and hits it. Yes, success.

Mom again inputs the information. Now she is reading back the credit-card number to the caller. Daughter with the phonics book is now occupied with son number three playing tag in the living room. Son number three screeches good-naturedly at a near miss of his sister's hand. Baby is finished at the breast and begins to throw papers off the computer desk onto floor.

The noise from the tag game escalates. Mom snaps her fingers for their attention. When they look her way, she puts her fingers to her lips. The children are quiet for the next three seconds. Just enough time to read the credit-card number back to the customer and end the call. *Whew!*

"Thank you, and God bless!" Mom says as she replaces the receiver. She turns to the noisemakers. "Guys, please, please, when I'm on the phone, could you be quiet?"

"Yes, Mom," comes a chorus of replies. Mom knows: it will be the same next time. "Now, Mary, what did you need help with?" Mom asks as she picks up the phonics book.

No, I will never have one of those video cameras recording every move I make for everyone to see. I'm not into reality television, just reality. I figure God is recording every move I make, and he's the only one I have to answer to.

Running a family business/apostolate is very demanding and very rewarding. It's kind of like homeschooling itself. In fact, our home business is a very integral part of our homeschooling, since we publish books. I've tried to incorporate my writing into our school curriculum. For example, two years ago, when I wrote *Kat Finds a Friend*, about a shoemaker's daughter who wishes to attend Mother Seton's school, we did extensive research on shoemaking. My son ended up collecting antique shoemaking supplies, putting together a shoemaking presentation and building a web page on shoemaking.

This year I'm writing a St. John Neumann book. John Neumann took the Erie Canal to Buffalo, New York, in 1836, so the unit study in the back of the book is on the Erie Canal. My oldest daughter built a set of model locks to present at her history fair. We also have canal folk songs playing in the background to inspire both mother and daughter.

The home business/apostolate truly permeates our whole home. It has become part of us, not something separate that Mom does. Everyone gets involved in the work and the play. The boys load and unload boxes of books, presentation supplies, and other materials. The girls help me with the dolls and kits, story ideas, and what we call "kerchunking." Kerchunking is punching and binding the books. The older children do this for extra spending money.

Another way we have integrated the home business/apostolate is to involve all the children in a presentation on American saints. We go around to schools, parishes, homeschool groups, girls' and boys' clubs, and so forth, doing our presentation. Each child has a part, although sometimes you'd think that part is to heckle the one who's speaking at the time. The children have grown so much in doing the presentations. Once, when we were performing in front of four hundred school children, my son was asked by another teenager if he was afraid to talk in front of so many people. He replied, "No, why would I be?"

Usually, when people hear that I have eight children, homeschool, and own a business, they ask, "How do you do it all?" The truthful, and simple, answer would be, "Grace." But I know that everybody reading this already knows that, especially if they already homeschool. I'm convinced that you couldn't get through a day without the grace of God.

If you're thinking about starting a home business/apostolate, there are a few tricks I've learned that I'd like to share with you. First, I always have to remind myself that my business is an apostolate. It's a ministry. My goal is serving others while doing the work of Christ. Having your apostolate also a business helps in building it. If you can legitimately collect money for goods and services, your apostolate will grow more efficiently. You can also apply business practices to streamline your apostolate for effectiveness and growth. Conversely, if you're a generous, ethical employer, your presence in the business world spreads the message of Christ in that sphere of influence.

Choosing Your Business/Apostolate

Do what you love. I've always loved writing. I've always loved history. I love the Catholic Church with my whole heart. I love homeschooling. I love researching. I love saints' stories. When I write this all out, I know that I love my business/apostolate. This is really important. You'll get frustrated and burned out if you don't love what you're doing.

Look at the talents God gave you. Do you write? Do you act? Do you sew? Do you cook? Look at the needs of others. Homeschoolers need good Catholic materials. What needs do you perceive that fit your talents? Are you a scientist who could write on Catholics in your field, or give a presentation to Catholics about science? Are you a cook who could put together a cookbook of liturgical recipes for children to use in our homeschools and parishes? Interested in politics? I would love to see a Catholic civics book for use in homeschools and parishes.

Get Organized — Get Scheduled

There's no doubt about it: if you homeschool, if you run a large household, or if you volunteer, you have to be organized. The same goes for a home business/apostolate. I use files to keep my projects straight. I use the computer extensively to keep my records up to date. I back up my finances and important writing projects on a separate hard drive. I keep all receipts. They're in a shoebox, but I have them. Find a system that works for you, and work with it.

The most effective tool I've used in combining homeschooling and the business/apostolate is the schedule. Using Terry Maxwell's *Managers of Their Homes*, I've composed a master schedule for every member of the family, except Dad. Everyone has something he's supposed to do so that Mom isn't pulled in seven directions at one time. I, too, have my time scheduled so that I don't waste it. I see the schedule as a tool, though. We use it for the construction of our day. We use it in a way that builds the best day we can possibly have. We don't let it build us. In other words, it's flexible.

When making up the schedule, I purposely didn't put any time in it for useless things like watching television. I realized there are too few hours in a day and that if they were spent in front of the television, I wouldn't get anything done. I still spend way too much time on the computer doing what I convince myself is "research."

Lower the Bar . . . Again!

Remember when you wanted to homeschool and people who did it told you that you'd have to lower your standards on some things, like ironing your husband's underwear or having all your ceiling fans cobweb-free? With every baby, my bar seems to get that much lower. With a business/apostolate, it's so low that they call me the limbo champ. I don't do any ironing now, unless something is really wrinkly, and there's nothing else to wear that Sunday morning to Mass. I've assigned more jobs as the children get older, but it takes a while until the blinders they're born with fall from their eyes and they see *all* the mess, not just the mess in the middle of the floor.

Involve the Whole Family, Especially Dad!

My dear husband has been the greatest asset to our home business/apostolate. He doesn't do saint presentations, he doesn't write books, he doesn't even kerchunk. What he does is far more valuable. He helps me with business decisions and supports me every step of the way. When the bar is so low that it's touching the ground, he helps pull it up to a reasonable level. He encourages me in so many ways to be the best mom, wife, writer, and businesswoman I can be. Without his wise counsel, our business/apostolate wouldn't have made it through the first year.

I've already enumerated the ways the children help. They are truly the inspiration for everything I do. Sometimes, in moments of frustration, I wish I could have an hour without them to work on something uninterrupted. Then the Holy Spirit whispers in my ear that they're the reason I'm doing what I'm doing. If I didn't have children who needed good saint books to integrate into their curriculum, I probably wouldn't have written those books. At that realization, I usually leave what I'm working on and pick up a storybook to read to the preschoolers, or ask the older girls if they want to bake cookies with me.

Most of All, Keep Your Eyes on Jesus

Just as for those taking on homeschooling, those taking on the task of a business/apostolate need Jesus, the Church he instituted, and the sacraments he gave us. Prayer time must be constant and consistent.

There are some days when my frustration level rises so high because of the constant interruptions, the constant noise, and the constant give-and-take of everyday life with children, that it makes me want to scream. But good moms never scream, right? This was one of the reasons I named my business/apostolate Ecce Homo Press. *Ecce Homo* is Latin for "Behold the Man," from the words Pilate spoke in John 19:5 after he had had Christ scourged. I knew that this undertaking would be bigger than I, and if I relied on my own efforts, I'd fail miserably. I feel the name of the business/apostolate is a constant reminder to look to Christ for every daily struggle. Our salvation is going through it with Christ, one minute, one hour, and one day at a time.

No, I don't want that camera on me twenty-four/seven. God sees my every move. My business/apostolate won't make me as rich and famous as surviving a reality-television drama. I'm more concerned about getting kicked out of Heaven than kicked off the island.

"The characteristic of the lay state being a life led in the midst of the world and of secular affairs, lay people are called by God to make of their apostolate, through the vigor of their Christian spirit, a leaven in the world."

Catechism of the Catholic Church, 940

Homeschooling While
Suffering Chronic Illness

Rachel Watkins

There are times in my life when I feel kindred to Moses, in particular the Moses of Numbers, chapter 11. In this chapter, Moses has one of his intimate conversations with God. He pulls no punches but clearly states how overwhelmed he feels at the life that God expects him to live. This was not the life he expected, and he feels ill-prepared for it.

There are days in my life when I feel as he does when he cries out, "I am not able to carry all this people alone; the burden is too heavy for me. If thou wilt deal thus with me, kill me at once, if I find favor in thy sight, that I may not see my wretchedness" (Num. 11:14-15).

Little that I'm currently doing is what I expected when I first got married. I'm at home full-time, although I had expected to have an important career. My husband, Matt, and I are expecting our eighth child, although we had begun our marriage as contracepting Catholics. I'm homeschooling, although I had been looking forward to being a PTA parent and eventually the school-board president, just as my father had been for over fifteen years. Finally, multiple sclerosis (MS), a chronic and often debilitating disease, was never on my personal radar screen. And while all of the above situations send me to my knees for help from the Lord, it's the MS that makes me cry out like Moses, "Please do me the favor of killing me at once."

I'd never give back a single one of the children that the Lord has blessed us with, and I can regularly see the blessings of our decision to homeschool. My MS, however, has no value to me at all. Yes, I realize the theological value of sharing in the suffering of Christ's cross and such, but making that head knowledge seep into my soul and heart is a constant struggle. Moses and I repeat together, "I need no longer face this distress."

Then I jump to verse 17, where the Lord tells Moses, "And I will come down and talk with you there; and I will take some of the spirit which is upon you and put it upon them; and they shall bear the burden of the people with you, that you may not bear it yourself alone." Oh, how I cling to those words telling me that I won't have to bear it by myself. Homeschooling and raising a larger-than-average family is hard for all of us. Having to struggle with a chronic illness or another handicap requires something extra that I don't always have, and it requires that others share it with me. But over the past eleven years of diagnosis and eight years of homeschooling, I've discovered some tricks.

Like most chronic illnesses — fibromyalgia, Epstein-Barr's Syndrome, and even diabetes — multiple sclerosis has as many faces as it has victims. My own progression is different from others I know with the same disease, and it's never quite the same from day to day or from week to week. The variety of symptoms and irregularity of symptoms makes flexibility a key to successful management. I'm getting better at realizing what can set me off on an exacerbation of symptoms (driving for more than an hour, for instance) and what helps me battle my constant fatigue (healthful snacks throughout the day and a quick nap after 2 p.m. if possible). Living with this disease has affected my marriage, family plans, and certainly homeschooling.

Homeschooling While Suffering Chronic Illness

When I was first introduced to homeschooling, I was still in denial of my diagnosis, having had only a few bad episodes. Thus I went into homeschooling with a perception of being "normal." Like most new homeschoolers I over-bought, over-scheduled, and overwhelmed myself and my children those first few years. It took about three years and two more babies before I began to know my disease better and my own teaching style.

I began homeschooling by creating my own curriculum for all the children, and then spent a year using a packaged curriculum, but always judged myself by what I saw other mothers accomplishing. I never felt I was doing all I could do and should do with my children. While the fatigue and pain of my illness prevented me from doing any more than I was doing, I never pointed the finger at my MS; rather, I pointed it at myself. I spent too many hours at Mass, in prayer, and in the confessional beating myself up for not pushing myself harder and expecting more of myself and my children.

I'll admit that in the dark days of my illness, I looked toward traditional school with a great longing. I'd welcome a break from the rigors of educating, caring for, and feeding my crew. This was especially hard in the house we moved into in 1999, where the elementary, middle, and high schools are within walking distance of my home. (The Lord has such a great sense of humor.) Even today, on days when both my spirit and body are weak, I look out at these buildings and think, "It wouldn't be too bad, would it?"

However, the time spent homeschooling has introduced me to people and methods to lean on when I'm not so strong. God has given me others to share the burden. Although I'm without a support group within my hometown, a group I left in Baltimore continues to be my support via telephone and e-mail. This electronic group includes friends from Missouri, Florida, and more. I would have packed my children's lunches long ago had not these friends been my support.

I believe that never knowing what the day will bring has made me more flexible than many other homeschoolers. I set weekly goals using the Mother of Divine Grace curriculum as a guide for my older girls, but allow for the fact that I might require more help with the little ones and housework. The needs of the entire family have sometimes made the needs of an individual child take a backseat. On any given day, if I'm unable to walk well, it means that the children over the age of five might not meet all of the week's goals, as they help me with the set of children under the age of five. But by God's grace and their determination, they're able to get all their work done over a month's time.

The downside to this flexibility is that I sometimes hesitate to commit my children to any activity that might require regular attendance (especially if money is involved and it's during the day). Their activities are limited by what Matt can get them to (evening sport teams only) or what they can walk to (library and church programs). It's the other side of the Lord's joke that the house he has blessed us with is also a short walk to both our town's library and our parish. When the activities are during the day and require a lengthy travel time for me, I'll make sure the rest of the week is light, to allow myself to recover. But at other times, people God has prepared to share my burden will often call to invite my children along for the ride to an activity that's too hard for me to get to. Or I humble myself and call on them to help us out.

I admit I can be almost harsh when someone wants to introduce me to a new curriculum idea. I've found that I get really stressed when I think that there's something better out there than what I'm doing! This stress of finding the best, brightest, and newest is a quick way to bring on an exacerbation of my symptoms. Instead, I'll listen to their enthusiasm but cling to the rocks that have taught four children, so far, to read, write, and do math. I rely mostly on the recommendations of the Mother of Divine Grace and throw a little bit of other stuff in for fun. This tight hold I have is only because I've found what works for my family and my children and I know how to teach it.

On the other hand, I always need to stretch myself for the little ones, whose attention span is as small as they are. My stash of games, ideas, and stories changes regularly with the seasons (puzzles are out only during the winter months, and painting is saved for outside during the spring). I use the library for books, tapes, and videos to help them get through the day. The videos are used a bit more when I'm not very strong. I'm also eternally grateful that the Lord has provided the finances for a good computer and some great games. Here again, I rely on the older ones. Like most mothers who are homeschooling a large family, I have an older child occupying the younger ones for a while so I can have one-on-one time with another child. While some of this is just standard homeschooling advice, it's necessary advice when your body isn't giving you the support you expect.

At some point, a relative asked me how I could possibly even consider homeschooling with my MS. It was only through the inspiration of the Holy Spirit that I came up with the answer: it was because of my MS that I was still homeschooling, and am still doing so. Homeschooling carries a great deal of responsibility and expectations, but unlike traditional school activities, all of it matters. My responsibilities have an eternal goal, not just trying to get through another semester of school.

Besides, the responsibilities of traditional school would be too much of a burden on me. I couldn't possibly consider getting my older ones out the door at 7:30 a.m. for school, dressed, fed, and lunches in hand every day. At that hour, the children are usually still in their pajamas, helping each other get breakfast while Mom is struggling to get her body going. I could never put the family through the hassle of all those sales of pizza, wrapping paper, candy, and magazines. My strength and memory can handle only so much, and the endless paper details of public school would drown me. My children don't need an extra few dollars or a permission slip for our field trips, and I won't be surprised some evening by the demand of baking two dozen cupcakes by morning.

I've come to accept that every day will not be the same, and I need to rely more on the long-term goals that Matt and I have set for our family and children, rather than on the daily goals. Matt and I jumped into homeschooling with both feet when introduced to it. Actually, we were more like lemmings that dive off the cliff and into the water because everyone else is diving!

Matt continues to keep both feet and hands in the middle of what we are doing. While he hasn't been a regular teacher, he has become more hands-on with our oldest as she has begun advanced mathematics (anything beyond multiplying and dividing is advanced for me) and science (I'm still struggling with nightmares from my high school chemistry. What is an ion?).

But Matt's help isn't a really big surprise. He did surprise me years ago during a retreat for married couples, however, when he shared the thought that my disease was the best thing that had ever happened to our marriage. As I sat next to him in shock, he continued that without my illness, he would have been a couch-potato dad, content to let me raise the family and provide him with three meals, an occasional beer, and total ownership of the television remote. He put icing on this cake when, in private, he told me that he had decided that since I had firm control of the sickness part of our wedding vow, he would take over the healthy part. His sharing of the burden is what we hope all homeschooling mothers get, but that isn't the reality. Even if he never taught, just knowing that he trusted what I was doing does much to help me continue.

Most importantly, I realize my children have something that even I can't explain, because they have a mother who is differently-abled (as our Holy Father said during his Jubilee Mass for the Disabled). This goes beyond their acceptance of the canes or wheelchairs that I've used; rather, it's a tenderness toward anyone who is "just a bit not regular," as my one son put it. That is irreplaceable and almost makes my disease worth it.

On those dark days when I wake up only to discover that I can't feel my left side, and I'm not sure how long it's going to last, and I realize that I'm still just as tired as when I went to bed, I don't always cry out like Moses in Numbers 11. Instead I try to remember Moses at the end of his unexpected life as he composes the Song of Moses, a recounting of God's care for his people Israel: "He found him in a desert land, and in the howling waste of the wilderness; he encircled him, he cared for him, he kept him as the apple of his eye" (Deut. 32:10). I read only that one verse because the rest of the Song of Moses has him reminding the Israelites of how rebellious they were, and I hope and pray never to be that rebellious again. I like that verse since I'm not a working mom, a PTA mom, a rebellious Catholic mom, or even a very healthy mom. I'm my children's teacher, who sometimes takes quite a few sick days without the help of a substitute, and I've never gotten an apple on my desk. Regardless of the life I thought I would have, if doing what I'm doing, MS and all, keeps me as the apple of the Lord's eye, I can be content.

"My grace is sufficient for you,
for my power is made perfect in weakness."

2 Corinthians 12:9

How I Homeschool My Children
While Keeping a Full-Time Job

Nicola Martinez

I work full-time as a freelance writer, serve as secretary and book-keeper for my husband's business, and do freelance publication design and editing. I put in twelve to fourteen hours a day, which means that homeschooling my children has required scheduling a regimen that must be both strict and flexible.

There are many mothers who work outside the home who would love to homeschool their children but feel they don't have time. Either they're single parents, their household requires two incomes, or time just seems to evaporate during the day. I'm here to tell you that it can be done. You can bring home the bacon, fry it up in a pan, and give your children a complete education. In fact, you might be surprised to find out that you're likely already homeschooling your children in a variety of subjects: health, shop, horticulture, humanity, and morality. If you want to teach them reading, writing, arithmetic, and science to boot, there's plenty of time throughout the day to add that to your repertoire.

"Not enough time," like "not enough" anything, is a relative term. Statistics show that in public school, students receive an average of only fifteen minutes of actual instruction per forty-five minute class. The other thirty minutes are made up of settling down the students at the beginning of class, wrapping up the lesson, and giving out homework. And of course, there's the time spent dealing with the inevitable distractions of twenty to thirty children being in one room.

If you give your child fifteen minutes of instruction per subject every evening (math, grammar, writing, science, and history), it would take only an hour and fifteen minutes to teach all the lessons for a given day. I've seen a mother work two jobs and give her children more than an hour and fifteen minutes. Unlike in conventional classrooms, where one teacher has to divide his time among thirty or so students, homeschooled children don't have to wait while the teacher helps or disciplines other children. Therefore, homeschooled children require only three to five hours a day to complete the same schedule of study as public-school children.

Even if you work from eight to five, have dinner on the table by six and cleared by seven, you'll have three hours before ten (an average bed-time) to get school in.

But wait. What if you don't finish dinner until eight, or you live in a state like South Carolina that requires four and a half hours, including lunch and recess, of daily schooling? That is where "creative" (not to be confused with "illegal" or "inadequate") homeschooling comes in.

For example, home economics is a school subject. If I lived in a state that required a certain number of hours per day for schooling, I'd have my children help with supper, with setting and clearing the table, and with the dishes. That's home economics, and it counts as time spent schooling. When the children practice adding, subtracting, and doing fractions while measuring ingredients in a recipe, they're getting some arithmetic as well as home economics.

What about baseball, softball, and basketball down at the Boys' and Girls' club? Any athletics in which your child participates counts as physical education. Other physical activities, such as bicycling, rollerblading, and skiing, also count as physical education. Piano and violin lessons count as music education.

What about Mass and CCD? That's religious education and counts as time schooled. When you go to the local museum, that's a field trip. Rent a movie on the Civil War, and have your children write a short paper on it. That's both history and composition. All of these suggestions count as time schooled without taking any extra time — and your children still learn valuable lessons.

One mother I know had a vacuum-cleaner salesman come and clean her carpet. It took an hour of her time. She got her carpets cleaned, and she taught her children, step by step, about high- and low-pressure sales. Her children enjoyed the lesson and learned something they never would have learned in school. By the way, that lesson counted as "free enterprise and business economics."

No state that I could find dictates what time of the day or night you must teach your children — merely that you do. Teenagers who don't require baby-sitting can do their assignments during the day while you're at work. You can use your evenings to teach them the following day's lesson and to go over the work they completed while you were out earning a buck. Besides, homeschooling doesn't have to have a concrete start and stop time. Teach one subject in the morning and the rest at night. If you can, come home for lunch and go over multiplication tables, or give a spelling test.

Like anything, homeschooling takes scheduling and discipline, but if you're pulling a full-time job, you already know about that. In my own homeschooling circle, there are parents who work it all kinds of ways. Part-time and shift workers adjust schooling around their schedules. Mothers and fathers who work different schedules share the homeschooling. I've even heard of a schoolteacher who teaches other children all day and then goes home to teach his own children in the evenings.

If you're considering homeschooling as an option but aren't sure you can do it, think again. Find out the requirements in your state. If you live in a state that requires 180 days of school per year, as I do, weekends count if you use them (as well as summer days). We do. My work schedule has to be flexible. Sometimes I have a writing deadline and work extra hours to get the job done, while other times I have a lull in activity. There are weekdays when we postpone schoolwork, only to make up time on the weekends after I've met my deadlines and can think clearly again.

It's perfectly okay to give your children their break while you're at work, and then school them when you're home. Even though most states require the parent or guardian to do the actual teaching, it doesn't mean you can't instruct your children in the lesson and have them complete the work while they're at a caregiver's home.

As long as your children are adequately learning the three Rs and you're supervising their schooling, your schedule can be as flexible as you need it to be. So go ahead and bring home the bacon, fry it up in the pan, and when your children help you wash the dishes afterward, record that as half an hour of home economics.

"With God all things are possible."
Matthew 19:26

Chapter Seven

The Father's Perspective

"Hear, my son, your father's instruction,
and reject not your mother's teaching."

Proverbs 1:8

Reading Aloud as a Family: A Role for Dad

Fredrick Cabell, Jr., Esq.

A creative or motivated father can find many ways to be involved with his children's education: everything from reviewing his children's work on a periodic basis, to teaching a particular subject or planning the curriculum and reviewing the texts. He can serve as an encouragement and give assistance to his wife and children. I recommend all of these practices. For me, one function stands above all the rest: reading aloud to my family.

All true pleasures in life seem to be enhanced by sharing them. Who has not, time and again, enjoyed the experience of sharing a meal, a movie, an athletic event, or other activity with someone they love? The experience, no matter how enjoyable in its own right, is enhanced by the sharing of it. Reading aloud as a family helps to foster an abundance of such moments.

Outside of worshiping together, I know of no more wholesome and bonding experience a family can share than reading great literature aloud. The shared emotions — joy, cheer, sorrow, fear — generate a deep and satisfying sense of togetherness. Memories are created that will last a lifetime. A good book makes an imprint on the heart and mind, and when experienced together, it becomes a shared memory.

The benefits of reading together as a family are many. As mentioned, there's the simple pleasure of a shared experience and the bond it creates. Reading aloud also develops the skill of recollection: being still with one's body and soul, while concentrating the mind on the matter at hand. While this skill can be, and I daresay must be, developed as part of one's prayer life, it can be further developed through listening as someone reads. Many children today live in a world of whirring activity and almost ceaseless noise. Reading aloud helps children learn to be still and listen attentively.

Further, reading aloud stimulates a child's imagination. Unlike television or motion pictures, a book doesn't fill in all the details. A book creates a general picture, but the listener still needs to fully develop the image of what he hears in his own mind. Watching is passive, while listening is active. One dulls the mind, while the other sharpens it. Through learning active listening, even the pleasure to be derived from passive watching can be enhanced. Ironically, it has been my experience that my children oftentimes enjoy a motion picture to a much greater extent than other children do. I've sat in a movie theater and watched my children laugh or cry in response to a truly funny or a sad scene, where other children seem bored or distracted.

Children with well-developed imaginations can understand subtle messages and symbolic images, and thus can penetrate more deeply into the truths of our Faith. Also, a well-developed imagination allows them to empathize with the human condition in all its manifestations.

Our world is sorely in need of great and good writers and artists, and such talent usually springs from a mind that has a good imagination. If we are to win the world for Christ, we must help our children to have bold imaginations and deep human emotions. Good literature enriches the mind and expands the soul. Reading to your family guarantees that the whole family will experience good literature.

Reading aloud also assists your children in acquiring the knowledge they need, both practical and academic, to be well-formed adults. Of course, your children learn as they read by themselves. But, reading aloud lets you bring them farther and faster than they could go on their own. You are there guiding them. You define the words that are hard to understand. You explain the complexities of the situations. You provide the commentary that puts the information in context and perspective. Many children, when they read, are anxious to get to the essence or the heart of a book. When you read aloud to them, you can teach them to *savor* a book.

As parents, we want to prepare our children to fight the good fight. In essence, we hope, through homeschooling, to prepare them to win the world for Christ. Yes, we are sheltering them, although not to keep them from the world forever; rather, it is to prepare them to challenge the world when they're sufficiently strong. In every endeavor that involves acquired skill, there's a period of preparation. Whether it's boot camp for soldiers or practice for football players, there's a period in which there's a controlled and simulated version of the ultimate reality to be faced.

Reading aloud can serve as a type of trial run of life. Through reading aloud, children get to experience a wide variety of life experiences from the safety of their living room and with the guidance of their parents. We can use books to teach them what is an appropriate Christian approach to different aspects of life. We can use books to show them the effects of God's grace on individuals. We can use books to show them the folly and disaster that are caused by sin. They can experience bravery and cowardice. They can feel the pain of loss. They can sense the joy of true love. They can fight a battle or follow a quest. They can discover the entire world. And they can have you alongside to help them understand and appreciate it all.

Of all the reasons for reading aloud, I believe the best reason is that it demonstrates to your children that you really care about them. You want to be with them. You want to share time with them. You want to teach them. When you're old and gray and your children have left your home, I believe you won't regret one minute you spent reading to your family. This simple act, night after night, says again and again, "I love you." The memories your children will have of your family huddled together around a good book will bring forth in them the love of what is right, and strengthen them to love heroically.

Reading aloud, however, is much more than just picking up any old book and reading. There are several issues to be considered when you decide to begin reading together as a family. Most important, it should go without saying that the books chosen must be of high quality and morally appropriate. Since most of us aren't experts in children's literature, we must rely on the expertise of others. At the end of this essay, I recommend several book lists that are quite comprehensive and give a general idea of the appropriate reading level. Such lists are invaluable.

For reading aloud to be enjoyable and effective, a proper ambiance must be established. This can be quite difficult, especially when there are young children who won't be interested in listening. Children must learn, sooner or later, to be relatively quiet at times. Reading aloud is a good place to start. It's best to provide the younger children with some other activity while Dad is reading. When our son was four, we would let him do puzzles or play while I was reading, as long as he remained relatively quiet. Within two weeks, he no longer wanted to play. Instead he sat and listened to the story. Not everyone will be this fortunate, but it's important to decree firmly that reading time is quiet time. Parents must also honor this pledge. If the phone rings, ignore it. Better yet, turn off the ringer.

During reading time, everyone should be comfortable, but not lounging. Attention should be focused on the book. Even an adult with a well-developed attention span focused on interesting material can sometimes lapse into distraction; a child can't do better. I try to glance at my children occasionally, and if I think they're drifting, I modify my tone of voice or attempt some other action to bring them back into focus. Sometimes a gentle "ahem" can do the trick. If this happens too often, it could be the book. So choose your books wisely.

It's important to keep a certain flow when reading a book. While at times it might be necessary to stop and explain a passage, or do a "reality check," such pauses should be minimized. If the book is written with an abundance of difficult words, try skimming the material beforehand and define the words before you start reading. Even in children's literature, there will be times when you need to look for a definition of a word. To keep things moving, my wife volunteers to look in the dictionary while I continue to read. When she finds the word, she raises her hand, and then I stop and she reads the definition. (It's actually smoother than it sounds.) Of course, the dictionary should always be within easy reach.

Make an effort to read in a way that's enjoyable for the listener. Don't read too quickly or too slowly. Be careful to articulate the words, especially uncommon or easily misconstrued words. Make sure you read at a volume all can hear, without bursting your family's eardrums. When reading, try to match the inflection of your voice with the mood of a passage. A scary passage should be read in a different manner than a funny or adventurous passage. Sometimes slow down for dramatic effect, and sometimes speed up.

When read aloud, dialogue among several characters at the same time can be a bit confusing. Using a slightly different voice for each character can make such a passage more understandable. Follow your best instincts, but don't ham it up too much. Over-acting can be as bad as a dull drone.

In our often-hectic lives, it isn't always possible to keep a firm schedule. To keep myself on my toes, I keep a log of the books we're reading and the number of pages we read each night. I make my entry the moment I put down the book. Some might think this is excessive or unnecessary, and for some that might be the case. Nonetheless, I find that this serves as a reminder to me that too many nights missed while reading a book can cause the experience to be ruined. Also, it serves as an excellent motivator to keep to the schedule. Entries in your log don't lie.

We try to read at least four out of seven nights in a week. We find anything less creates gaps in our reading that diminishes our ability to recall and enjoy the story. In some states, the law requires that you keep a journal of your child's lessons. Since this is the case in our state, we always photocopy our log and place it in our children's portfolios.

Once a year, prior to the beginning of the academic year, I review book lists and do a rough plan of the books we'll be reading. As you near the end of a particular book, make sure you have available the next book on your list. If you're reading a series, such as the venerable Chronicles of Narnia or Little House books, I think it's best to read the series straight through, especially if the children are enjoying it.

Reading together is one of my family's greatest joys. But be forewarned: reading aloud will cause your children to complain a great deal. Almost every night, my children begin moaning as soon as I close the book. It's a complaint I love to hear. May God bless you as you read as a family.

Fredrick Cabell's List of Books About Books

The following books and book lists are available from Emmanuel Books (see Appendix A).

A *Mother's List of Books*, by Theresa Fagin: in my opinion, the best book list on the market. A comprehensive and well-researched list covering more than a thousand books, grouped into four age categories, for ages two to seventeen.

Children's Literature List, by Lisanne Bales: this is another excellent literature list. Her selections for read-alouds are particularly helpful.

Honey for a Child's Heart, by Gladys Hunt: this resource assists parents in determining what to look for in children's literature and contains recommendations for over three hundred books.

A Landscape with Dragons, by Michael O'Brien: although I don't agree with all of Mr. O'Brien's conclusions, this is an excellent book for assisting parents in discerning the content of children's literature, and it contains an excellent book list.

"Finally, brethren, whatever is true, whatever is honorable, whatever is just, whatever is pure, whatever is lovely, whatever is gracious, if there is any excellence, if there is anything worthy of praise, think about these things."

Philippians 4:8

Twenty-One Things
Fathers Can Do
for Their Homeschool

Steve Wood

Fathers are vitally important to the long-term success of a homeschool. There will be several times a homeschooling mother feels like throwing in the towel and quitting. At such critical times, a good husband and father can help his wife over the humps. Even without doing a lot of the actual teaching, a husband can reduce the stress load on his wife and help create a family environment conducive to homeschooling success — right through the high school years.

1. *Marry a good woman.* I can't tell you how important this is. When Karen and I were married, we didn't know anything about homeschooling. It was only after we had two preschool-aged children that we discovered it. I'm very thankful to God for having given me a wife who is godly and a good homeschooling mother. If you'd like to see your grandchildren homeschooled, you need to teach your own children how to select a mate who will be a good teacher, ready to make all the sacrifices necessary to establish a successful homeschool. Fathers need to teach their sons how to choose a virtuous wife. If homeschooling is what your grown

children will want to do in their own families, it needs to be a conscious part of the spouse-selection process.

2. *Along with your wife, be open to life.* Bring new students into your homeschool. As you cooperate with God in the high calling of bringing children into this world, God will enlarge your hearts and your ability to financially support and educate them. Don't project your current ability to educate or support into the future without also taking into account the fact that both God's blessings and the abilities he gives to parents increase with each new child.

3. *Work hard, and increase your skills to support your family on a single paycheck.* Family finances are not peripheral to homeschooling: you must recognize that they play a central role. For a homeschool to succeed, a father needs to excel in his job performance and regularly improve his work skills so that he can support a growing family, either on a single paycheck or on his pay plus part-time employment by his wife. Consumer debt needs to be vigorously resisted, and other forms of debt need to be absolutely minimized. Most families simply can't carry a large debt load and homeschool at the same time. Over 95 percent of the younger families I know who are able to manage debt well also tithe regularly. To those who regularly give back to God the first portion of their financial increase, God seems to give the grace to resist excessive debt.

4. *Train and discipline your children, especially those between eighteen months and five years old.* The number-one cause of homeschool burnout is lack of discipline in the home. A dad can prepare the home for education long before the children actually start formal schooling, because the bulk of this training and discipline is done between the ages of about eighteen months and five years. During this formative time, a father plays a central role in teaching his

children respect, obedience, and a proper attitude toward all those in authority. A wise father lays the foundation for a successful homeschool before his children even begin their education.

5. *Be the principal of your homeschool.* This is how you apply child training and discipline to homeschooling. Every school needs a principal. In the Wood homeschool, I'm the principal.

As a young single Christian, in my Protestant days, I was in charge of one of the largest, fastest-growing Christian-education ministries in southern California. My main job was to recruit Christian education teachers. Yet my number-one problem was that the teachers were quitting faster than I could recruit them.

Just then there was a young psychologist in the Los Angeles area who had written a book called *Dare to Discipline.* He was James Dobson. I got hold of that book and realized that the main reason all of my Sunday-school teachers were quitting was the discipline problem. So I went around to each of my teachers and said to them, "Listen, you handle the minor discipline problems, but for any medium to significant problems, I will take responsibility. You just contact me, and I will take care of it." The number of teachers quitting dropped to a relative trickle, and I simply concentrated on working with the discipline problems. Dads, you would be wise to remember this experience of mine.

In our homeschool, we have a few discipline problems from time to time. My wife, Karen, has a direct phone line to me at my office. If there's a problem, particularly at the beginning of the school year, I drive home and take care of the situation. I look my children right in the eye and tell them, "This is not puff, and I am utterly serious that this homeschool will succeed. I am deeply appreciative of your mother teaching you, and *nothing* you do is going to get in the way of that. I want you to know that I guarantee that. Therefore, this foolishness is going to stop." Some years I've had to make two or three trips home. These few brief trips saved my wife hours, weeks, and months of discipline headaches. Once your children realize that you're willing to leave work and come home to straighten things out, it's amazing what a brief phone call from the principal will do.

Before you say, "I can't take this time off from work," consider this: it has taken me only about ninety minutes total to keep our homeschool on a successful track for fifteen years. This is a very small price to pay for keeping my children from becoming entangled in the peer culture present in practically every modern classroom. It's the emotional overload from discipline problems that makes moms want to quit homeschooling. You need to take it off your wife's shoulders if you want lasting success in your homeschool.

6. *Don't set unachievable academic goals for your homeschool.* We want our children to get to heaven, not necessarily to Harvard. Heaven is graduation. Anything else is secondary. A lot of parents have that backward. You must do what God calls you to do.

In our home, my youngest son was born with a medical problem that required surgery in his first year of life. He had two surgeries, and for about ten to fourteen days after each operation, he couldn't be left alone at all, day or night. Karen was with him constantly, and nothing was done in our homeschool during that period. And, of course, that was the time of year just before our older children were to undergo standardized testing.

That year our children did better on their standardized testing than they have ever done in fifteen years of homeschooling. You see, we were simply doing what God called us to do: taking care of the little guy, who just needed some love and physical attention. The homeschool took care of itself. That was the grace of God; it wasn't us.

7. *Protect your family from trash coming into your home.* As St. Joseph is the guardian of the Holy Family, so fathers are the protectors

of their families. If you go to all the trouble of homeschooling, make sure that your efforts are not subverted by trash from the Internet and the media, or by bad neighborhood influences.

At the beginning of this last school year, we had some new neighbors. One of the little girls came over and wanted to tell my daughters dirty jokes she had heard at school. Quite frankly, I was concerned and somewhat nervous about what to do about her. The next night, as I drove up the driveway, there she was, playing with my daughters. I got down on her level, spoke her name, and said, "We really enjoy having you come over and play at our house, but I do not want you telling any more dirty jokes to my children — ever. Do you understand what I'm talking about?" Then I said, "We really want you to come over here, we really want you to play, but we cannot have those type of jokes if you are coming over here to play. Do you understand that?" That was it.

That is the kind of thing a dad needs to do. You don't terrify a child; you must be very kind, but be firm and direct. Don't allow the benefits of homeschooling to be undermined. You must be the protector of your children's virtue.

8. *Encourage your teens and pre-teens to be chaste.* Millions of Catholic teens cease practicing their faith every year, in large part due to a loss of chastity. A stern warning in the book of Proverbs says that sexual immorality not only leads a person away from God, but also creates a huge stumbling block in regaining the paths of life (Prov. 2:16-19). A dad is responsible for warning both his daughters and his sons against the consequences of immorality.

One effective way to do this is to show them the statistics proving that premarital relations and cohabitation lead to a dramatic increase in the probability of divorce later in life. (For such statistics, see my book *The ABCs of Choosing a Good Husband* [Family Life Center Publications], chapter 5, "Extinguishing *Real* Love — Before Your Marriage Begins."

Young people are eager to find lasting love in our divorce-prone world. Another highly effective way to preserve chastity in your children is to encourage courtship, rather than recreational dating, as the wisest path leading to lifelong love and marriage.

Finally, if you want your children to be chaste, then be chaste yourself. In many ways, the dad is the trendsetter in the family. Children will imitate a chaste and virtuous dad.

9. *Take an interest in the homeschool, and put a spark under some tardy assignments.* Dads need to demonstrate verbal and physical interest in the homeschool. A dad can express his interest simply by asking, "How did school go today? What did you learn?"

Homeschooling groups often have an annual ceremony where the children are progressed from grade to grade. There's a too-large number of Catholic dads who don't show up to witness their child's grade advancement. Such a lack of visible support can be very discouraging to homeschooling wives.

Dad, you need to express your appreciation; you need to take an interest in your homeschool. It doesn't mean you have to take a major teaching responsibility, but it does miracles for your wife when you simply take an active interest in what's going on.

You can also put a spark under some tardy assignments. Tell your children, "There is going to be no computer, no Friday night videos, no going out. In fact, the universe is going to collapse unless you get that assignment in on time to Seton [or wherever]." And, you know, they get it done.

10. *Be the religious leader of your home.* Read the scriptures, and lead in prayer. This is essential, because the primary reason you're homeschooling is to see a legacy of faith passed down the generations of your family. You don't have to be a theologian, nor do you have to turn your home into a monastery. Rather, being the religious leader in your home requires just a few minutes each

day, a few actions each week, and some special times during the year.

11. *Provide the necessary equipment, curricula, and materials for the homeschool.* Don't be a tightwad. All too many men think this about homeschooling: "Okay, if the kids are attending a private or parochial school, it costs me about $8,000 a year. Now my wife is talking to me about homeschooling. I'm not really excited about it, but the cost is zero." It's damaging to the temporal and eternal welfare of your children to expense homeschooling anywhere near zero. To finance your homeschool, you need to think of a comfortable budget somewhere between zero and the cost of private education.

I'm so thankful that my wife wants to homeschool. If she wants something that's necessary, she will get it — whether it's bookshelves, a blackboard, curricula, used books, whatever. You should be supplying your wife with these things. If you need a new pickup truck, go ahead and buy it, but at the same time make sure your wife has what she needs for the homeschool.

A wife should have what she needs to get the job done, and this includes dedicated space in your home. All of us give space in our homes to what we feel is important. If you don't have the space, then you can make it. I love figuring out how to create homeschooling space when it isn't readily apparent. We once had a dumpy junk-filled garage that I turned into a premier homeschool classroom. Interestingly, when we sold that house, it went to the first prospective buyer after only fifteen minutes. Along with the Lord's blessing, it was our homeschool garage that helped sell our house so quickly. In our next house, we gave up our dining room and made that into our homeschool space.

Our present home has a large upper loft that was a seldom-used game room. I told the previous owner, "We'll buy the house if you get rid of the pool table." We felt the homeschool space was more important than the pool table. Nothing wrong with pool tables, just first things first. Homeschooling should have a priority in the family budget and space in your home.

12. *Get some good educational computer programs.* Make sure your homeschool has a reasonably fast computer along with good educational software. Computers are great for drilling in certain subjects, teaching typing, writing papers, and research projects. Educational software can keep a child productively engaged while Mom is busy teaching another sibling. Every child needs computer literacy to be ready for the workplace. Remember to use filtering software if your computer is connected to the Internet.

13. *Recruit older children to teach the younger ones.* Hire a tutor if necessary. Teaching reading takes a lot of time. Nuns, many with only high school diplomas, used to teach reading to the children going through Catholic schools. You don't need a master's degree to teach reading to the average child. You just need to do it the right way. One of my daughters wants to be a teacher, so we hired her to teach. All it took was the incentive of a shopping spree at JC Penney to interest her in the job. If any of your older children are gifted in a particular subject, hire them to do the teaching.

If there are some subjects that are creating a logjam in your homeschool, it would be worthwhile to hire an outside tutor. Hiring a tutor is still cheaper than sending the children to a parochial or private school, and it's certainly worth doing if it keeps your homeschool going.

14. *Look for ways to streamline your home life and to increase the efficiency of the homeschool.* Men, you need to listen to your wives regularly. There were several times when Karen was ready to quit, saying, "We are not going to do this next year." When you hear the

first hints of such talk, start looking for ways to keep your home-school going. Men are usually good at analytical thought.

One significant way to help your wife is to find out her most difficult problem and turn it into her easiest task. For instance, purchase a video course for the most difficult and time-consuming subject. By doing things like this, you'll keep the subject load for several children from crushing your wife, particularly during the high school years.

15. *Teach your children how to earn a living.* I believe that a homeschooled child should be able to support himself by the time he graduates from high school. Unfortunately, a lot of children today can't do so, even when they graduate from college. The next generation of homeschoolers will probably face an unfriendly economy. Fathers need to teach their sons breadwinning skills early and well in order to be prepared to support the second generation of homeschool families.

A vital part of Jesus' formation within the Holy Family was his work in the carpenter shop. You should seek ways to incorporate your children in your business, profession, or home-based enterprise. If you can't offer any work opportunities, you might be able to arrange a work internship with a friend of the family. Until the Industrial Revolution in the nineteenth century, work was normally within the context of family life, in or near the home.

When I started the Family Life Center, I couldn't afford to hire adults to assist me. So my children started working with me when they were about eleven years old. I dare say my oldest three teens could probably run an apostolate on their own right now as a result of their work experiences. They've been involved in a variety of outreaches that have brought people back to the Faith, caused it to come alive in others, and helped bring converts into the Church.

I can't say enough good things about the concept of work within the family circle. For me, it was born of necessity, but looking back, if I had to do it over again, I would try to do it intentionally. Through our family work relationship, we have had meaningful interaction; we have accomplished real things together, not just spent time consuming entertainment together.

Think hard about how to incorporate family work into your homeschool. Homeschoolers usually live on a single paycheck in an economy that no longer recognizes a family wage. A home-based business that would enable your family to work together provides far more than needed income; it also provides the opportunity for a family to engage in meaningful activity together.

16. *Assist your children in determining their vocation skills and in choosing a major in college.* You can save yourself between $15,000 and $30,000 in college tuition if you keep your children from jumping majors — if you help them determine what their major should be before they start. A good vocational-interests diagnostic test, such as Cor, will help your child recognize what gifts, skills, and motivations God has placed in him, and costs only about $100. Clearly, this small investment in time and money can pay for itself many times over when your child is ready for college.

17. *If you can afford it, take your family on a vacation.* A homeschooling family needs a sanity check once in a while. The best way to do this is to go on vacation. Take a break, and get out of the house.

18. *Incorporate learning experiences into your family vacation.* Family trips can powerfully reinforce your studies. All of our children would agree that one of our best family vacations was when we studied the Civil War for a whole year in unit studies, and then toured the Virginia and Gettysburg battlefields. The result was

that I turned into a Civil War nut. Everybody else has gone on to other subjects, but I'm still fascinated by the Civil War.

19. *Encourage your wife*. Homeschooling at times can be a very heavy emotional load for a wife. Share that load by lessening her burden. Go on walks, talks, go out to dinner. Pray for her. Recognize her limits. Just listening, encouraging, and praying for her can make a big difference.

20. *Express appreciation for your wife's heroic efforts in home-schooling*. Proverbs 31:28 says, "Her children rise up and call her blessed. Her husband also, and he praises her." I believe that men need to verbally and publicly express appreciation for their wives in homeschooling. Although the wife is the primary teacher, the husband can and should be the primary facilitator, providing a context in which the entire venture can be a success. Part of this is recognizing the extra effort she's making.

I've had two daughters graduate from our homeschool, and at their graduation ceremonies, they asked their parents to say something. I said something to each of my daughters and gave them a Bible verse to ponder. I spent even more time talking about Karen, because the event was a dual graduation for both children and parents — especially for the mothers. A husband's timely and open appreciation of his wife, not just at graduation time but also throughout the school years, can help her get over the countless homeschooling hurdles.

21. *Develop a good sense of humor for those times when things get really crazy*. And they *will* get crazy!

EDITORS' NOTE: Steve has a tape series just for fathers on the topic of discipline: *The Training and Discipline of Children for Fathers*. These tapes will give Dad a short course in discipline in three hours of drive time. Tapes can be ordered by calling (800) 705-6131 or by visiting Steve's website at www.dads.org.

"Fathers, do not provoke your children to anger,
but bring them up in the discipline and
instruction of the Lord."

Ephesians 6:4

Seven Ways Mothers
Can Recruit Fathers

Steve Wood

There are a lot of Catholic mothers struggling alone in their homeschooling who could really use some support from the dads. How do you motivate men to be active in a Catholic homeschool?

Here are seven ways that mothers can recruit fathers to be active in homeschooling. Several of these steps will require serious rethinking among Catholic mothers. The alternatives are clear: either complain about husbands during support-group meetings, or develop a positive plan to incorporate the involvement of fathers in your own homeschool.

1. *Make a conscious effort to reach out to men.* Somebody should be ringing alarm bells for the lack of male involvement in the spiritual life of the Church. Yet little is actually being done to reach out to the generations of men born after World War II — namely, the "Baby Boomers" and "Generation X."

I've seen thousands of Catholic men respond to the challenges we put forth in St. Joseph's Covenant Keepers. This apostolate to Catholic men did not just happen. We made a very conscious effort to reach fathers, and dedicated a huge proportion of the resources in our family apostolate to this vital task.

Men can be brought back to active involvement in both church life and family life. But it won't just happen automatically. Instead of sitting around, asking, "When are the men going to get involved?" go out and do some things to get them involved.

2. Ask yourself, "How will this homeschool activity promote or hinder the involvement of Catholic fathers?" Before legislators pass a bill, they should ask themselves, "How will this piece of legislation help or hurt families?" In the same way, before you draw up the calendar for your homeschooler support group, ask yourself, for each item, "Is this activity going to make it easier or harder for the husbands to get involved with homeschooling?"

Make the involvement of fathers a high-priority item as you develop your support-group calendar and your annual conferences. I believe that getting dads involved in homeschooling is just as important as teaching children to read and write.

3. Do things that men are comfortable with. Basically, men like sports, food, and dirt, and if they can't have dirt, then at least something that makes them sweaty. Keep those things in mind the next time you're planning a homeschool gathering that resembles a Pampered Chef party. There's nothing wrong with Pampered Chef parties, but they're certainly not the best venue to attract fathers. For instance, men don't really go for those little quarter-size sandwiches. They prefer to eat something they can get their hands around.

If you're scheduling an event at the beginning of the school year, remember that this will be the first contact that some men will have with your group. Careful planning can help ensure that their first contact with homeschooling won't be their last. The same applies to an activity in the spring or early summer, for those families thinking about homeschooling during the next year. These and other special times are when you want to have something that's going to attract men.

Why not have a barbecue? Why not ask some of the dads to bring their grills and have a cook-off contest? Follow or precede the barbecue with a father and son/daughter softball game. Men usually like sports and feel comfortable relating to other men in sports activities. If a man tries to strike out some other dad who's up at bat, they'll both feel much more comfortable later sitting down and talking or praying the Rosary together.

Almost any type of outdoor activity is an ideal way to incorporate husbands in the Catholic homeschooling community. Wise wives should not only plan activities that are of interest to themselves and beneficial for their children, but should constantly place a high priority on activities that will get the dads involved.

Our homeschooler group decided to have a Presidential Fitness Day. I made a point of calling some of the dads who don't regularly participate in the support group, but who like sports, and they seemed eager to provide leadership and coaching for the event.

Another way of involving fathers is having a homeschool night at a local baseball game. Our town is the winter home of the Texas Rangers, and we also have a Triple-A team that plays during the summer. We use the homeschool phone tree to encourage families to gather on the free nights at the baseball park. The children love getting together, the wives can catch up on everything, and it's a great time for the guys to get to know each other in a comfortable setting.

Such activities can provide incentives for the dads to want to do other things with homeschooling families. These things aren't tough to do. Just keep alert for ways to encourage dads' involvement.

4. *Affirm and thank your husband for his heroic support of your family on a single paycheck.* Thanking a father for his bread-winning role is something that should be done by the children as well as the mother. Supporting a family on a single paycheck takes heroic effort in today's economy.

Last Father's Day, my wife, Karen, thanked me for supporting our family so we could have a homeschool. Then my children took turns thanking me for things I do for the family. We give a similar "thank you" to Karen on Mother's Day. Since a huge part of a father's life is devoted to the financial support of his family, he should be thanked for all his work. Breadwinning isn't something outside the umbrella of practicing the Catholic life. It's a vital part of family life and homeschooling, and thus should be frequently affirmed.

A Catholic homeschooling wife once wrote to me, saying that she was upset because her husband "did not do one little thing" in their homeschool. She did admit that he works very hard, provides well for the family, leads the family Rosary, and goes to Mass every Sunday. That particular week, I had helped a wife whose husband had left her, and I had also counseled another wife in a far-worse situation, and I think that I may have been too curt when I said, "You need to start being thankful for what you have. You have it 97 percent better than all the other wives I know about!" But she later wrote back to me, "Thank you, thank you, thank you. I just forgot what I have."

Start thanking your husband just for his breadwinner role — for getting up early, working hard, and bringing home a paycheck. You might be amazed at the results. A man needs to know that his work is vital support for the homeschool.

5. Pay attention to your marriage; don't be a Martha Stewart homeschooler. Martha Stewart has the perfect house, the perfect table settings, perfect decorations, and yet she lacks a husband to share her home. Always remember that your husband is an important part of your home and your homeschooling efforts. Don't fall into the trap of becoming thoroughly exhausted, striving to have a perfect Catholic homeschool, while neglecting your husband.

Save time, energy, and effort for your marriage and for your husband. I believe this is one of the most important things you could do for your homeschool. Homeschooling should not drive a wedge between spouses. If you really care about the long-term success of your homeschool, then save some of yourself to invest in your marriage. It will pay rich dividends in your family life.

6. *Encourage a spiritual life for dads as well as moms.* In one part of the country, I know of a particular orthodox Catholic group that came in and recruited about 90 percent of the homeschool mothers. Of course, the mothers were all excited about this spiritual movement. Yet when I asked how many of the dads were involved, "not a single one," was the answer.

It's a mistake for wives to continually go to retreats and conferences and develop their spiritual lives without their husbands. This only increases the distance between them. Although this arrangement might seem fine when you have only elementary-school-age children, when these children reach their teens, it will be vital for good old Dad to be around, on board, on duty, and active in every spiritual aspect of family life.

There's a need to develop TEAM spirituality between parents: "Together Everyone Accomplishes More." It's worth the time and effort to recruit husbands. Unfortunately, some people are trying to build family movements while bypassing the dads.

Shortly after I started an international family organization, I put it on pause, because I realized there was a significant absence of involved fathers in family life. That's when we started St. Joseph's Covenant Keepers as a special outreach for fathers. We felt that, for Catholic family life at this moment in history, it was a necessary thing to do. Cursillo is another group that wisely puts a priority on reaching the husbands. A husband must make his Cursillo retreat first, before a wife is allowed to go. The result is couple participation throughout the movement.

Many homeschoolers have neglected to develop TEAM spirituality between spouses. The result has been a lot of women who are languishing and complaining about their husbands' lack of involvement. Of course, much of this non-involvement is solely the husbands' doing; nevertheless, wives should ask themselves if their husbands' lack of involvement might be attributable to some of their own actions. There's obviously nothing wrong with encouraging women's spiritual life. It just shouldn't be done while neglecting the husbands' spirituality.

7. *Send your husband to a St. Joseph's Covenant Keepers conference.* At almost every one of these conferences, designed to encourage and equip men to become successful Catholic fathers, I say, "Please thank your wives on my behalf, for registering you for this conference," and all the men laugh. Over two-thirds of the registrations come in from Catholic wives. They're the ones who have fueled St. Joseph's Covenant Keepers throughout the United States.

A wise wife recognizes that she doesn't make a good preacher to her husband. Proverbs says that "iron sharpens iron," and there is a certain dynamic by which men don't mind being challenged by another man. Most husbands want a spiritual challenge that's straight, strong, and direct, but they usually don't want it coming from their wives. Be of service to your family by gracefully encouraging your husband to participate in St. Joseph's Covenant Keepers. Your prayerful support is the key to the success of any outreach to Catholic fathers.

"A good wife who can find?
She is far more precious than jewels."
Proverbs 31:10

Homeschooling and Teaching About Marital Intimacy

Ed Rivet

If the title of this essay strikes you as unusual, imagine your reaction had you read "Homeschooling and Sex Education" as its title! One of the great aspects of homeschooling is being able to avoid the detrimental effects of secular-educational thinking on sex. For the most part, homeschooling literature ignores this subject as something left entirely to the discretion of parents — as well it should be.

However, that doesn't mean that parents wouldn't appreciate some affirmation or a little insight in their effort to form their children's values and consciences. Crucial to this whole subject is *context*; hence the title "Marital Intimacy." Those two words create immediate definitions and parameters. What the world views as an activity open to all persons, we view as exclusive to marriage. While our culture focuses on the physical and the carnal, we see an intimacy that is relational, emotional, even spiritual.

As Catholic parents, we have the privilege of sharing with our children the most beautiful, thorough, and fulfilling moral and theological perspective on human sexuality. To understand the complete meaning of the physical love between man and woman in the sacramental bond of marriage is to have a glimpse of both divine reality and divine mystery. This is a profound irony, given the moral depravity that grips our country today. Living in the truth is beyond swimming upstream; it's like trying to cling to a rock in the midst of a torrent. But cling to the Rock we must. To whom else can we go?

The beauty of the homeschooling "curriculum" for this subject is that it is as much learned by life experience as it is by specific discussions of the "birds and bees." The complexity and subtlety of committed married life is such that it must be learned much like an art form, and passed on from mentor to student. Children's sexual perspectives are formed by thousands of little cues, unspoken messages, and demonstrated lessons.

I certainly don't mean to suggest that there's only one right way to approach teaching your children on this crucial matter. But there are some broad themes that parents might want to reflect on in developing their own approach to it.

Modesty

Now *there* is a word that is almost completely without context in our society today. The bombardment of sexual images in our culture has obliterated any sense of modesty. Television programs, movies, music videos, advertisements, and clothing fashions are obsessed with exposing the body and portraying sexuality. Parents have an enormous and difficult task in protecting their children from this unholy exposure. Sadly, monitoring TV watching has become an absolute necessity. Immediate and prudent response to situations where your children witness immodest exposure has a real impact. It's the ultimate teachable moment.

My wife and I were amazed to see how quickly our children learned to discern what is acceptable behavior or clothing. Once, while at a less-discerning neighbor's home, our six-year-old son told the mother, "My parents wouldn't let us watch this show. The women are not dressed right." The mother changed the channel.

Homeschooling and Teaching About Marital Intimacy

Our ten- and twelve-year-old children now use the remote to even cut away from immodest or suggestive television commercials.

Once learned, the lesson of modesty bears its own fruit. It's a lesson that also carries over in the way you as parents dress, and in the way you help your children purchase their own wardrobe. Children can spot inconsistency in a heartbeat. The best "textbook" is one that never graced a schoolroom: living and reflecting modesty.

Romance and Love

Here's another area where children need plenty of help from parents. For decades now, children — especially young girls — have had their ideas about romance and love shaped by the animation of Disney: *Cinderella, Snow White, Sleeping Beauty, The Little Mermaid,* and *Pocahontas.* Many of us have seen every one of these "classics." Over and over, the theme is played of a beautiful young woman looking for, or waiting for, the man of her dreams. Love between the leading characters is instantaneous. Taken to the absurd, the prince and Cinderella are eternally in love and they don't even know each other's names. Cinderella dreamily sings, "So this is love." You might want to scream out, "No way!" Love is infinitely more than a starry-eyed waltz. The "love" portrayed in these movies is only as skin-deep as the beauty of the characters. The swooning emotionalism of romance is passed off as love.

The stark contrast to these stories is Disney's *Beauty and the Beast.* Here two people look beyond romance, even look beyond the worst of faults, to discover the heart, soul, and potential of the other. Now, that is love. But this story is the exception, not the rule. Even here, an underlying theme of this story is breaking the spell of "beastliness" to restore a handsome prince. There's always a handsome prince and beautiful maiden; frequently she's not at all modestly portrayed.

Infatuation, not love, is presented in these movies and countless others that focus on superficial attraction and romance. Particularly troubling are the cultural forces (include teen magazines here) that lead thirteen- and fourteen-year-old girls to be intensely concerned with attracting male attention. It's nothing new to say that there's a direct correlation between the amount of genuine love and attention children get from their parents and the degree to which adolescent children focus on "romance." A child with enough sincere love at home will not go looking for it elsewhere. By contrast, children will actually learn more about love and romance as they learn about the role of chastity in relationships.

Chastity in Marriage

As children get older, the broader concept of chastity can be introduced and developed to its full understanding. Parents today readily focus on the task of presenting chastity until marriage as the standard for their children. In the wake of the AIDS and communicable-disease epidemic, abstinence for teens has become fashionable even in certain secular circles. But again, thinking in terms of a larger context, Catholic parents have the advantage of Church teachings, which allow children to develop more fully in their character and spirituality.

Catholic marriage is a sacramental vocation, as are the ordained and religious orders. Each vocation calls for some form of chastity and self-control. A whole range of circumstances can require married couples to refrain from physical relations for various lengths of time (e.g., illness, separation due to work or family commitments, a complicated pregnancy or birth). Following Church teaching through the use of Natural Family Planning (NFP) requires periodic abstinence if a couple has sufficiently serious reason to space their children. With checkout-lane magazine covers screaming the false promise of limitless sex, parents do their children a great favor by introducing the idea that abstinence is even part of marriage. Scripture tells us, "To everything, there is a season." Marital intimacy, too, has times for expression and times for refraining. Contrary to cultural messages, physical intimacy is not an everyday, always available reality. (This is hardly a revelation to any couple married for any length of time.)

It's specifically during those times of abstinence that couples express the true depth of their love for each other. They've put their physical relationship at the service of their larger relationship. Husband and wife can be more attentive to each other's non-physical needs. They can be more sensitive to their spouse's emotional and spiritual well-being. The dynamic of their non-physical love for each other will be demonstrated in those little cues and messages, spoken and unspoken. It's a type of romance akin to courting, but it's already within the context of a committed, ongoing relationship. Children will notice the extra relational attention a couple will pay each other while abstaining from sexual intimacy. Compare this example with superficial, "love at first sight" portrayals in the movies.

Modesty, chastity, and love that puts physical intimacy at the service of a vocational marriage create a context for "sex education" that is as countercultural as homeschooling itself. The opportunities for teaching our children are indeed plentiful as we live out our marriage vocation and provide guidance to our children about those cultural expressions of romance and sexuality which are contrary to God's design. By comparison, these two tasks seem more daunting than simply explaining how babies are made.

As married couples, we know that human sexuality is an extraordinary and beautiful gift from God. Teaching our children about it should be seen as our privilege rather than something to be dreaded. Best of all, it is a subject on which our faith and our Church has provided a rich and thorough "lesson plan." Perhaps your homeschooling experience has challenged you as to how to go about teaching math, science, or other subjects. But marital intimacy (sex education) is one area in which Catholic parents can be confident in knowing they have the very best curriculum available.

"This is my mission field: a child's heart
Where endless thoughts and actions start,
For in that heart through word and deed
I plant and water sacred seed."

Marcia Baldon

Faith of Our Fathers

Dan McGuire

A common complaint among homeschooling mothers is that they often don't receive adequate support from their husbands. Certainly many fathers are as actively involved in the homeschool as their jobs will allow. I even know of a few fathers who have arranged flexible work schedules so they can be hands-on instructors with their children. These positive examples are certainly inspiring, but this essay isn't necessarily for them; it's for the fathers who aren't involved at all, or aren't as involved as they could be.

There's a sense of urgency to addressing this problem, not simply because it seems so widespread, but mainly because the abdication of the father's role places an enormous burden on the mother. This burden, both physical and psychological, is harmful to the entire family and the marriage itself.

Lack of active involvement in the homeschool will generally stem from one of two basic causes. The first, and most serious, is a general malaise or lukewarmness about the Faith. In our culture, many men have abandoned even the pretense of practicing their faith. Within the homeschooling community it isn't uncommon to find fathers who are lukewarm toward their faith and uninterested in the homeschool. Among many men, there's a prevailing attitude that religion is a woman's thing and the sweet wife will take care of it while the husband watches football, goes golfing, works extra hours, or whatever.

In the beginning, it wasn't this way. Indeed, a quick check of sacred Scripture shows that it was a father's duty and responsibility to train his sons in the Faith:

- *Sirach 3:1-16:* Divine establishment of fathers' authority.
- *Sirach 48:10:* God sends his prophets to re-establish the proper function of the father within the family; which, in turn, revives all of society.
- *Proverbs, chapter 4:* A father's teaching is God's message for the child. The importance of hearing and obeying the father is the same as hearing and obeying God the Father.
- *Proverbs 1:1-8:* The first seven verses establish the importance of the entire book of Wisdom. Verse 8 charges the parents with teaching it to the child.
- *Proverbs 6:20:* The importance of listening to the teaching of the parents.
- *Joel 1:1-3; Isaiah 38:19:* Fathers charged with keeping the covenant alive through the generations.
- *John 5:19-20:* Fathers provide an example to their sons by what they do.
- *Luke 11:11-13; Matthew 7:9-12:* God's Fatherhood compared with man's.
- *1 John 2:12-14:* Fathers' role is as intermediary and conduit of knowledge of God.
- *1 Thessalonians 2:11-12:* St. Paul compares his instruction to that of a father.
- *Hebrews 12:7-9:* Fatherly discipline.
- *Ephesians 6:4:* Fathers' responsibility teach the Faith.

In both the Old and New Testaments, the message is quite clear: fathers have a responsibility to pass on the Faith in a uniquely masculine way. In the Old Testament, fathers were charged with passing on the entire cultural heritage of Israel — most importantly, the covenant with Yahweh.

Indeed, God's revelation of himself as a Father shows us the status and responsibility that belongs to the title of *father*. We can look to God's fully revealed relationship with man and see in it a model for the proper exercise of earthly fatherhood.

Yet, despite this close connection between God's fatherhood and our own, many fathers still reject their rightful spiritual duties, seeing religion as something irrational, fuzzy — and feminine.

But it's simply absurd that Catholics, in particular, would adopt this view. How can our doctrine, so firmly reinforced by philosophy and natural law, be perceived as mere subjective feelings? How can a faith illuminated by the brilliance of Aquinas and Augustine become seen as the dark home of mindless ritual? How can a Church built on the rock of St. Peter be confused with an edifice built on emotions?

Our Catholic faith is certainly not based on a warm fuzzy feeling, yet some of the discomfort men feel regarding matters of faith is perfectly natural. On a very fundamental level, faith has a distinctly feminine aspect. Faith requires receptivity, openness, and vulnerability. Didn't Mary, our exemplar in the faith, demonstrate all these? In our culture, masculinity and vulnerability aren't usually thought of together.

Viewed objectively, the human soul is always "feminine" with respect to God. The human soul is receptive to God's activity and is docile, or should be, in obedience to his will. The Church is always the bride, while Christ is always the Bridegroom. We know that all souls are drawn to life with God; that is where we truly live and move and have our being. Why, then, does it seem feminine? Shouldn't it naturally appeal to both men and women?

Although it might seem today that the interior life is more of an affective, feminine thing, it wasn't always thus. In the early centuries, the interior life was a distinctly male province. The interior life of the early monks was truly seen not only as a form of martyrdom, but as a *spiritual combat*. Men would enter the monastic life to do battle with the Devil and continue Christ's victory on earth. These battles, while primarily spiritual, sometimes resulted in actual physical wounds to the monks. Our faith is both feminine and masculine at the same time.

What about those fathers who are firm in their faith but are still cool toward homeschooling? What are the problems that cause these men to shrink from the role so clearly assigned them in Scripture?

Many fathers, particularly those who take their familial leadership seriously, are uncomfortable with homeschooling because they are in a subordinate role. While this seems like an ego problem, it really is the sign of a deeper misunderstanding. In the sacrament of Marriage, the man and woman truly do become one in the eyes of God. From God's perspective, there's a unity between man and woman that defies any earthly attempt at separation. Children are given by God to a husband and wife, and he charges them with the responsibility of raising and educating them.

To carry out this divine command, couples in our culture must adopt a division of labor. The parent who stays home is the primary teacher, while the one who works outside the home provides the financial support that makes the homeschool a viable option. This division is purely practical and secular. Each parent participates in the same response to the command of God in different but complimentary ways. Put simply, only in man's mind is his role subordinate; in God's eyes, there is simply one response.

The acceptance of this passive and supporting role is an exercise in humility. Like most of God's plans, this one is wonderfully simple; those most likely to chafe at the idea of a subordinate role are also those most in need of developing the virtues of humility and obedience.

Dads who refuse to take an active part in the spiritual development of their children are either unaware of God's call or are simply disobedient to it. To re-establish their proper role, fathers need to do a few things.

First, they need to figure out their priorities. They need to get rid of the "I don't have time" excuse. Dads, you have no higher priority; this matter concerns the salvation of at least two souls, yours and your child's. Whatever else you might think is important simply pales in comparison. Secondly, it doesn't take lots of time; it just takes real interest and leadership by example. Third, in order to provide that leadership, and to understand the priority issue, many of today's fathers must invest some preparatory time in educating themselves.

Most people ended their formal religious instruction about the time they were confirmed. It isn't surprising that an eighth-grade education in the faith is insufficient for adult-level responsibilities. This weak education explains why some Catholic men can believe that religion is all about feelings. The real meat and potatoes of the Faith, served up by the likes of Aquinas and Augustine, aren't on the typical eighth-grade menu. Why is it that the only subject we do not continue to study as we grow older is the one that, in the end, really matters? No one gets to heaven by knowing and living nuclear physics.

Can we fake it, and get by without the education and without a heartfelt commitment? Not a chance, for the simple reason that children have a built-in hypocrisy detector. You might be able to fool very young children by pretending that the Faith is important. As they grow, they will realize that there is a gulf between what Dad says and what he does. In time, this destroys the father's credibility and authority. By the time the children get into CCD or Catholic school — and our homeschools are indeed Catholic schools — the long-term patterns are largely set. After the kids have watched Dad ignore or pay lip service to God for several years, can anyone really expect a CCD teacher to fix their faith in one hour per week? The premise is preposterous. It's sad that parents will buy all the developmentally appropriate toys for their children because the first three years are so critical to proper brain development, yet all the time ignore the development of their soul.

Begin a family time of reading Scripture. Begin with a prayer to open your heart and mind:

> Eternal Father, enlighten my mind
> to understand what I am about to read,
> and help me to put it into practice.
> Help me to recognize in this reading
> an instrument of your grace,
> directing my soul to greater union with you,
> and through me, the souls of others
> with whom I share what you wish me to learn.

Christ is present in his Gospel. Visit him there, and ask him to help you. The results of a heartfelt prayer can be miraculous. Every person has a part to play in the mission of the Church. Fathers, don't neglect this responsibility. Personal sanctity and spiritual leadership are not options to be exercised if we feel like it. God has given explicit instruction that both are mandatory.

> "Immediately, the father of the child cried out
> and said, 'I believe; help my unbelief!' "
> Mark 9:24

Chapter Eight

Finding Inspiration

*"Many of life's failures are people who
did not realize how close they were
to success when they gave up."*

Thomas Edison

With the Eyes of the Soul

Cay A. Gibson

When we think of Helen Keller, we think of the highlight of her education: that almost indescribable moment when Annie Sullivan put Helen's hand under a running water faucet and formed a connection between the word *water* and the liquid. We don't often recall that her teacher spent the entire morning trying to make her understand the difference between water, mug, and doll. It was only during the break from daily lessons and frustrations that Helen realized what Miss Sullivan was trying to teach her. In this example lie many worthwhile lessons that all home-schoolers should note.

Parents can learn, for example, to take breaks with their children in the midst of the daily grind, and to enjoy nature. This episode in Helen's schooling can teach us not to depend entirely on workbooks and textbooks for our children's complete education. It can also teach us that education lies not only in the teaching of the mind, but also in the teaching of the soul.

Books definitely play a necessary role in education. I'm a dedicated user of workbooks and living books in our homeschool; don't think that I'm advocating a no-book policy. The main reason we have many books in the house is that I love books, and I want my children to love reading. It's well known that better students are insatiable readers. But there are some things that can be learned only from the world around us.

During her adulthood, Helen Keller was an insatiable reader and the writer of many books, articles, and letters. Her autobiography, *Helen Keller, The Story of My Life,*[1] is a summary of her educational experience under Annie Sullivan's gentle guidance. In reading it, you'll find numerous suggestions on how to make learning a joyful experience and a fond memory. Helen describes her teacher's ability to make a combination of words form sentences and how Helen learned to read when Miss Sullivan presented the lessons through an intellectual game of hide-and-seek.

Helen writes, "For a long time I had no regular lessons. Even when I studied most earnestly, it seemed more like play than work." She goes on to tell how Miss Sullivan would stop and talk about anything that delighted or interested Helen. She tells how they read and studied outside and how, "All my early lessons have in them the breath of the woods. . . . " She gives a beautiful description here. She describes how Annie Sullivan made her understand that the earth was divided into zones and had two poles by demonstrating with an orange, a stick for the poles, and twine to mark the zones.

A collection of fossils that someone sent to Helen was the basis of her education about the world of the dinosaurs. Annie Sullivan made raised maps out of clay and helped Helen build dams in the streams, so Helen could explore the concepts of islands and lakes and of "burning mountains, buried cities, moving rivers of ice."

---

[1] Chapter 7 of Helen Keller's autobiography is a must read for all parents who want to gain a sense of excitement, play, patience, and gentleness in their children's education. It shows what can be taught on the days when book work isn't going as planned or when we feel we're not teaching our children enough. It reminds us how to give our children insight to the world around us, not only with their eyes, but also with their soul.

Helen praised her teacher's "genius, her quick sympathy, her loving tact, which made the first years of my education so beautiful," and finished with this loving tribute: "All the best of me belongs to her — there is not a talent or an inspiration or a joy in me that has not awakened by her loving touch."

Many parents are hesitant about homeschooling because they feel they will lose patience with their children. We should take comfort that Annie Sullivan had bad days, too. After the first lesson in teaching Helen proper table manners, Miss Sullivan went directly to bed and stayed in her room the rest of the day with a severe headache. Sound familiar? Did she fail Helen and her education? Certainly not. She was human, but she never gave up, either on Helen or her own ideals. It is because of this brilliant teacher's perseverance that Helen Keller was able to write in her later years, "Knowledge is love and light and vision."

What would Helen have been able to do if she hadn't had a serious illness that left her blind and deaf? Some people say she would have been even greater than she actually became. Then again, she might not have lived up to her utmost potential and, certainly, wouldn't have influenced the world with the legacy she left behind. She might have taken her hearing and sight for granted, as so many of us do, and Annie Sullivan's teaching methods and influence might never have become known.

It's an awesome task to teach a blind and deaf child to understand the world around her. It's an incredible task to teach that child to read and write. And it's an amazing task to do all this and leave that child with a joyous sense of wonder and a love of learning. Yet one person did all this. As homeschooling mothers, we have the potential and opportunity to do something comparable.

Helen's early temper tantrums (before Annie Sullivan's arrival) came, not from a ruthless, wild child, but from an active child with a keen mind who had a desire to express herself and couldn't. She couldn't take in everything around her because she didn't understand it. This frustrated and angered her, and many people misunderstood her. Annie Sullivan's gentle, patient guidance was the key that unlocked Helen's mind to the world around her.

Homeschooling parents all possess this key. Frustration and anger are signs that a child doesn't understand something or is unable to express it. It doesn't mean the child is incapable of learning. These are the times when we must do as Annie Sullivan did. Take the child's hand and dip it into the cool refreshing wonders of the world around us, in hope of awakening something in his mind and soul. Don't let the textbook become your master. Look at what Helen learned without a math book. Look at what she taught the world. Allow your child to realize that, while a book is a necessary tool, all learning isn't found in books; much is found in the world around us

---

"Character cannot be developed in ease and quiet.
Only through experience of trial and suffering can the soul
be strengthened, ambition inspired, and success achieved."

Helen Keller

Reflections on Ice

Maureen and Robert Wittmann

There are many definitions of "unschooling." But by most any definition, I probably would not be labeled an unschooler. However, there have been times when my family has moved to an "unschooling mode" temporarily.

Life has a way of throwing wrenches into family plans. Since homeschooling, for us at least, revolves around family, any upset in the family schedule affects our homeschool. Lessons might need to be put aside temporarily in times of serious illness or a new baby.

As I neared the end of my sixth pregnancy, I moved from structured schooler to unschooler. In this particular instance, I had prepared in advance, having schooled lightly over the summer.

As winter approached and my abdomen grew, formal academics began to take a backseat. And as I moved out of the picture as homeschool teacher, my husband, Rob, moved in to fill the void — albeit in a more informal way.

Rob is an ice-skating and hockey enthusiast. He decided that year, when our sixth baby was developing inside my womb, that he and our children would build an outdoor ice-skating rink in the woods behind our home. This took an incredible amount of planning and work — so much work, in fact, that my husband sweated off twenty pounds that fall and winter.

The ground first had to be cleared of dead trees, small boulders, and brush. Bonfires raged as fallen trees and brush were disposed of. The children, along with their father, enjoyed roasted hot dogs and marshmallows through it all. On weekends the neighbors often joined us, supplying graham crackers and Hershey bars to make S'mores and providing the socialization we homeschoolers hear about so often. Although the children often came in smelling of smoke and covered in dust, I didn't really mind. The wash might have been overflowing, but so were the hearts and minds of my children

Then the leveling began. My darling husband rented surveying equipment for the job. The children learned to use the equipment alongside their father, and they were able to see firsthand the necessity of planning and doing a job right. (Years earlier, an attempt to build a rink by simply eyeing the lay of the land ended in a dismal failure.)

Next, side-boards had to be constructed. Since hockey would be played on this rink, the boards had to be high enough to stop pucks from flying into the woods. The children learned about measuring and construction.

To fill the rink with water, Rob rented a pump to pull water from the creek that ran parallel to the rink. My husband never does anything small; the rink was a whopping 90 by 45 feet. (It has since been expanded to 110 by 50 feet.) Renting the pump was much cheaper than filling the rink from our outside tap. It was also much faster. The children were now learning about conservation and how to think "outside the box."

One of the most difficult parts of the project was the laying of the plastic liner. It needed to be cut to size and stapled to the side-boards. This isn't as easy as it sounds. If cut too small or ripped accidentally, $175 would be wasted.

Rob wired lights for night skating and music for choreographing figure-skating routines. So there were lessons in electricity.

My dining room was turned into a hose room. To keep the ice skateable, Rob would need to spray a little water on the ice from time to time. The rink was far into the woods, so 250 feet of hose was needed. Since Rob didn't want his hoses freezing up, he decided to keep them in the house through the winter. This time, the lesson the children learned was from their mother. They learned about patience and what it means to love one's husband.

Lessons in thrift were also learned. As a family living on a limited income, we couldn't afford to buy brand-new ice skates for the children. However, we knew the importance of buying upper-end skates with good ankle support. Cheap skates aren't worth the expense. We scoured the used-sporting-goods stores and garage sales for high-quality equipment at reasonable prices.

Through the whole process the children were involved. They loved helping Dad chop down the dead trees, learning about surveying, and hammering in the stakes to hold the hockey boards.

Most important, they learned about enjoying the fruits of their efforts. They spent the winter skating up a storm. No one could claim that our children were in need of socialization that winter, as our home was filled with guests on most days. One unschooling family must have spent three or four days a week at our house.

And at the end of it all, on February 16, we had a little girl join our family. Margaret Rose Wittmann has many a skating season ahead of her, and Rob looks forward to her joining his hockey team.

EDITORS' NOTE: For more about backyard ice rinks, read *Home Ice: Reflections on Backyard Rinks and Frozen Ponds*, by Jack Falla. To view and learn more about the Wittmann ice rink, visit www.hpurchase.com/rwittmann03.htm.

"It is wonderful how ice can be so warm. . . ."
Bobby Orr

The February Funk:
How to Make It Up Through the Downs

Nicola Martinez

Wow! Labor Day came and went, and the school year got off to a great start. Summer ended, and your children were really enthusiastic about plunging into their new books. You had just spent the last month and a half preparing lesson plans and getting your files together, things clicked right into place, and you figured that this homeschooling thing was a cinch. You and your children rolled through Columbus Day. Veterans' Day gave everybody a break, and then Thanksgiving hit, making lunch preparation a no-brainer: turkey sandwiches until Christmas. Advent tripped on the heels of Thanksgiving, instilling an atypical spark into the usual routine of the day. Then the excitement of Christmas lit up December like the night sky on the Fourth of July. But wait, you haven't reached July yet.

You've just hit New Year's Day. Winter has eclipsed fall and settled into everyone's bones. No one wants to get out of bed in the morning to shower and dress in the cold, and now, when school is finished by early afternoon, your children can't go out to ride their bicycles. No jogging around the block. No playing on the swingset. No gardening. No nothing. By the third week in February, your children are bored. School is now a drag, and your children are sluggish and inattentive. They need a break, they say. After all, they haven't had a holiday in over a month. Just the day-to-day drudgery of routine: breakfast, prayer, school, breakfast, prayer, school, breakfast, prayer, school. What's worse, there's no end in sight. Spring break won't arrive for another six weeks. Your children are now convinced they'll be dead by spring, and the more they whine, the more convinced you become that they're right — because you're ready to kill them.

It doesn't matter what you suggest to make their day more appealing and productive. Those educational computer games that were a hit on Christmas Day are now old news. The house echoes with lamentations of, "But Mooooommmm, we've watched every video we own a hundred times!" Siblings fight. Babies cry. Children tug at you at every turn, and in the back of your mind, you're wondering if there is an Internet class available that teaches noose-tying. You'll decide later if the noose is for you or them.

The enthusiasm you had for homeschooling has soured into frustration and doubt. You prayed about homeschooling before taking the plunge, so you can't understand why it isn't going smoothly. Deep down you know God directed you to this, but doubts creep into your psyche. Perhaps you didn't get the right message. Perhaps public or parochial school would be better. Maybe you're not cut out for homeschooling after all. You've never felt compelled to yell at your children so much in their entire lives. This can't be healthy, you tell yourself. Something has to give, because your patience is stretched so taut that it's about to snap back and take someone's eye out.

There's rule I've come to live by: never make any homeschooling decisions in February.

Not to worry; you'll get through this. February is the worst month for homeschooling. No one in my circle knows why. We all speculate that it's the long winter and days of being cooped up, but regardless of the reason, February is the month most mothers want to throw in the towel and head for the ropes. The first year I homeschooled, I wanted to quit in February. The second year I homeschooled, I wanted to quit in February. The third year . . . Do you see the pattern starting to develop?

Each February, my sister-in-law patiently listens to me rant and rave about my children being uncooperative. She sits silently while I lay all my doubts on the table, and throw a pity-party about *me* having to do it *all* and *nobody* appreciating my efforts. When I'm finished, she always says, "You know it's February, don't you?" and the cloud lifts from my shoulders.

Getting through February is one of the most challenging things about homeschooling. I won't lie to you. It's time for serious prayer, diligence, and frequent visits to the Most Blessed Sacrament. It's a time to bolster that virtue called patience, and occasionally it's a time to lock yourself in the bedroom and count to ten.

Of course, it might be well and good to tell you about February, but you need something concrete to get you through the month.

The best way that I've found to get through the February Funk is to revise your teaching schedule. Being able to create a flexible schedule is one of the greatest gifts of homeschooling. Knowing in advance that the Funk is coming is an excellent way to dissipate the effect it will have on you and your children.

For example, arrange your lesson plans so that you begin the school year a week early, or finish a week late. Beginning early is usually an easier sell, at least with my children, so we can take days off in February. Save Monday, Tuesday, Thursday, and Friday for school activities, and leave Wednesday for fun activities, activities that get you out of the house, but not necessarily into the cold. Perhaps plan your field trips to the museum or theater for February.

Begin a novena, but go to the church to pray it. That will not only help build spirituality in your children, but it will get you all up and moving, and activity is the number-one cure for boredom.

Each day at three-o'clock, take thirty minutes to pray the Divine Mercy, or conduct an age-appropriate Bible study.

Short breaks, taken often, will alleviate the drudgery of the homeschool routine. Start school a little later in the day, perhaps 9:30 instead of 8:30, and break after lunch to play a board game with your pre-teen, or read a story to your kindergartner. Anything that breaks the routine of the day-in, day-out grind will help you get through even the worst February Funk.

And if the Funk does seep in and start to steal your enthusiasm, look at the calendar. Remember that it's February, and think of the one rule: never make any homeschooling decisions in February.

"Love is patient and kind;
love is not jealous or boastful."
1 Corinthians. 13:4

Flags of Doubt

Janet Cassidy

Whether it's the intimidation of walking into a school hallway decorated with creative assignments, or hearing about activities, programs, and prom nights, every homeschooler has experiences that raise the flag of doubt.

How will we handle graduation? Where can we get a diploma? Will I be able to handle high school math? Are they writing enough? Am I giving typical assignments for their grade? Am I too soft? Too strict? How should they be tested? Tutored? Tortured?

Many of us just forge ahead without a teaching degree, self-confidence, or knowledge of what the future holds. We move forward strictly on faith. Without faith, the tough days, subjects, and fears would be formidable obstacles to our success.

Why is it that so many of us are successful? In fact, *very* successful?

We often begin homeschooling with the idea that we can educate our children by teaching them the required subjects. After homeschooling awhile, we develop personal philosophies, which evolve from the question, "What do our children — or any of us, for that matter — truly need to know?" Although we retain educational standards and evaluate progress, we slowly discover that the answer isn't found in the content of the materials we use. We do, of course, help our children accomplish mastery of their subjects, but we learn that there's so much more to educating a child. It's the *so much more* that makes us successful.

For example: Our children discover that seeking answers is as important as finding them. They often become independent learners and form opinions of their own. They learn that different approaches work for different people. They watch us grow and learn, discovering therein a lifelong process for themselves. They watch us scale various hurdles and learn much about perseverance.

Our children encounter forgiveness when impatience prevails. They see Scripture come alive through daily application and prayer. They experience our commitment to them. They develop respect for others and receive it themselves.

They learn about adaptation, and not only in science. They find that sometimes a break is more important than continuing. Or that sitting with a friend is an act of cooperation with God's will. They learn that sometimes English can be enhanced by silliness, or tense moments lightened by hugs. Our children know that we don't have an endless supply of energy, yet they see us diligently striving to meet our responsibilities.

I keep a poster above our computer that has a quote by Theodore Roosevelt: "Do what you can, with what you have, where you are." For me, it may be translated, "What can I do this day, with this time, or this child, or this situation?" Facing the reality of what this day brings and learning how to respond to it is uniquely educational — even if a test score can't measure it.

And what about that flag of doubt that flies on occasion?

As homeschoolers, we must face the reality that we can't always imitate the best that schools have to offer. Fortunately, we don't have to. Unfortunately, we often beat ourselves up over this. We have a lot to offer our children as home educators, even if we don't have an authentic science lab. This isn't a competition; it's about schools and families doing the best they can.

For most of us, homeschooling comes from our belief that this is what God wants for our family at this time. This means that we can be assured of his strength and wisdom in accomplishing it. Homeschooling can't be successful if we try to do it alone. It isn't an isolated activity.

With full days of teaching and parenting, we must make time to seek God's will in our efforts. Sometimes this discernment comes in the form of words from a friend or a spontaneous idea, or an answer in prayer. Prayer can revitalize us. It can make all things possible. It can help us see the hidden and aid us in working through the difficult.

I remember one time I was struggling with a dilemma in math. It was through brainstorming with a friend and through prayer that I found a solution. That solution, to my great surprise, meant moving forward in a very illogical way. I was trying to find a method of math that would work without the automatic recall of facts. Flash cards and all of the typical methods weren't working. How could we move forward in math without rote memorization? You just can't work in double digits if you haven't first accomplished the basics, right?

It was so hard to go forward in a way that was out of the ordinary, but I trusted that God was directing me, so I moved ahead, crazy as it seemed. It didn't make any sense to me, nor did it agree with any method for teaching math I had seen, but I was compelled to do it, so I did.

Now, several years later, I can say it was the right way to go. We found a method and an aid that worked for us, but only because we trusted the Holy Spirit's promptings and moved forward on faith.

What is that saying about God drawing straight with crooked lines? He does indeed.

Successful homeschooling comes through shifts in our understanding of what our children need. It comes with personal growth — theirs and ours. By discovering a God who loves and directs us, we experience tangible grace. Through God's blessings, we enjoy the fruits of labor. We have a wonderful opportunity to stand outside the vacuum that encourages our children to labor for things that are fleeting.

We encourage our children to ask, quite simply, "How can I use the gifts God has given me?" and "What does God want me to do with my life?"

And then, by their side, we pray, and wait, and work. In doing so, I believe, we give them that "so much more" in the process.

"To be successful, the first thing to do is to fall in love with your work."

Sr. Mary Lauretta

The Golden Years

Susie Lloyd

Scene: A recurring dream. The year is 2066. I'm one hundred years old. I'm in my seventy-fifth consecutive year of homeschooling.

I'm at the bank on a Friday morning with five children, ages thirteen through two. The teller hands out five lollipops and says, "Don't you have school today?" to Child Four, youngest of the articulate type. Sinister of her — trying to buy information from a six-year-old with a penny sucker. Not to mention cheap.

Child Four (looks at me and shrugs): "Um, I don't know."

Instantly a chorus erupts:

Child One: "We don't go to school."

Child Two: "Don't say that. We do, too. We're homeschooled."

Child Three: "Except we don't have to take a bus from the bedroom to the kitchen. Ha ha."

Child One: "We're on lunch. Is that right, Mom? Or are we just taking the rest of the day off again?"

Chorus: "Please, please! Oh pretty please!"

Child Two: "That's not fair. I did math in the car."

Child Three: "We could count this as a field trip. We go on a lot of field trips."

Teller frowns slightly.

Me: "Would you believe it's a snow day?"

Teller glances out the window. May.

Me: "What I mean is, we still have three snow days to make up. After all, we must keep up with state standards."

Teller: "I was just wondering one thing. What are you planning to do when someday your children go out into the Real World?"

Me: "How many times have you been in this dream, lady? Haven't you figured out yet that this is never going to end? This is the past, the present, the future! These kids are never going to grow up. I'm trapped in homeschool Jumangi. With every turn, we get deeper into workbooks, extracurricular activities, and pregnancy. My husband and I will never retire. We'll never have a second honeymoon in our golden years. And you know what? It's all your fault. All these years I hand over a wad of cash, and you never give me a lollipop. Maybe if just once you gave me one, it would break the spell."

Child One: "Want a lick of mine?"

Child Two: "I haven't finished mine yet. You can have the rest, Mom."

Child Three: "Take mine! I was saving it for you. I
    didn't really want it anyway. It's only half-licked."

Child Four hands me a wet stick.

Child Five: "Crunch."

Teller (smiles at the kids, pulls out her stash, and holds
    a lollipop out to me): "You've earned it."

But suddenly I don't want it. In fact, everything I thought I
wanted I would now trade for five wet lollipop sticks.

Me: "No, thanks. I don't want out of this dream after
    all. I don't want to wake up and find that my kids
    are grown, and that my job is done. What I've got
    is the Real World."

I pick up my toddler, extend a second hand to our six-year-old,
and with a third beckon the other kids to follow. We all leave for
home.
    These are the golden years.

---

*"My mother had a great deal of trouble with me,
but I think she enjoyed it."*

Mark Twain

Chapter Nine

Homeschooling Community and Support

"For where two or three are gathered in my name,
there am I in the midst of them."

Matthew 18:20

Sharing the Joy of Homeschooling with Others

Annie Kitching

One of the fears many parents have as they begin homeschooling is whether others will accept their decision. If their child has been enrolled in a Catholic school, or in a parish's religious-education program, new homeschooling parents might wonder how their friends and acquaintances from the parish will react. They might even be concerned that they will be looked on askance by their pastor and parish staff. As many families have discovered, these fears aren't entirely groundless. As a homeschooling mother who is also on the staff of a Catholic parish, I believe there are a number of things that homeschooling families can do that will make their transition smoother and also serve in a substantial but very delicate way to promote homeschooling.

• *Be proud.* Surely we have all noticed that the happier and more confident people are, the more we're drawn to them. The same is true about homeschooling families. Families who are secretive about their homeschooling don't engender trust in others, particularly in those who are unfamiliar with homeschooling. Unless there's a real, substantial reason for homeschoolers to be covert, it will make a much better impression if we're cheerful and open about it, even when we're not entirely sure what the reaction will be. When people ask questions about our homeschooling, or about our curriculum, we should remember that they're probably asking simply because they're not familiar with homeschooling — not to express disapproval. When we're tight-lipped and uncommunicative, we might give the impression that we're doing something unwholesome.

• *Be positive*. Many of us might have chosen to homeschool because we weren't satisfied with the education offered at our local public or parish school. Few parents are unreservedly happy with the school choice they've made for their children. There are, in fact, almost no educational choices that don't have a few flaws or downsides. (Even homeschoolers have days when we consider throwing in the towel.) For this reason, most parents we talk to will be able to identify on some level with our decision to homeschool.

On the other hand, while loving their children as dearly as we love ours, these parents have made a different choice. Therefore, dwelling on our dissatisfaction with the educational options they have chosen can be perceived as personal criticism. Dwelling on negatives is simply not the best way to endear us to others or build unity among parents and families. Not only might our dissatisfaction cause other parents to argue the benefits of their own child's school, but it might also make them view homeschoolers as a bunch of complainers who have chosen homeschooling for negative reasons.

When others ask us why we homeschool, it's as easy for us to sound positive and proactive as it is to sound negative and reactionary — and it gives a much more upbeat view of homeschooling. Compare the impression these statements will make: "We didn't like the fact that the teachers weren't really Catholic and my child got no personal attention" versus "We just love the opportunity to go to daily Mass together, and it's really good for my son to be able to progress at his own speed."

• *Make connections.* Homeschooling families have a lot to offer a parish. Get to know your parish staff. Of course, it makes sense to find a parish in which you feel comfortable. Yet even in a parish that you love, you might still find some resistance on the part of the priests or staff. It's best to assume that the resistance is due to the fact that they don't understand homeschooling. Just let them see that you're ready to be a positive and active member of the parish, and that your children are well-behaved and well-educated. It certainly never hurts to invite the priests to dinner, or to go by the parish offices and formally introduce yourself.

Better yet, get involved. There are many volunteer jobs that a homeschooling family can undertake: folding programs, serving at weekday Masses, visiting the elderly, taking care of the flowers or candles, helping with the nursery, cleaning the church. Find out where you and your children can be of service. Your participation will benefit your parish and your family. Bit by bit, you'll find opportunities to explain what homeschooling is all about.

Take advantage of the positive things your parish has to offer. Many homeschooling parents in our parish have their children in regular religious-education classes. Several of these parents have volunteered as catechists. They might put in one hour a week with their children and other parish children. The hour is certainly not all the religious instruction their children get, but it's a way for them to make friends their own age in the parish and broaden their peers' understanding of homeschooling. Your parish may have a children's choir, sports teams, or clubs that your children can join. Parents, meanwhile, should consider taking advantage of the parish library or Bible studies.

Your participation will make your homeschooling community as well known and well respected as the other sub-communities in the parish. The more people are aware of your existence, the more your needs will be considered and met.

• *Be proactive.* There might be some issues on which you and your parish staff won't agree. There may be long-standing policies made without homeschoolers in mind that don't fit your situation. However, if you've previously formed warm relationships and been supportive of the decision-makers, you'll find your difficulties are more easily surmounted. If the director of religious education likes and respects you, it isn't unlikely she'll listen to you as you share your opinion of certain books in the parish library. If the pastor sees you at weekday Mass and chats with you as you water the plants each week, it's much more likely that he'll understand why you might like to prepare your child for First Communion at home. On the other hand, if the first time you meet the parish staff, you show up with strong complaints or requests that no one else has made before, it's more likely you'll meet the natural resistance that many human beings put up in such situations.

• *Find an advocate.* One important thing that area homeschooling groups can do is find a priest who understands homeschooling and is well-respected among his peers, to serve as their group's chaplain. In fact, it's a *very* good idea to find or form a Catholic homeschooling support group. Sharing a few homeschooling Masses each year will build a sense of community in such a group. It's nice if your eighth-graders and high school graduates can be celebrated at a graduation Mass each spring. If problems should arise with diocesan staff or individual priests, your chaplain might be able to calm the troubled waters. At the very least, he can give you advice, encouragement, and support.

• *Make suggestions.* Once you're established in your parish as homeschoolers, especially if there are a number of homeschooling families, don't hesitate to suggest ways in which your parish can support you. Often, a staff person unfamiliar with homeschooling might not realize how he can help. You can suggest one of the easiest and most welcoming things they can do, which is to remember homeschoolers when announcements are made and invitations are given. If childcare is offered during the day for preschool children, so mothers can attend studies or events, it isn't difficult to arrange for a study area serving homeschooled children. One service our parish offers to homeschooling families is the opportunity to borrow religious-education videos and textbooks. Some Catholic schools might be open to including homeschooled children in certain special events or sports teams. Parishes might be able to provide space for homeschooling families to have science classes, speakers, or a monthly social.

Then observe as the parish benefits. As my parish became more sensitive to homeschooling families, it has actually benefitted other families as well. The success and ease with which our homeschooling families prepared their children for sacraments has led us to encourage all parish families who wish to take on this responsibility, based on their child's readiness, rather than on their grade level. When we began to provide religious-education materials and assistance for our homeschooling families, it occurred to us that we should offer the same support for public-school families. In almost everything, we've become more flexible and more respectful of the role of parents as primary educators. All this has come about through the opportunity we've had to get to know and appreciate the homeschooling families in our parish.

---

*"For thou lovest all things that exist,
and hast loathing for none of the things
which thou hast made, for thou wouldst not
have made anything if thou hadst hated it."*

Wisdom 11:24

How to Throw an All Saints' Bash

Lynne Cimorelli

Support groups are not only a great resource for homeschooling parents to swap curriculum and method ideas; they also offer opportunities for homeschooled children to get together and have fun. They can even learn a few things along the way. A support group is only as good as its members make it. I suggest that members get together to plan meetings and brainstorm some creative, fun activities for the children.

Some of the activities my group has done are a science fair, a talent show, park days, a monthly book club, a homemaking class, Little Flowers club for girls and Blue Knights club for boys (Ecce Homo Press; see Appendix A), lots of field trips, and my personal favorite: the All Saints' Party. You can have a very simple All Saints' Party where people dress up as their favorite saint, everyone tries to guess who they are, and there are piñatas full of candy. One year, our group went the extra mile and turned it into not only a great party, but also a learning opportunity on par with a unit study.

I was asked to head up the party, so first I chose a theme, which was "Saints of the Early Church." I found a fabulous website that has a saints' timeline with brief biographies of each saint on the list: www.catholic-forum.com/saints. I looked at the biographies of various saints from the first three centuries and settled on fourteen saints. I then designed a simple game or set of clues for each saint that was related to the website biography. Each family who was coming to the party was assigned one saint. They were asked to bring a game of my design, a small sign that gave a clue and that invited each child to guess the saint's name, and a bowl of candy to be used as a reward for a correct guess.

The key to success here was that the games were pre-designed so that the members only had to gather the materials and make a sign. We also had some people bring apple cider, cups, and napkins. Everyone was given the website and the list of saints a month before the party and asked to print out those pages so their children could familiarize themselves with these early-Church heroes and be able to guess them correctly. In addition, most families included their children in the design of their assigned game and sign, so it became a fun way for everyone to participate actively in the party. Here were some of the chosen saints and the clues that went with them:

• St. Mark. His biography stated that he's often portrayed with lions, so the game was "Pin the Tail on the Lion." The sign read, "I am a first-century saint who wrote the second Gospel and am often portrayed with lions. Who am I?"

• St. Peter. A treasure box was filled with candy, padlocked shut, and then the children had to find the correct key out of several on a key ring to get to the treasure. The sign read, "I lived in the first century, was given the keys to the Kingdom, and became the first Pope. Who am I?"

• St. Stephen. The game here was tossing stones at a target and trying to hit the bull's-eye. The sign read, "I was a first-century saint who was stoned to death. Who am I?"

• *St. Paul.* Different objects were placed in a velvet bag and the children had to reach in, blindfolded, and try to figure out what the objects were. The sign read, "I was a first-century saint who was blinded by lightning on the road to Damascus and then converted. Who am I?" An alternate game for this one is a javelin toss, using a homemade javelin with a lightning bolt painted on the side of it.

• *St. Polycarp of Smyrna.* The clue was a picture of a man standing amid flames. The sign read, "I was a second-century martyr whom they tried to burn alive. Who am I?"

• *St. Eustachius.* The clue here was a large tree branch that was fashioned into antlers with a yellow cross in the middle of it. The sign read, "I was a second-century martyr who was converted when I saw a glowing cross between the antlers of a stag while on a hunting trip. Who am I?" The "antlers" could be turned into a ring-toss game, too.

• *St. Ignatius of Antioch.* The clue for this one was a bowl of animal crackers, which were given out as prizes if the saint was guessed correctly. The sign read, "I was a second-century martyr who was killed by wild animals. Who am I?"

• *St. Helena.* The clue was a little brown cross made of construction paper, on which was written, "The True Cross," and each child was given a cross to put in his goody bag. The sign read, "I was a third-century saint, Constantine the Great's mother, and I found the True Cross. Who am I?"

• *St. Felix of Nola.* The game had spider webs strung up between a couple of posts, and the children threw plastic spiders at the web, trying to make them stick. Spiders and webs are easy to find in the stores around Halloween. The sign read, "I was a third-century saint who was protected from the soldiers by a spider that spun a web over the door. Who am I?"

For a bonus game, we had an angel halo toss, and the children were asked to name the nine choirs of angels. We used a ring toss owned by one of our members that had a girl holding the post on which you throw the rings. She was modified by the addition of some wings into an angel, hence the "halo toss."

We all gathered at a local park that had a sheltered table area, and we set up our games on picnic tables, with a bowl of candy next to each game. The parent who made the game manned the "booth" to hand out the candy to the correct guessers. Then we set up a station at the beginning with paper bags and markers for the children to decorate their own saintly goody bags. The children came dressed as first-, second-, and third-century saints, and took their goody bags to each station to play the games and try to guess the saints. Of course, they had the list of the fourteen saints and the website on which to look up the information well ahead of time, so those who had studied breezed right through, guessing correctly and collecting lots of candy.

After the games, we had a costume-guessing contest, where each person told a little about the saint he was dressed as, and everyone else tried to guess the saint. To make the dressing up a little easier, I recommended wearing a sheet belted on over their play clothes as a robe (to capture that ancient look) and then attaching a clue of some sort (e.g., if you were going to be St. Peter, you might hang a bunch of keys around your neck; if you were St. Matthew, you might carry a sack of coins). I suggested that if they didn't want to come as someone on the list, they could come as anyone out of the New Testament, especially for the girls, as there were only two female saints on the list.

Everyone had a great time, and there was a lot of learning involved, too. One of the moms told me that she had her children split up the list of saints, and they each accessed the website, looked up their saints, printed their information, and then shared it with each other. They all gained some computer and Internet skills as well as learning about new saints. She commented happily that she and her children had learned more religion in preparing for that party than in several years of religious education. In my mind, that comment alone is what makes the time and effort in putting together a party like this so worthwhile. That's what support groups are all about.

"It is not merely by the title of example that we cherish the memory of those in heaven; we seek, rather, that by this devotion to the exercise of fraternal charity the union of the whole Church in the Spirit may be strengthened. Exactly as Christian communion among our fellow pilgrims brings us closer to Christ, so our communion with the saints joins us to Christ, from whom, as from its fountain and head, issues all grace, and the life of the People of God itself."

Catechism of the Catholic Church, 957

Field Trips

Maureen Wittmann

One of the many advantages of homeschooling is the ability to get out of the classroom and into the community. The children are able to take the knowledge they've gained through their studies and apply them to real life. As a home educator, I needn't worry about finding chaperones, scheduling transportation, covering insurance risks, or gathering permission slips. I simply buckle the children into the family van and go.

Staying on Budget

In our home, cost is always a consideration in planning field trips. My husband is the sole wage earner for our growing family, so we don't have a lot of expendable cash. Even on a budget, however, we have many options for field trips. Free trip locales include the post office, factories, bakeries, local television or radio stations, fire stations, and so on. A visit to a political campaign office could provide important lessons in civic duty. Trips to nursing homes, soup kitchens, and hospitals not only offer educational benefits, but also demonstrate Christianity and charity in action. Monasteries, seminaries, historical churches, and shrines can be pilgrimages that give glory to God. What a joy it is to share our faith with our children, whether it be in our homes or on a family excursion.

When visiting museums, symphonies, and zoos, always check for discounts. For example, our local zoo has free admission on Tuesdays. Museums and such often offer discounts for large groups and educational outings, so consider organizing a trip with friends to save money.

Finally, when making field-trip plans, weigh the educational benefits and make sure that they're worth your time, money, and energy.

Field Trips with Dad

Field trips give Dad the perfect opportunity to become involved in the family's homeschool. Dad can share his expertise or special interests. My husband loves the outdoors and has made many bird-watching, hiking, and camping excursions with our children. The educational benefits of their outings have been tremendous. In addition, the benefits of shared family time can't begin to be measured. Whether Dad's interest is in cars, sports, model-making, or horses, he shouldn't pass up the opportunity to invite the children into his world.

Dad doesn't have to wait until the weekend or evenings to take the children on a field trip either; his place of work can make for an educational visit. For example, a dear friend's husband works for the lieutenant governor of our state. He invited his children and their friends on a tour of the state capitol building. Because of his job, the children saw a lot more than they would have on the standard public tour. He was able to take us onto the floor of the Senate and the House. He took us behind the scenes of the governor's and the lieutenant governor's offices. It was a very rich and rewarding trip for all involved.

Field Trips with Large Groups

Many larger homeschooling support groups have an official coordinator for field trips. If someone else is putting together a trip that you'll be going on, please be considerate of his time and hard work. Make sure to let the coordinator know if you're coming and how many will be in your party. Large-group field trips are more enjoyable when deadlines are honored and participants are on time. Also, do your best to keep your children under control, and never use field trips for babysitting.

If you're the support group's field-trip coordinator, consider the "reverse field trip." Invite, for instance, a priest, scientist, or local weatherman to give a lecture or demonstration to your group. Recently our support group invited an expert on reptiles to its regular monthly get-together. The children loved seeing and touching the animals, and they gained a wealth of information about our cold-blooded friends.

Take into account the ages of the children attending. Teens and little ones are light years apart in understanding and interests, as well as the ability to listen and participate. Some support groups designate separate coordinators for teenagers and young children. Think about exchanging babysitting time with another home-schooling parent, so that small children aren't dragged on trips where they'll be bored.

Before embarking upon your group field trip, take a few minutes to cover all of the basic rules of conduct. Most of us know the rules, but it helps children to be reminded in advance to stay with the group at all times, to pay attention when spoken to by adults, to ask before touching, and to raise their hands before asking questions. With small children, use a buddy system; that is, each child finds a buddy, and they hold hands. This way, they're less likely to become separated from the group.

Once your field trip has ended, encourage parents and children to write thank-you notes. When your hosts receive thank-you cards, they will not only be open to inviting your group back again, but they'll also be likely to help spread the good news of homeschooling.

Advance Preparation

Before a field trip, encourage your children to read related books. By doing some advance research on their own, they'll be more likely to retain the information received on the trip. A visit to your local library should help you find all of the books and reference materials you need. Don't be afraid to ask the librarian for help. Sometimes a librarian will come up with something special that you would have never found by yourself. Tapping into the Internet can also provide an abundance of maps, interesting facts, and resource information.

Encourage your children to ask lots of questions. In fact, have them prepare some questions in advance. Asking probing questions is a skill that will benefit your children as they grow into adults. It's easier for them to find the answers and lessons of their experiences when they first learn to ask the right questions.

Prepare a field-trip scrapbook. The scrapbook can be filled with reports, pictures, and souvenirs. Not only will the scrapbook make a nice keepsake for years to come, but it will also provide the opportunity to go back and review the information learned on your field trips. Also, if your state requires record-keeping, the scrapbook provides tangible proof of your educational excursions.

Impromptu Trips

Not all field trips require advance planning. When you find yourself, or your children, overwhelmed by boredom or cabin fever, get outdoors and go on an impromptu field trip. If you're studying ancient Egypt and you find that your local museum is having a King Tut exhibit, load the children into the car and go. At times, a break is just what we need to get back on track in our homeschool.

Sometimes an impromptu trip is called for when schoolwork is going great and you feel that the children deserve a reward for their hard work. Instead of heading to McDonald's playland, consider a fun field trip. When reading our local newspaper, I keep my eyes open for fun, yet educational, events in the area. That way, I'm prepared, should I feel the need to keep the children motivated. Getting out of the house might be just the thing.

Family vacations can also be turned into field trips. It's fun to make a side trip to cultural events, monuments, or parks while traveling to other cities. We especially enjoy visiting the natural wonders of our land. My husband scours topographical maps from the library to find waterfalls, swamps, and such, so that we can do some off-road exploring when traveling cross-country.

I can't begin to count the number of times that people who don't homeschool have questioned whether or not my home-schooled children are being properly socialized. Yet the very nature of homeschooling lends itself to teaching our young ones social skills. One-on-one tutoring takes much less time than teaching in a large-classroom setting; therefore we're able to get out into the community and associate with people of all ages, races, and creeds. In fact, we've the wonderful opportunity to bring real-life experiences into our homeschools.

"As the family goes, so goes the nation and so goes the whole world in which we live."

Pope John Paul II

Staying Within Parish
Sacramental Guidelines

Maureen Wittmann

One fall day, I began receiving phone calls from local Catholic homeschoolers with news that our Catholic diocese was about to implement sacramental guidelines for homeschoolers. After fielding three or four calls in one day, I sat down and prayed. I didn't want this to take place in my diocese. Knowing that such guidelines are a political hot button, an issue that has divided Catholic homeschoolers across the country, I didn't want to be in the middle of such a controversy. I begged God for his guidance and for his help.

Our local support group has no hierarchy of leadership. As editor of our newsletter, I'm the one whom concerned homeschoolers were calling for help. It became obvious that I wasn't going to be able to ignore the proposed guidelines, and I was expected to do something about the situation. Fortunately, God was working on answering my prayer, and the answer came in the form of a very holy and wise priest by the name of Fr. George, who was the spiritual advisor of our support group. Father called me and filled me in on all the details.

The diocese had been getting numerous calls from DREs asking if homeschooled children were required to attend parish religion programs in order to receive the sacraments. They didn't know if their home religion programs were sufficient. The diocese decided that some kind of guidelines needed to be in place in order to help parishes minister to homeschoolers. Father went on to tell me that a committee had been put together, and proposed guidelines had already been drawn up. The committee had mailed the proposed guidelines to every parish in the diocese, asking for the input of pastors, DREs, and school principals. Comments and suggestions were to be returned to the committee in less than a month.

The sacramental guidelines that were being proposed were a bureaucratic nightmare, for homeschoolers and for parish staff. They were lengthy and cumbersome. They requested that parents report to their pastor any intention to homeschool. They requested that homeschooling parents be certified catechists. They requested that the diocese approve all religious materials used by homeschoolers. Worst of all was the implication that homeschoolers isolated themselves from their Catholic community.

I contacted homeschoolers in other dioceses to find out whether anyone had been able to keep guidelines out of their diocese completely, and the answer was negative. It began to sink in that the guidelines were here to stay. The best we could do was to lobby for guidelines that were workable for our families and parishes.

Fortunately, Fr. George was always looking out for us homeschoolers. As our spiritual advisor, he wrote inspiring articles for our newsletter, suggested having a Back-to-School Mass each year, dressed as St. Nicholas every December 1, and celebrated the Graduation Mass each May. Now he was helping us in another way.

Homeschoolers hadn't been invited to participate in drafting the sacramental guidelines, so now was the time to get our concerns heard. If we were to make a difference, we needed to act fast and we needed to act smart. Father instructed us first to pray. We were to ask the Holy Spirit for guidance, not only for ourselves, but also for the individual members of the guideline committee and for our beloved bishop. Then we were to work through our pastors, DREs, and parish-school principals. Father asked us not to contact the bishop or the committee directly.

Since there were only a few weeks to respond, we didn't have time to get news of the guidelines into our monthly newsletter. Fortunately, I keep a list of email addresses of families in our local support group. I was able to email copies of the proposed guidelines to nearly sixty families. For those without email, we made phone calls. Our Back-to-School Mass took place during this time frame, so we were able to get the news out at the potluck that followed the Mass.

We prayed a novena to the Holy Spirit. Then families contacted their parishes with their concerns. Personal meetings were scheduled and letters written. I volunteered help to anyone who needed assistance in writing letters. Father stressed that we needed to be charitable in our approach, and everyone complied.

Father also asked that we give our parish contacts a copy of the sacramental guidelines issued by the Pittsburgh Diocese, *Faith Education in the Home*, and a copy of Edward N. Peters's book *Home Schooling and the New Code of Canon Law* (Christendom College Press). *Faith Education in the Home* is a beautiful document that reaffirms the homeschooling parents' vocation as primary educator (found at www.diopitt.org/education/homertf.zip). *Home Schooling and the New Code of Canon Law* lays out all of the legal reasons why undue conditions cannot be placed on homeschooling parents who are seeking the sacraments for their children.

It was also during this time that the Catholic Homeschool Network of America (CHSNA) published its booklet *Responsibilities and Rights of Parents in Religious Education*. Our statewide organization was able to get this new booklet into the hands of the committee.

Father always stressed the importance of parish involvement. Now that involvement was paying off. Our pastors, DREs, and even parish-school principals took our concerns to the committee. They really went to bat for us.

My own experience was incredible. When I first began homeschooling, I wasn't sure how to approach preparation for the sacraments. I went to the DRE of my parish and asked her if I needed to enroll my children in CCD in order for my children to receive the sacraments. She looked at me with astonishment and commented "Maureen, your children already go to Catholic school. Why would you want to put them in parish religion class?" Unfortunately, I couldn't take my concerns to her, as she was no longer the DRE of our parish and her replacement quit unexpectedly the day before I arrived to talk about the guidelines. I couldn't go to my pastor because he was out of town. My only recourse was the principal of the parish school.

After the principal had reviewed the proposed guidelines and the Pittsburgh guidelines, I met with him. He was very supportive and had already contacted members of the guideline committee. He let them know of my concerns and added his own concern that the guidelines would create undue work for pastors and DREs.

I live in an urban parish with a school that's barely able to keep its doors open, due to dwindling enrollment. I asked the principal of this struggling school if he looked at my large family and wished that my children were enrolled in his school. He had me in tears when he responded, "In my history as an educator, there have been many wonderful families who, like you and Bob, have decided that homeschooling was the best alternative for them. I have always found people, like yourselves, most interesting and more spiritually grounded than most. I think you're both a gift and a treasure to the mission of the Church."

I know that not all homeschoolers will have the positive experience I had in my parish, but when an organized group of Catholic homeschoolers come together in prayer and act reasonably, the results can be amazing. The final guidelines didn't resemble the original draft in any way. Instead they reaffirm the parents' role as primary educators of their children. In fact, they were almost identical to the suggested guidelines laid out in CHSNA's booklet *Responsibilities and Rights of Parents in Religious Education*. I don't know how it all came about and what it was exactly that changed the hearts of the homeschooling guideline committee, but I'm willing to bet that the Holy Spirit had something to do with it.

"Parents are under grave obligation to see to the religious and moral education of their children, as well as to their physical and civic training, as far as they can, and moreover to provide for their temporal well-being."

Code of Canon Law 1917, Canon 1113

Homeschooling, Canon Law,
and the Right to Receive the Sacraments

Pete Vere, JCL

"Our son is ready to be confirmed, but he received his religious education at home, rather than through the parish CCD program. What are my canonical rights?"

Even during my student days in canon law, such questions often came my way from concerned homeschooling parents. Busy as I then was, I could seldom afford to give more than a brief answer. Yet in most cases, only a brief answer was necessary, coupled with a quick phone call to the pastor in question. I found most pastors good men who unfortunately received their formation in canon law sometime between the closing of Vatican II and the introduction of the 1983 *Code of Canon Law* — a time when canon law was in a serious state of flux. This meant priests from that era were not as clear on canon law as previous and subsequent generations. And thus, as a student, I found that the topic of homeschooling and canon law kept coming my way, particularly where the right of homeschooled children to the sacraments was involved. In fact, I always hoped to return to this topic after graduation.

Before I begin, a brief definition of canon law is probably in order for those unfamiliar with this subject. Basically, canon law is the internal legal system of the Catholic Church. It's the system of laws and regulations through which the Church maintains order and discipline among its adherents. The word *canon* originally comes from the Greek word *kanon*, meaning "rules by which to live." Therefore, canon law is the Church's internal legal system by which we as Catholics are expected to conduct our day-to-day affairs. This legal system is broken down into individual rules of conduct, which we normally call *canons*. A large portion of these rules are collected into seven books of legislation that, together, are known as the *Code of Canon Law*.

Homeschooling and Catechesis

Let's now turn our attention to the question that lies before us. Namely, how does canon law help the homeschooling family resolve certain problems that might arise within the everyday practice of their faith?

Well, before answering this question directly, let's first look at how the *Code of Canon Law* defines parental rights and obligations in the area of catechesis. For the following canon prepares the foundation through which subsequent canons concerning Catholic homeschooling will be interpreted:

> *Canon 774 §1:* The care for catechesis, under the direction of lawful ecclesiastical authority, extends to all members of the Church, to each according to his or her role.
>
> *§2:* Before all others, parents are bound to form their children, by word and example, in faith and in Christian living. The same obligation binds godparents and those who take the place of parents.

Now, to break this down into lay language, the first paragraph teaches us that catechesis, or the teaching of basic Catholic truths, is everyone's business within the Church. However, it must come under the direction of the lawful ecclesiastical authority. In other words, as Catholics, we're expected to receive guidance from our priests and bishops when carrying out the great work of teaching the Faith to others. Furthermore, our duty concerning catechesis differs depending upon our role in life. For example, a priest has a greater responsibility to ensure that the faithful of his parish are properly catechized than would the new convert. Basically, our rights and obligations with regard to religious formation depend upon our state in life.

Now, the state in life of Catholic parents, as noted in the canon's second paragraph, binds them to ensuring the catechetical formation of their children. This is not simply a canonical right, or a legal option the parent may or may not fulfill at his own choosing. Rather, under canon law an *obligation* exists requiring parents, by the very fact that they are Catholics bringing children into the world, to form their children in the truths and teachings of the Catholic Faith. Furthermore, parents are bound to this obligation before all others, meaning parents bear more responsibility for the religious upbringing of their children than anyone else. In such a way, parents are bound both in word and in example, meaning they must live according to the Catholic Faith as well. Of course, as the canon concludes, the obligation placed upon parents extends to godparents and those who take the place of parents in a given situation.

Homeschooling and Catholic Education

At this point, you're probably wondering how all this canonical teaching directly relates to the topic of homeschooling. To answer this question, let's look at the introductory canon under the title *Catholic Education* from the Code of Canon Law:

> *Canon 793 §1:* Parents, and those who take their place, have both the obligation and the right to educate their children. Catholic parents have also the duty and the right to choose those means and institutes which, in their local circumstances, can best promote the Catholic education of their children.

So, according to the first paragraph of canon 793, parents have both the right and the obligation to educate their children. By virtue of the fact that they have brought children into the world, Catholic parents may and must educate their children to the best of their ability. This right and obligation also applies to those who would take the place of parents, such as foster parents and other legal guardians. In fact, if we go deeper into the canon, the right and obligation of parents to educate their offspring is of Natural Law. In other words, the Church as an institution does not concede this right, but rather the Church upholds this right as part of a higher law. Basically, the right to educate one's children is like the right to life; the Church does not grant it, but simply upholds it. In its genesis, this right originates from God.

Now, the canon's second sentence clearly expands upon this natural right and obligation. Taking into account local circumstances, the canon gives parents both the right and the duty of choosing the best means of Catholic education for their children. Of course, one possible means of educating one's children in the Catholic Faith is homeschooling. Therefore, it simply follows that the *Code of Canon Law* upholds the right of Catholic parents, should they choose to homeschool their children.

"However," some will object, "the canon you quoted doesn't explicitly state homeschooling as an option. On this basis, couldn't the diocesan bishop or the parish priest, therefore, either deny or severely limit my right as a Catholic parent to homeschool my children?"

If we examine the *Code of Canon Law* carefully, the resounding answer is "NO!" For as canon 18 clearly states, "Laws which prescribe a penalty, or restrict the free exercise of rights, or contain an exception to the law, are to be interpreted strictly." Because a Church law limiting homeschooled families would be a restriction upon the right of Catholic parents to homeschool their children, such laws would have to be strictly interpreted. What canon law means by "strict interpretation" is not our rigid adherence to the law restricting our rights. Rather, it is the law that is restricted, in that it applies only within as few cases as possible. Therefore, Catholic parents needn't fear canon law in this case, for the law works in their favor by preventing authorities within the Church from unduly restricting the right of such parents to homeschool their children.

Homeschooling and the Sacraments

Yet the right to homeschool doesn't necessarily mean the right to receive the sacraments; therefore is the right of homeschooled children to the sacraments protected by canon law?

Indeed it is, according to canon 213, which clearly states, "Christ's faithful have the right to be assisted by their Pastors from the spiritual riches of the Church, especially by the word of God and the sacraments." In other words, like any other member of the Church, homeschooled children have the right to be nourished from the Church's spiritual treasury. With regards to the word of God and the reception of the sacraments, their rights are particularly protected under canon law. Since what belongs to homeschooled children is a right, and not merely a privilege, the Church's pastors must assist homeschooled children in the reception of the sacraments.

The Canonical Right to Confirmation

In my limited experience as a canonist working with homeschooling families, the most contested sacramental issue I've come across is the right of homeschooled children to receive the sacrament of Confirmation in a timely manner. This is why, over and above the broad rights given in canon 213, homeschooling parents must be aware of their children's specific canonical rights concerning this sacrament. For along with Holy Communion, receiving the sacrament of Confirmation is one right of homeschooled children strongly protected by the *Code of Canon Law*. A defense of this right begins with restating canon 885 §1: "The diocesan Bishop is bound to ensure that the sacrament of Confirmation is conferred upon his subjects who duly and reasonably request it." What constitutes a reasonable request from Catholic homeschooling families? Canons 889 and 890 succinctly answer this question as follows:

> *Canon 889 §1*: Every baptized person who is not confirmed, and only such a person, is capable of receiving Confirmation.
>
> *§2*: Apart from the danger of death, to receive Confirmation lawfully, a person who has the use of reason must be suitably instructed, properly disposed and able to renew the baptismal promises.

In short, the conditions constituting a reasonable request are that the candidate not be confirmed already (since this sacrament cannot be repeated) and that the candidate be capable of receiving the sacrament. Most homeschooled children seeking to receive the sacrament of Confirmation fulfill these conditions.

"Capacity" is clarified in the canon's second paragraph as possessing the use of reason, suitably instructed in the meaning and significance of the sacrament, properly disposed toward receiving the grace of the sacrament, and able to renew one's baptismal promises. Even then, none of these conditions oblige the homeschooled child in danger of death; however, this is a separate discussion.

With regard to the topic at hand, although homeschooling parents have little control over when their children will attain the use of reason, within the homeschooling curricula, such parents are able to prepare their children properly in the latter three criteria constituting capacity. Therefore, such children have the canonical right to receive the sacrament of Confirmation, and their parents must ensure the protection of this right.

The Right to Receive the Sacraments

In fact, as seen from the following canon, the protection of this canonical right is one homeschooling parents mutually share with their parish priest:

> *Canon 890:* The faithful are bound to receive this sacrament at the proper time. Parents and pastors of souls, especially parish priests, are to see that the faithful are properly instructed to receive the sacrament and come to it at the opportune time.

In summarizing this section, we see that homeschooled children, like any other member of the Church, have a canonical right to the sacrament of Confirmation, provided certain conditions are fulfilled. When this right is challenged, the *Code of Canon Law* obliges both parents and pastors to protect it.

Homeschooling families needn't fear canon law. For contrary to what many believe, the *Code of Canon Law* is a great friend to homeschooling families. Its canons uphold the right of parents to homeschool their children and the right of homeschooled children to receive the sacraments, particularly Confirmation. Homeschooling families should be aware of the canonical rights of both parents and children, and parents should be prepared to defend their family's canonical rights, if necessary. As the last canon of the Code reminds us, in interpreting canon law, we must always observe canonical equity and keep in mind the salvation of souls, "which in the Church must always be the supreme law" (canon 1752).

EDITORS' NOTE: For more on this topic, Pete Vere recommends *Home Schooling and the New Code of Canon Law*, by Edward N. Peters (Christendom College Press).

———————

"Wrong is wrong even if everyone else is doing it;
right is right even if no one else is doing it."

St. Augustine

Chapter Ten

Home Management

"Disorder in society is the result
of disorder in the family."

St. Angela Merici

Escape the Clutter and Find Peace

Sue Kreiner

We all would love to be better organized, but the thought of wading through all our stuff is so overwhelming, we tell ourselves, "Maybe next year!" Nevertheless, the rewards of organizing your life make it well worth the effort. It puts you in control of your home and gives you more free time to enjoy other things.

I highly recommend doing a very thorough decluttering. Devoting an entire week (or more, if necessary) to purging your possessions ruthlessly will eliminate a lot of future work. Once you've decided to purge, make a list of your highest priorities. Begin with an obvious area in your home that you see every day, an area that bothers you — your biggest eyesore. Eliminate as many distractions and interruptions as possible. You might even ask a friend to come and help, and to give you moral support.

As you go from item to item, ask yourself, "Is this something I can live without?" If you answer yes, throw it away immediately, or put in a "give away" box. Then make sure you do in fact give it away. If your answer is maybe, start a "maybe" box. Write the date on the box and put it in an unobtrusive place, such as your basement or attic. If you haven't missed any of the items in six months or a year, your "maybe" box turns into a "give away" box. Set a deadline, and mark your calendar, for the "give away" decision.

Now you have to find a method of organizing all the necessary items you plan to keep. Remember: the simpler the better.

One of my worst problem areas used to be my bedroom dresser. Things such as broken toys, mending, and outgrown clothing always ended up on my dresser to be dealt with later. When my mother passed away about six years ago, none of my sisters were interested in her gold-edged dresser mirror with unique perfume bottles. I wasn't sure that I wanted it either, as I had too much stuff on my dresser already. I finally did decide to keep it, requiring me to clean off all the other stuff. I put my mother's beautiful mirror and bottles on the dresser, and it looked so nice that I haven't been tempted to clutter it since. Your worst cluttered areas can look beautiful, if you focus on what you really want to keep.

Ask your husband and children to help you keep the house neat and uncluttered. Invite them to keep their personal belongings in their own rooms. If possible, have an area near the entrance of your home where coats can hang on hooks at the children's height. Place boots and shoes nearby in stacking bins or lined neatly under the coat rack.

Have a specific place on your desk for school papers and correspondence. Discipline yourself to take care of these papers daily. File away just a few of your child's best papers, and throw the rest away (best done when they're not looking). Do, however, keep a portfolio for each child with their chapter tests and other important papers that show his progress throughout the year.

Use see-through storage containers or ice-cream pails to organize toys, art supplies, and games. You can tape a picture of the contents to the box to remind your children where things should go. At my house, I control the bucket of Legos and other games. I will get just one thing out at a time, only after the children have their chores done and other toys put away. When they're done playing with the Legos, I put them up high in my closet until the next time. I also keep only one large container of toys in the house at a time. We have another container of toys in storage. When the children become bored with what's in the house, we trade our in-house toys with our stored toys. This rotation system works very well for us.

Outside toys — such as bats, balls, rollerblades, skates, and so forth — need never come into the house as long as you have a large basket or catch-all just inside the garage door or in a corner of the porch.

When you attempt to tackle a very large project such as spring-cleaning your entire house, focus on just one room or job at a time. Make a list with every room in the house on it, then a job list for each room. Then tackle as many jobs as possible on the list. What a joy it is to cross these jobs off your list! When cleaning an entire house, looking at the big picture can be overwhelming, but taking it a little at a time makes it much more manageable. 2 Chronicles 15:7 tells us, "But you, take courage! Do not let your hands be weak, for your work shall be rewarded."

If you do find yourself becoming discouraged partway through a project, give yourself a ten- to fifteen-minute break. Pray and ask God for perseverance in finishing your project, and offer yourself a treat when it's finished. An incentive can help renew your enthusiasm and energy.

One book I highly recommend is *Simplicity*, by John Michael Talbot, with Dan O'Neill (Servant Pub.). It isn't a how-to manual for cleaning and decluttering (like Don Aslett's book *Clutter's Last Stand*). Rather, *Simplicity* focuses on having an inner attitude of humility and obedience to God, and on changing the way we think and live in regard to our material possessions. Talbot quotes the timeless words of Gandhi: "Live simply so that others may simply live." Accepting this challenge to simplify has been very liberating and has made my life more peaceful.

As good as it is to pursue our goals faithfully, remember to be content with doing your best. If we keep our focus on Jesus Christ, our Lord and Redeemer, we'll go far beyond what we could otherwise accomplish. He alone can give us the strength to persevere and bless us with peace, contentment, and joy.

"Have no anxiety about anything, but in everything,
by prayer and supplication with thanksgiving,
let your requests be made known to God.
And the peace of God, which passes all understanding,
will keep your hearts and your minds in Christ Jesus."

Philippians 4:6-7

A Place of Function and Beauty:
Getting Our Homes in Order

Holly Pierlot

I firmly believe that the way we keep our homes deeply affects the quality of our homeschooling. The home ought to be both *functional*, to meet our needs, and *beautiful*, to inspire our spirits. When God created the Garden of Eden, he did so in order to provide Adam and Eve with a place where their essential human needs would be met. But he also created a paradise, a place of great beauty, for their enjoyment. And so we, too, are called to bring about these dual aspects of function and beauty in our homes.

Each room in the house is meant to serve a specific purpose, with "a place for everything and everything in its place." This seems like an obvious truth, of course, yet we homeschoolers frequently lose sight of it. How often do we discover our possessions scattered all over the house in the strangest places, like a history novel behind the toilet? How often do we find ourselves hunting in vain for socks or keys, or muttering viciously as we search for crayons — again?! How often are we unable to locate that pen and paper when we want to copy a message from an important phone call?

So much of the difficulty in our home comes from not having it set up to meet our real needs. If we want to have order in our homes (and thus in our homeschools), we need to determine which furniture and items must be in each room, according to its designated purpose. It's very simple really: if people come in at the back door, I don't put my coat hanger at the front door. If I'm homeschooling in the kitchen, I need most of my supplies accessible where I am — not stored across the house on the porch.

In addition to having order and functionality, we want to create a place of beauty for our family, for their enjoyment. This doesn't mean that we need to spend a small fortune on decorating costs, but it does mean maintaining standards of cleanliness and tidiness and also trying to add in little bits of beauty and the personal touch. Our house must be a *home*; as Pius XII once said, even our pictures and trinkets should be a reflection of the happy memories and shared common life we live together.

Of course, each family will have its own expression of beauty. While some might call it gaudy, my family and I really liked some bright yellow-cloth black-eyed susans I had on the kitchen table for years. It was our way of keeping "sunshine" in the house on dreary winter days. It was also an instant toy, as the toddlers loved to pull all the flowers off the stems, scattering "sunshine" all over the kitchen! My children also loved prisms in the kitchen window, and in late afternoon it wasn't unusual to see someone sitting on the counter making "rainbows dance" on the walls by twisting the strings.

A Room Analysis

There are some easy steps you can follow, to set up your home in a fashion that will bring about both function and beauty. Start with a "Room Analysis," whereby you go through your rooms with a sheet of paper and *think* about your home before actually working on it. To conduct your own Room Analysis, divide your paper into the following sections and answer the questions for each room:

• *Room's intended purpose.* In this section, write down what you want to see happen in this room. *What exactly is going to go on here?* For example, Child #1 Bedroom: if sleeping and clothing storage is all I want to happen here, then I write this out and that will determine what is put in this room. But if I want my child also to play, read, listen to music, and do homework here, the room will require different types of furniture and supplies.

• *What needs to be removed?* In this section, write down *everything in the room that doesn't need to be there because it doesn't fit with the purpose of the room.* This is what you'll remove. For example, if the porch is to be merely a place for coats, hats, boots, keys, and purses, then nothing else except the tools or furniture for those purposes needs to be there. Get rid of the cleaners and toys!

This small, simple step will add up to a big change when repeated throughout the house.

It also helps practically to have a "transfer room" in your house while you're re-arranging — a place where you can put stuff temporarily as you get most of the rooms in order. Then tackle this room last.

• *What furniture and supplies need to be there?* In this section, according to the purpose of your room, determine *exactly what you need in that room to accomplish its purpose.* For example, if I want the family to read in the living room, I need to put bookshelves and books in the living room. If we pray there, then we need our rosaries, prayer books, and so on in that room.

• *What repairs need to be done?* While you're at it, glance about the room and write down all the items and areas that need to be fixed in the room: the broken cabinet latches, burned-out light bulbs, peeling paint, and so on. Write a big U for "urgent" beside absolute and immediate musts.

• *Beautifying projects.* Keeping in mind often-limited budgets, write down any projects you would like to do to make the room more beautiful and enjoyable for your family members: make new curtains, build a new bookshelf, finish the wallpapering, and so on. Remember, it doesn't have to be a palatial suite — only beautiful to you!

• *Room chores.* Now analyze what chores *need* to be done — daily, weekly, and monthly or seasonally — to keep the room functional and beautiful. Write these down. Once you have your rooms the way you want them, maintenance will be the key to organization.

• *Home and property analysis.* It helps to use these same questions for the outside of your house, too — the lawns, the garage, the shed, the garden, and so forth. You or your husband can also go through these lists and see what needs to be done to bring order to these places as well.

• *Clothing and laundry.* Since clothing can so often look like part of the furniture in a messy home, it, too, needs to be brought to order:
  - ❑ How much clothing do I think is reasonable for each member of the family to have?
  - ❑ Is there adequate bureau and closet space for proper storage and maintenance of this clothing?
  - ❑ What do I need for storage of seasonal clothing?
  - ❑ Where are we to put laundry waiting to be washed?
  - ❑ How often does laundry need to be done in our home?
  - ❑ How can I arrange for laundry to be brought to the washing machine and returned after it's washed?
  - ❑ What articles of clothing need to be repaired?
  - ❑ What articles of clothing must be bought for each person's daily and seasonal needs?

Once you've gone through all your rooms:
• Move the furniture and supplies around
    according to your plan.
• Get rid of everything you don't need.
• Classify your purchase needs on lists entitled
    "Urgent," "Soon" and "Can Wait."
• Write up daily and weekly chore charts for main-
    taining the order you have just brought about.
• Teach your husband and children where everything
    goes and where and how everything will be done!

The Family Must Care for the Home

The work of keeping the home functional and beautiful is the responsibility of the family who lives there. A 100-percent surefire way for me, as a homeschooling mother, to burn out *fast* is to try to do it all myself. In reality, it's impossible, even in the best of situations.

Every member of the family who lives in the home must share responsibility for keeping it up. It's only logical, then, to begin with the list of jobs that need to be done in the home and then to divide these up among all the family members according to talent and ability and time. Yes, that includes husband and children! The work of the home is not something other members do to help Mommy, but something they do because they, too, are stewards of God's creation, and stewardship begins with where we live.

There are many practical benefits to this, too. First, spreading the workload over many people (even toddlers) results in a much happier Mommy! Second, as an old saying goes, "Idleness is the Devil's workshop." Having balanced, moderate work helps keep little bodies busy and active with less time to get into trouble. Third, having kids help out inspires a work ethic and helps de-velop character, and is actually a form of training for adulthood — for the care they will have to provide for their own families someday. In this way, housework and maintaining order not only make homeschooling easier, but also make our home a school of virtue.

"Like the sun rising in the heights of the Lord,
so is the beauty of a good wife
in her well-ordered home."

Sirach 26:16

Dinner Is on the Table!
Meal Planning

Maureen Wittmann

I know that, if I'm to be effective in homeschooling, I need to be effective in managing my home and my finances. (I've seen more than one family leave homeschooling and place their children into site-based schools because they were overwhelmed by housework or because they couldn't make ends meet.) I've found that with a little preplanning, for example, I can save money on my grocery bill and save time in managing my home.

On Monday mornings, I spend one hour at my dining-room table with the grocery ads, coupons, and my favorite recipes. Based on the week's sales, I make out a menu for the week's evening meals. My friends tease me when they see my menu taped to the refrigerator, but I'm saving money and time.

By planning ahead, I save money, because I don't have to make quick trips to the store for missing ingredients for the evening's meal. In such cases, we would stop at the convenience store just down the road, instead of the out-of-the-way, cost-cutting grocery store.

I save time, because I know what I'm going to make a week in advance. If I plan ahead and put a roast and few vegetables in the oven at 4:00, I'm not trying to figure out what to cook just minutes before my husband walks in the door and then rushing to get everything together.

On days when I know that I'll be on the run all day, I plan ahead by utilizing my crockpot. It's a nice feeling to come home to a prepared dinner after a long day. Using my crockpot saves on frustration and money. Even the toughest, cheapest cuts of meat come out delicious in the crockpot.

Some families save time by creating freezer meals, sometimes a month in advance. I own the book *Once a Month Cooking*, but I've never taken on the endeavor. Cooking a month's worth of meals in one day just sounds too daunting to me. However, I do make freezer meals in advance. For example, if chicken roasters are on sale at a rock-bottom price, I will cook several at one time, serve one for dinner and freeze the rest. I've done the same with meatloaf, lasagna, and other main dishes. Another way I save time is to chop all the vegetables that I have at once, use what I need at the time and put the rest in an airtight container for use later in the week.

I've also been able to get into a mind set that's always looking for ways to save money in my kitchen. If chuck roast is on the menu, then, after the table has been cleared, I'll put the beef bone into a pot with some seasonings and an onion and let it simmer. In a few hours, I have a very nice broth with almost no work. I do the same with vegetables — the parts that are usually discarded after chopping. If I don't have an adequate amount to make broth, I'll put the vegetables into the refrigerator or freezer until I have enough.

Leftover vegetables from dinner sometimes go into a Tupperware dish in the freezer. Once the Tupperware dish is full, we have "leftover soup." I combine the homemade broth, the frozen vegetables, and some rice or pasta, and we have a delicious soup.

For breakfast the children fend for themselves. They have cereal except for my one child who can't eat wheat products; he has fresh fruit or yogurt. For lunch we keep it very simple. Summer-time lunches often consist of vegetable dippers and fresh fruit, many times from our own garden. In the winter, leftover soup, pasta, or grilled-cheese sandwiches all make a quick and delicious lunch.

Remember to keep things easy so that you'll be able to spend more time homeschooling and less time cooking

To keep dinner simple, here are some crockpot recipes:

BARBECUED SPARERIBS
3 pounds country-style ribs
½ cup thinly sliced celery
1 medium onion, diced
1 cup barbecue sauce
½ cup corn syrup

Combine in crockpot and cook on
low for eight to ten hours (or on
high for three to four hours)
Serves eight.

7-UP STEW
2 pounds stew meat
1 can cream of mushroom soup
1 package onion-soup mix
1 cup lemon-lime soda (I've also made
this with caffeine-free cola)

Combine in crockpot, and cook on
low for eight to ten hours (or on
high for three to four hours).
Makes a nice gravy to serve with
egg noodles or mashed potatoes.
Serves eight.

SPICY ITALIAN ROAST

Large roast (the cheaper the better)
1 package dry Italian-dressing mix
1 small can beef broth
small jar pepperoncini (with the juice)

Combine in crockpot, and cook on
low for eight to ten hours (or on
high for three to four hours).
Variation: If you don't like spicy,
substitute a can of stewed
tomatoes for the pepperoncini.
Serves eight.

CHICKEN BURRITOS
1 to 2 pounds chicken
1 package burrito-seasoning mix
1¼ cups water
tortillas

Mix water and seasoning mix in crockpot.
Add chicken and cook on low for six to
eight hours. Remove the skin and
bones from the chicken. Shred meat
with two forks and serve on warm tortillas.
Optional toppings: shredded cheese,
lettuce, sour cream, rice.
Serves four. Easily doubled.

CHICKEN AND STUFFING

2 to 3 pounds chicken
1²/₃ cup water
1 can cream soup of your choice
1 box stuffing mix

Combine chicken, water, and soup in crockpot
on low for four to five hours. Remove the skin
and bones from the chicken. Cut meat
into bite-size pieces. Mix in stuffing
mix. Cook on low for one more hour.
Serves eight.

Toasted on One Side and Crusty on the Other?
Five Fireproofing Secrets for Preventing Burnout

Gregory K. Popcak, MSW

The despair was palpable. Even though I was talking to her on the phone, I could almost see the anguished expression on Deann's face as she exhaled sharply.

"I just can't do it anymore," she said. "I always wanted to home-school, and I think I made a good run at it, but maybe I'm just not cut out for this anymore."

As a psychotherapist, and director of the Pastoral Solutions Institute (www.exceptionalmarriages.com), I regularly counsel Catholics across the country on how to apply their faith to tough marriage, family, and personal problems. And because I'm a home-schooling father, over the years I've had the opportunity to work with many families who teach their children at home.

In many ways, Deann was very typical of many of the home-schooling mothers I've known. Married for twelve years, she's a mother of four with a deep love for her children and an even deeper faith. Yet here she was, in counseling with me for a problem that had all the earmarks of a clinical depression — a problem that had her questioning some of the most important decisions of her life. Deann was burned out. What went wrong? And how can you make sure it doesn't happen to you?

Burnout: What Is It?

In a sense, burnout is depression's obnoxious little sister. Not quite strong enough to knock you out completely, it slowly drains your energy by picking, picking, picking at you all day long. While stress is a normal part of life and everyone has days that are harder than others, you know you're getting burned out when you begin consistently getting irritated over every little thing; when, day after day, even simple requests by your children start eliciting a disgusted reaction; when formerly simple interactions between you and your children begin turning into constant power struggles; and when you start looking for almost any excuse to "take another day off" from school because you can't bring yourself to face another lesson plan. ("Hey kids, it's . . . uh . . . Greek Orthodox Groundhog Day — yeah, that's it. Why don't you go play for a while? Mommy's going to lie down. . . .")

Left unchecked, burnout can lead to a depressive disorder known as dysthymia, a kind of emotional walking pneumonia that allows you to function, but sucks all the joy out of your day and makes you wish you could run away from home.

The good news is that burnout (even the more sinister forms of it) can be prevented or cured fairly readily. In the following pages, we will take a look at what it takes to burnout-proof your homeschool.

How Does It Happen?

Nobody wakes up one morning and decides, "Gee, I'll think I'll get burned out today." So how does it happen? How does a dedicated, loving, and faithful homeschooling parent get the legs knocked out from under her? Well, come to think of it, that's exactly what happens.

Imagine that you're sitting on a five-legged stool. Each leg represents one aspect of a healthy homeschool, a homeschool that's burnout-proof. Specifically, these five legs stand for: a partnership marriage, a good discipline system (good rapport plus consistent rules and consequences), a healthy family-based spirituality, good self-care (mental and physical), and a curriculum that's suited to both the teacher and the students. To sit comfortably, you need all five legs of the stool. Now, you might be able to get by if the legs aren't exactly even, or perhaps if one or two of the legs are missing entirely, but the fact is, unless all five legs are present to a more or less equal degree, you're going to feel constantly off balance. It won't take much to knock you off your seat, and into burnout.

Let's take a closer look at each of these five legs with an eye toward burnout-proofing your homeschool.

A Partnership Marriage

There's much to be said about having a healthy Christian marriage, but for our purposes, we must boil it all down to the need to understand and respect the unique dynamic of the homeschooling marriage.

What do I mean? Well, it might surprise you to discover that homeschooling couples actually have much more in common with two-career couples than with other traditional marriages. In traditional stay-at-home families, roles are fairly rigidly defined. The husband is the primary breadwinner, and the wife has primary charge over keeping the home running smoothly. In such a dynamic, the husband may occasionally "help" his wife with the home and the children, but that's all it is: "Helping her do her job." With the occasional hiccup, this arrangement works well enough for the average stay-at-home mother.

But to homeschool effectively, the roles can't be so rigidly defined without risking burnout. You need a marriage *partner*, who's willing to jump in and pick up the slack around the home, and I'm not just referring to the domestic chores, but the relationship tasks as well (making sure you know you're appreciated and loved, planning dates, and so on). Homeschooling is a full-time job and must be respected as such. You can't try to squeeze lessons in among cleaning the house, running errands, serving on community and church committees, and all the other things that primarily occupy the time of other stay-at-home mothers. That isn't to say that you can't do these things, too, if you have the time, but the fact is, if you want to homeschool well and in a manner that will prevent you from burning out, every daytime activity other than home-schooling has to come second, including housework.

Both the husband and wife have to be willing to accept this basic fact of homeschooling life. Teaching children at home is a different career choice than that of the average stay-at-home mother, and this important difference needs to be appreciated. As one prominent homeschooling mother and speaker has put it, "I can pay someone else to teach my children while I stay home and clean the toilets, or I can teach my children at home and pay *someone else* to clean the toilets. I would prefer to do the latter."

While there are many conflicted two-career families in which the mother has to labor at her day job and then work what sociologist Arlie Hochschild called "the second shift" at home, in happy two-career families — and this applies to happy homeschooling families as well — the husband and the wife see to it that they're true *partners* in caring for the home, for the children, and for each other, and whatever they can't do themselves, they must be willing to either hire out or let go. Homeschooling families who are joyful experience this kind of partnership marriage.

In homeschooling families that aren't as joyful, and therefore are more susceptible to burnout, husbands expect to come home from a long day at work to find a house perfectly kept, children perfectly well-educated, a meal perfectly well prepared, and a wife who is perfectly happy to keep her needs for intimacy and help to herself.

While there are many things involved in creating a partnership marriage that can approach all the tasks of domestic life with grace, you can get a good start by walking through the following formula:

a. Of all the hours you're awake, how many hours per week can you *comfortably* work without beginning to feel frayed (the most important word here is *comfortably*)?

Write the number here. _____

b. Now ask yourself the following, "In a week, how much time does it take me to *really teach my children well?*" Subtract this number from your answer to "a" above.

Write the total here. _____

c. Now ask yourself the following: "How many hours per week would it take to run my home well?" Subtract that number from the total in "b" above.

Write the total here. _____

d. Did you get a negative number? If not, wonderful — you're truly on top of things. But if you did get a negative number, this number represents the *amount of time you simply cannot work by yourself without burning out.* With your spouse, discuss creative ways the two of you can work together, or get additional help, or adjust your expectations accordingly, to make up the difference and at least break even.

A Good Discipline System

The second most frequent reason homeschooling families call me in desperation is because there's a significant breakdown of discipline in the home.

"I can't get him to listen to me."

"She just won't do her work!"

"Every little thing has to be a battle."

"I started homeschooling because I wanted us to be close to each other. Now, the only thing we're close to is killing each other!"

Each of the above comments has been made to me, at one time or another, by a well-meaning but frustrated homeschooling parent. Good discipline is an essential part of preventing homeschool burnout, and I don't mean the heavy-handed "Vee Have Vays of Making You LEARN" kind of discipline either.

Discipline comes from the Latin word *discipulus*, meaning "disciple" or "student." A good discipline system has three components: good rapport, consistent rules, and logical consequences.

• *Good rapport* is essential to effective discipline. In fact, it's the foundation for it. Just as Jesus "commands" our obedience by entering into an intimate relationship with us and then becoming our servant (as the children's song says, "Oh, how I love Jesus, because he first loved me!"), so too must we "command" our children's obedience by being loving servants to them. We can't just be content to teach our children and boss them around all day; we must take the time to build a relationship with them, to "catch them being good," to be generous with affection and genuine compliments, and to make time to do things one-on-one with them. Without these rapport-building activities, the only way to make our children mind us is to make them fear us, and this fear-based obedience is a serious affront to the "community of love" Pope John Paul II called all families to build and celebrate. Besides, having to chase your children around all day as if you were the family policeman is exhausting, and it leads to burnout.

By contrast, when rapport is strong, children are more likely to obey because they don't wish to offend the relationship they have with you. St. Thérèse, the Little Flower, wrote in *The Story of a Soul* that she never wanted to be disobedient to her parents, because they were so attentive to her needs that they deserved nothing less than her best. There is a psalm that says, "How can I repay the Lord for all the good he has done for me?" (Ps. 116:12). This is the model of Christian obedience that invites our children to say, "How can I repay my mom and dad for all the good they have done for me?"

• *Clear and consistent rules.* Assuming that parent-child rapport is solid, the second part of good discipline is clear and consistent rules. I once spoke with a mother of seven who said to me, "I've realized lately how much I've slacked off over the years. I used to have very specific rules and consequences laid out for my first two or three children, but as time went by, I just assumed that the babies would catch on by watching their brothers and sisters. Somehow I forgot that I needed *to teach each one* how to behave!"

Don't assume everyone knows the rules. Don't assume you do either. Ask yourself, "What five things need to happen in order for there to be more peace in my home?" Review these five things with the children and then post them as rules on the refrigerator or in another public place. While the family is learning them, review them every day over breakfast, and then review them again when the children's behavior starts fraying around the edges. Also, instead of telling your child the rule whenever he breaks it, point to the sign and say, "Please look at the list and tell me the rule." This beats lecturing them all day.

Likewise, make sure you enforce the rules consistently, because if you don't care enough about your own rules to enforce them, then your children, your disciples, can't be expected to care enough to learn and follow them.

• *Logical consequences.* Now that you have clear and consistent rules posted, let's look at the third part of effective discipline: logical consequences. A logical consequence has three characteristics: it immediately follows the problem behavior, it inconveniences your child more than it inconveniences you, and it teaches your child what to do (instead of merely what to stop doing). If what you're doing to correct your child's behavior doesn't meet these three criteria, you're not using logical consequences.

Finally, a logical consequence is always just, in that it does no more or less than to require the child to clean up the literal or figurative mess he has made. If the consequence applied doesn't "clean up the mess," then the consequence isn't severe enough. If, on the other hand, the consequence requires the child to "clean up the mess" and then also jump through twenty other hoops just to prove to you that he has learned his lesson once and for all, then the consequence is too severe. There's no such thing as "once and for all" when it comes to disciplining children. There's only over and over and over and over until, finally, it sticks all on its own. The sooner a parent gets over the "once and for all" fantasy, the happier that parent will be.

Let me give you some practical illustrations of what a logical consequence looks like. Say your child talks back to you. In this case, it makes no sense to take away his bicycle. It is, however, a perfectly logical consequence to require the child to repeat what he just said in a more respectful manner and a more respectful tone, and keep asking him to repeat it until he gets it right (after which you can compliment him for his delivery). Likewise, if your child breaks something, either in anger or in a fit of mindless high-spiritedness, it makes no sense to spank him, but it does make sense to require him to apologize, clean up the mess, and make some kind of real restitution (either by replacing the item or by working off the debt).

To recap, logical consequences are always concerned first and foremost with teaching the child what to do *instead of* the offensive thing he just did.

The more solid your rapport, the clearer your expectations, and the more logical your consequences are, then the more compliant your children will be, the more peaceful your home will feel, and the more burnout-proof you will become.

Five Fireproofing Secrets for Preventing Burnout

A Healthy Family-Based Spirituality

Too many homeschooling parents burn up a lot of energy feeling guilty because they don't have time to engage in the kinds of formal prayer from which they have drawn comfort in the past. This isn't good, because guilt, especially spiritual guilt, can lead to burnout.

But if we know how to live out the vocation of marriage properly, prayer doesn't have to be something we do; it can become something we *are*. Did you ever stop to think that every time you give your children a glass of water, or dress them, or make a meal, or maintain your home, you're performing a corporal work of mercy (giving drink to the thirsty, feeding the hungry, clothing the naked, sheltering the homeless, and so on)? Likewise, every time you let a child slide on a less serious offense, correct the more serious ones, teach your child a new skill, or wipe your child's tears, you're performing a spiritual work of mercy (bearing wrongs patiently, admonishing the sinner, counseling the ignorant, comforting the sorrowing, and so on)?

There are two main schools of spirituality in Catholicism: the Benedictine model and the Salesian model. St. Benedict wrote about the importance of prayer and work. In this model, there are lines drawn between time spent in work and time spent in prayer, and prayer is seen as something you have to leave your work to do.

St. Francis de Sales, however, wrote about how work *is* prayer, if it's done in the right spirit. You don't have to say a fifteen-decade Rosary every day, or even make it to daily Mass if that just isn't possible (although these things are certainly noble exercises). You can nurture your spiritual life by simply appreciating the spiritual value and significance of the work you do, and pray that every day God will give you the grace to manifest his love to your children so that perhaps, someday (a very good day indeed) they will look at you and get just a little hint of how much their Lord loves them.

Learn how to "pray your marriage," and you'll begin to appreciate every little act of service as a mortification worthy of the most devout Christian, you'll see every joy as an opportunity to celebrate God's providence, and you'll experience every intimate moment between you and your children and between you and your spouse as a foretaste and promise of the intimacy God wishes to share with you. After all, he is the one who put these people in your life. If you can manage this much, and really acknowledge the true spiritual significance the Lord places on your role, you'll move one step closer to being burnout-proof.

Good Self-Care

In our family Scripture study, I've been struck recently by how many times Jesus slips off in an attempt to get some alone time. Regularly, the Son of God momentarily sets aside the overwhelming responsibility of saving the world from itself, and goes off to be alone with his thoughts, to sit with his Father and to recharge his batteries, if I may put it that way.

If even Jesus needed a few minutes to compose himself now and then, why do we find it so difficult, so guilt-inspiring, to take the time we need to care for our bodies, minds, and spirits?

In order to prevent burnout, you have to keep your "machine" and all its respective parts well oiled and in good working order. You've often heard it said that we're the temples of the Holy Spirit. Don't we care for and reverence the churches in which the Precious Body and Blood dwells? How much more, then, should we care for the body whose flesh has become one with the Divine Flesh, whose blood is intimately mixed with his Precious Blood? To care for our physical, emotional, and spiritual needs is not fussiness on our parts. As long as it's done with prudence and modesty, caring for ourselves is a spiritual obligation; it's an act that expresses our gratitude to the Creator for having made us, as the psalm says, so fearfully and wonderfully.

Five Fireproofing Secrets for Preventing Burnout

Are you a good steward of the gift that is your body, mind, and spirit? Consider the following: what do you need to do to feel positive about your appearance on a daily basis? When you get ready in the morning, do you dress in a manner that you feel is attractive? Or do you just throw on anything because "nobody" (read: only your children) is going to see you today? Do you have good nutrition? Or do you eat over the sink while you're getting lunch for the children? Do you read books that interest and stimulate you, or is your intellectual stimulation limited to your son's fourth-grade science text? Do you seek out someone to talk to and support you in your homeschooling (like your husband, for example, or a good homeschooling group), or do you feel isolated from other grown-ups? Do you occasionally take classes or lessons to hone your skills, develop your talents, or discover other God-given, yet still-hidden gifts? Or do you allow the treasure that God planted in you to remain buried? Do you take time to remember that you're a thinking, feeling, passionate, committed woman, and celebrate all that that means, or do you catch yourself thinking, "I'm just a mom"?

Done with the right spirit, healthy self-care has a spiritual import. Through our baptism, we're given the threefold mission of being priest, prophet, *and king*. Of course, we're priests because we're given the privilege of offering ourselves in sacrifice for the good of others, and we're prophets, because we're empowered to proclaim God's truth. But we're *kings* because God dwells in us and shares his nobility with us, and just as we would respect and make a fuss over any other noble, royal, personage we encountered, so, too, do we deserve — by God's good grace — to command the respect of others and have at least a modest fuss made over us.

But isn't that prideful? Isn't that self-indulgent? In a word, no. Pride is the sin of making yourself out to be more than you are and denying the source (God) of whatever goodness you have. True humility, however, doesn't come from denying your goodness and nobility, but from gladly acknowledging the gifts you've been given and honoring the giver. Even a humble king, one who acknowledges that any privilege and worth he has comes by the grace of God, is still a king — and carries himself as such.

By the grace of your baptism, you're entitled to celebrate your kingship by caring for the good, noble creature that you are. Remember, one of the best ways to honor the Creator is by being a good steward of his creation.

A Curriculum Suited to the
Needs of the Teacher and Students

Finally, to prevent homeschool burnout, you need to make sure that the curriculum and guides you're using are really meeting the needs of the teacher and students utilizing them.

Even if you've been teaching for a while, you should reevaluate your materials from time to time. Ask yourself:

- ❏ Do I enjoy the curriculum I use, and get at least a little excited when I take it out each day?
- ❏ Do my children seem motivated by the materials I use, or are they bored, overwhelmed, or having difficulty staying on task?
- ❏ Am I pleased with the subjects covered by my curricula as well as the depth with which those subjects are addressed?
- ❏ Does my curriculum respect the need to foster academics, spirituality, and the relationship between teacher and student — without overemphasizing any one of these?

Another point to consider is the match of the curriculum you use to the learning styles of your children. For example, children with a *visual learning style* do best with materials that emphasize reading, drawing, and writing. They learn well with pictures and illustrations, and tend to be fairly communicative. *Auditory learners* do best with materials that emphasize direct teaching and the spoken word. They need to be talked through tasks to understand them, and they learn best by discussion and debate. Likewise they often enjoy mnemonic songs and poems. *Kinesthetic learners* however, tend to learn best by doing. They work best with hands-on projects and manipulatives. If they can do it or act it out, they can learn it. However, if you try to talk to them too much, or ask them to read too much, their eyes glaze over.

Does the curriculum you're using emphasize the learning style your child exhibits? If not, you might be setting your child up for failure and yourself up for frustration.

Resist the temptation to settle on a curriculum that "everybody says" is the best. The best curriculum is the one that sets fire to the imaginations of your children, and helps them learn to their potential. Likewise, resist the temptation to find one thing and stick with it no matter what. As far as curricula go, it's true that familiarity can breed contempt — in both you and your children. Always keep your eyes open for interesting and challenging new ideas to keep your homeschool on the cutting edge. Doing so will help you remain proud of the work you do and help you feel like the professional homeschooling parent you are.

The Community of Love

Ultimately, the more your home is an example of the "community of love" that the Church calls all Catholic families to be, the less you (or, for that matter, your children) will be at risk for burnout. If, generally speaking, there is conflict in your marriage, discord between your children, power struggles over discipline, frustration over unfulfilled expectations, and a general lack of teamwork, then your homeschool will suffer. You don't homeschool in a vacuum. Your homeschool will reflect, celebrate, or suffer from the same dynamics that you experience in every other aspect of daily life as a family.

Nurture your relationships. Seek out the resources and counsel you need to overcome any barriers to joy, open dialogue, love, and cooperation in your family. Build rapport with your children. Celebrate and deepen your marital intimacy. Care for the gift that is your body, mind, and spirit. Create an environment for learning, and pray for the grace to experience the spiritual significance of every part of your day. Finally, give yourself a pat on the back for doing the most important work in the world: raising your children and teaching them how to become the people God is calling them to be.

"Ah! There is nothing like staying home for comfort."

Jane Austen

Scheduling:
Finding Order in Chaos

Maureen Wittmann

When my children were young, I spent very little time scheduling course work and looked instead for teachable moments. I let the Holy Spirit guide us, and it worked beautifully.

That doesn't mean that I threw caution to the wind and simply "hoped for the best." I provided my children with a healthy environment that encouraged learning. Our bookshelves were filled with great books, the television stayed off, and I furnished them with plenty of stimulating activities.

Although I didn't keep written schedules, I did have a plan worked out in my mind. By reading books and magazines on homeschooling, attending summer conferences, and belonging to local and online support groups, I had the advantage of finding out what worked for other Catholic homeschoolers. In doing all this, I possessed a good idea of what I wanted to accomplish each school year and how to go about doing it. Although I was relaxed in my approach, I was able to guide my children toward the academic goals that I deemed important. For example, they loved their read-aloud time with Mom, so history consisted of real books read aloud with little ones surrounding me on the couch. We began with Bible stories, then moved to the Ancient Egyptians, then the

Ancient Greeks, and so on. This was all done in a very natural setting.

However, as the size of my family grew and my little children became big children, everything changed. In my case, waiting for teachable moments with seven children is daunting at best. It might be better described as chaos. Inevitably, everyone needs me at once to look at this book or comment on that building project or change a diaper. I decided that I needed to find a balance between a relaxed environment that promoted a strong desire to learn, and an environment run on strict schedules that promoted personal discipline.

I began by sitting down at my computer, and making up some schedules on my word processor. (See www.catholictreasury.com to download free scheduling forms.) I borrowed several ideas from my friend Susan, who successfully implemented a scheduling system in her homeschool. I took her schedule forms and pruned them for my family dynamic.

Now, at the beginning of the school year, I put together a course of study. I write down our goals, textbooks to be used, and ideas for additional enrichment. I'm able to do this fairly easily, as I already have an idea of what I want to accomplish for the year. This is because I take time to read everything I can on homeschooling, glean everything I can from my homeschooling friends, and learn from the conferences I attend.

Next I look at those goals and break them down by month. By looking at the year, month by month, I can make arrangements for holidays and pre-planned events. For example, last year I knew that I'd be having a baby in April, which would disrupt our regular schedule. So I made the decision to extend our formal academics later into the year. I also made plans for activities that could be done at home without much input from Mother, while canceling activities outside of our home, such as gymnastics and Scrabble Club, during the months of March, April, and May.

Scheduling: Finding Order in Chaos

At the beginning of each quarter, I write out a quarterly course of study, similar to what I did at the beginning of the year, only more detailed. This gives me the opportunity to review our current course and make adjustments for previously unforeseen changes. No matter how much we plan, life has a way of happening and the best-laid plans sometimes fall by the wayside. I need the quarterly review to make sure that we're on track with our goals for the year. Also, children's intellectual development doesn't always coincide with even the best-planned curriculum. If a child is advancing faster or slower than we expect, we need to make adjustments. A good example is my severely dyslexic son. I found that teaching him to read would take much longer than I ever imagined and plans had to be changed. On the other hand, plans also changed when he excelled in math and science more so than expected.

There is one more scheduling form that I use. That is my weekly planner. Every Sunday evening, I sit down at my computer and fill out itineraries for each day of the week. This is perhaps the most important of all my planning tools. If I fail to give the children a schedule for the week, little is accomplished. I have one for each of my children, second grade and above. I still maintain a relaxed mode for the younger children and don't provide schedules for them.

On Monday morning, each child is given an itinerary. The children are then responsible for completing the work assigned. We begin our school day at nine, after breakfast and morning chores have been completed. By lunchtime the younger children are usually finished and can work on their special interests. The children in fifth grade and up take an hour break at lunchtime, and then usually finish their work by three.

I never schedule extracurricular activities or club meetings before lunch. Although our homeschool group offers many wonderful morning educational activities, the children and I are unable to keep to our schedule if we put off schoolwork until the afternoon.

Unfortunately, I'm not disciplined enough to get back on track when a wrench is thrown into our plans.

It should be noted that I don't completely dictate my children's day to them. Although they're responsible for completing the work assigned to them, they can choose the order in which they do their schoolwork, as well as when they do it. I strongly encourage them to complete their work first thing in the morning, and they comply. It took only a couple of incidents of working late into the evening for them to realize the advantages of completing their work as soon as possible. The faster they complete their assignments, the sooner they can play, read for enjoyment, or pursue their special interests.

They also have some say in their course work. For example, I have a second-grader who loves spelling, and so, at her request, I schedule spelling for her every day. Another child loves adventure stories, so his history reading usually consists of action-packed historical fiction. I also ask the children to help me in choosing their textbooks. While most of my children use *Voyages in English*, I have one child who prefers *Simply Grammar*. For my children who love to write, I make sure to give them ample computer time to compose their endless stories.

It is in this way that I found compromise between the relaxed and the strict. I do keep schedules, I do write out my goals, and yet I give my children ample time to explore on their own. I give them a say in their studies and in how they approach those studies. And it's working beautifully for our family.

"All things should be done decently and in order."
1 Corinthians 14:40

Chapter Eleven

Homeschool Students and Graduates

"Rule your mind or it will rule you."
Horace

Unschooling at Its Best

Michael Aquilina III

I guess you could say that I'm an unschooler — that is, if you have a clear idea of what an unschooler is.

If you believe *The New York Times*, unschoolers are the radical fringe of homeschooling. Whenever the media are forced to report on high-achieving, spelling-bee-winning, and well-behaved homeschoolers, they'll often bring up unschooling as the dark side of the movement. They conjure up homes with hippie parents, living-room furniture on the front porch, a TV constantly on and tuned to the Cartoon Network, and unsupervised, socially misfit children.

However, my family and I have a different view of things. In fact, I find it hard to believe that there are any real unschooling families like the ones suggested by the media.

If you ask different unschooling families, "What is unschooling?" you're likely to get many different answers. In this short essay, I don't hope to give you the ultimate definition of unschooling. In fact, there's no real definition of unschooling, because the method of unschooling depends on the family's goals. Instead, I'll tell you what unschooling is to me.

I'm thirteen years old, and the oldest of six children. I've never been enrolled in a school. But I wasn't always an unschooler. In fact, during my first few years of homeschooling, my mother did her best to emulate a school environment by buying as many textbooks and workbooks as humanly possible.

I didn't always take very well to the books she bought. Even in kindergarten, I'd concentrate on the things that interested me and not do as well in subjects I cared less about. I finished my religion workbook in one night and my phonics workbook in a week.

After a while, I started to rebel against using the prepared workbooks that my parents bought for me. And even my mother had to admit that some of the worksheets were just silly. I think that it got pretty tough to teach me anything but the subjects in which I was interested. Yet at the same time, she noticed that I was learning. I had started to buy computer manuals at bookstores, and I'd spend my nights poring over them, learning new things every night. I was a pretty strange little kid.

It's even stranger if you consider that at the time, when I was in the first grade, I was terrified of our home computer. Tales of crashes, power surges, and viruses scared me half to death. I refused to touch the computer. But I still loved to read computer books. Then, one day, my Dad experienced an enormous computer problem. He called everyone he knew to try to figure out the solution, and nobody seemed to know what to do. Then I overheard him on the phone, and went into the room and explained how to fix the problem. I knew the solution because I had read it in one of my computer books. After that victory, I began to lose my fear of computers, and within two years I was doing some basic programming.

Around that time, my parents started to loosen up on the prepared textbooks and worksheets, although we were still using a set curriculum.

At the end of my fifth-grade year, my parents told me that I could try unschooling the next school year if my standardized test scores, which are required by the state, came back well. At first, I knew nothing about it, and I thought that the idea of learning without any textbooks was a little strange, but I really did enjoy subjects that were off the beaten path of worksheets, so I decided to go with it.

In my seventh-grade year, I got interested in amateur "ham" radio, and I passed a Federal Communications Commission radio-license examination that covered math, electronics, physics, civics, and more. I started volunteering two afternoons a week at the town library. I also decided to write my first book. I've always had a devotion to St. Jude, so I decided to write about him. On a weeklong trip to my grandparents, I wrote my first book, *St. Jude: A Friend in Need*. I soon started offering it to different publishers, and in the process wrote up a marketing plan for it. One of the publishers wrote, "I am impressed with the grace and lucidity with which you write. We receive many manuscripts from adults (even from prominent authors) who cannot write as well as you or with as much color and interest." Finally, after many encouraging rejections, the book was accepted by Pauline Books and Media and was published in early 2004.

My first year as an unschooler was a success, at least to my parents and me (and to the publisher and the Federal Communications Commission). However, others disagreed. In my home state of Pennsylvania, the laws about homeschooling are very strict. Among other rules and regulations, you must hand in a portfolio of work samples to be checked by your local school district every year. I handed in my book and radio license, among many other things, as samples in my portfolio, but the school district returned them, saying that I hadn't received an "appropriate education." The middle-school principal seemed quite shocked that there were no worksheets in the portfolio. My parents firmly disagreed, and eventually the principal backed down.

The next year, I started my own computer consulting business, designing websites, repairing and installing computers, configuring networks, and giving advice on computer purchases for home users, small businesses, and nonprofit organizations. This was perfect for me, as in the seven years since I had discovered computer manuals at my local bookstore, I had used almost every version of the Macintosh and Windows operating systems, designed over ten websites for myself, read hundreds of computer books, written software programs, and fixed my family's computer problems. I know that there was no way I could have done that without the time I spent as a small child reading computer books. If I had been using a textbook computer course, like those used in a school, I probably wouldn't know much more than anyone else about computers now.

This school year, I'll be starting high school. In preparation for college, I'll be using a more standard course of study. While my parents are still trying to keep the spirit of freedom, even within the constraints, I know I'll always look back fondly on my unschooling days.

Unschooling isn't for everyone. If the thought of learning without textbooks makes you queasy, then unschooling is not for you. But if you'd like a more open-ended way of learning, then unschooling might well be for you.

I think there's a little bit of unschooling in all homeschoolers. The school system of textbooks, worksheets, and fill-in-the-blank forms works very well for its purpose — teaching a large amount of students a large amount of stuff. But in a homeschool setting, there isn't really any point in using books that were made for teaching a whole group of children in a school setting, crowded into a place far from home. When we decide to homeschool, we're set free from these limits. How far we go with that freedom is our choice.

No matter how far you decide to take unschooling, rest assured that unschooling definitely isn't the radical dark side of homeschooling. Unschoolers have no lack of friends and are usually good students. What's more, we learn, and we achieve.

My unschooling experience has been really great, and I encourage anyone else who's interested to try it out. It might change your life forever, as it did mine.

---

*"Education rears disciples, imitators,
and routinists, not pioneers of new ideas
and creative geniuses. The schools are not
nurseries of progress and improvement,
but conservatories of tradition and
unvarying modes of thought."*

Ludwig von Mises

Homeschooling with a Disability

Colin Fry

Nine years ago, when all my friends went off on the bus to kindergarten, I was at the kitchen table. It was on this day that my mom introduced me to a whole new way of learning, and I jumped right in. My name is Colin Fry. I'm in the ninth grade now and have always been homeschooled. I have to say that it has been a great experience.

I have spina bifida, which is caused when the neural tube doesn't close before birth. One of the consequences of spina bifida is paralysis. I walk with crutches or use a wheelchair. I've had many surgeries to repair nerve damage.

Although I have this disability, I love to be active. During the school year, I play on an adult basketball team called the Sun Wheelers. Every two months or so, we travel to tournaments in our region. When we were stationed in Texas, I traveled to two national competitions with my track team. Fishing and just being outdoors are other things I like to do. Having a disability has not held me back athletically.

Being homeschooled has been great when it comes to my schedule. If my team is going to leave for a game in the middle of the day, I don't have to miss out. Going to church during the week isn't a problem either. Also, I don't lose school time because of my doctor appointments or the many things I have to do at the hospital. Instead of being tied down to the public-school schedule, I can work when it's best for me.

Our family has tried many approaches to homeschooling over the years, trying to find the perfect program. We've struggled through strenuous textbook programs. With each of us doing our own thing and Mom running back and forth, giving each of us a new lesson, these programs took up too much of our day, and we didn't get anything else done. It was also boring doing everything by ourselves.

Now we use a more relaxed approach with unit studies. My mom gives us our lessons altogether and answers any questions we might have. Then we gather the supplies we need for the day and go to work. Mom checks on us periodically. We record everything we've done in our day planners when we're done. On Thursdays we get together with other families in our homeschool group to present memory work and do thematic projects. We finish up with recorder class. Mom checks our day planners on Friday and makes sure everything has been finished and filed away.

What we're doing is great, and I hope that it will keep working for us. I like hearing ideas from other family members about the subjects we're studying. A text gives me just a brief overview of what happened and when. Using library books and other resources besides texts gives more interesting, more in-depth information on the subject.

I'm much closer to my family than I think I would have been if I were away at school. My mom is the one giving us instruction, instead of a stranger. We talk about many different things during the day, such as politics, historical events and what we think about them, and our beliefs. My dad takes care of my math classes and chauffeurs me everywhere.

I'm very close to my siblings. Very close. We do get into each other's hair at times. We joke around at the table sometimes, which can get us off track. However, being together every day has also helped us solve personal problems instead of running from them. Our relationship is much stronger because of this. Being at home has also brought me closer to the littler children. This has given me incentive to set a good example and make the right choices.

Homeschooling has increased my love for my religion, my family, and my education. We're not just sitting around in our pajamas all day. We are working and growing as a family. Instead of being shut up in a classroom, we're able to get out in the real world for field trips, classes, and travel. I feel blessed to have been given this opportunity.

"Children in turn contribute to the growth in holiness
of their parents. Each and every one should be generous
and tireless in forgiving one another for offenses, quarrels,
injustices, and neglect. Mutual affection suggests this.
The charity of Christ demands it."
Catechism of the Catholic Church, 2227

Homeschooled K Through 12

Clare Ruth Glomski

"Clare knows everybody," Lisa said in a feigned whisper. Lisa was a freshman on campus, and her younger sister was visiting. "Everyone and everything," she added, giving me a big smile. I couldn't help but smile. If she could have seen me a year earlier!

After twelve grades in homeschool, I decided it was time to try something different. I decided to go to college. That part wasn't hard; everyone expected that. There was very little more I could accomplish at home. I also decided to move out. That was a little harder. A million doubts and questions came at me from every side. Would I be safe? How would I afford it? How much of a shock would it really be to go from home to the dorms? How would I manage?

I knew I had to try. I wanted to prove to myself, to my parents, to the world that I could do it. So many people expressed doubt that I could do it, that it felt almost like a dare. Maybe I was foolish to let that influence me. I also wanted to try something completely new. Going to college meant a complete change for me.

It was important to find a college I was comfortable with. I found a small Catholic liberal-arts school with an excellent education program. The biggest drawback was that it was ten hours from home, but I knew it was the best choice.

It wouldn't matter how perfect the school was if I couldn't afford it. I thank God everything fell together. More and more colleges, especially private ones, are looking at the complete profile of applicants. My test scores, transcripts, and portfolios took the place of a more traditional certified diploma. Many schools also have scholarship programs in place that automatically assign an award based on a student's GPA and SAT scores. A really good school will go beyond that and work with you to determine how much aid you need. My admissions counselor heard from me almost every week with a new question. She was my door to the system. She was invaluable in helping me understand university workings. She was also my voice at a college hundreds of miles away. She fought for me to get the money I needed, because she believed in me.

I knew inside myself that I was capable of succeeding academically. Homeschooling is really a lot closer to university life than a public high school. There's a similar amount of self-direction and independent work. You decide if you're going to make it.

Professors long for students who are willing to voice opinions and educated guesses they're willing to defend. This is second nature to a homeschooler, who is used to being the only student, not being able to just keep silent and hope someone else speaks up. Many traditional students, on the other hand, are used to there being one set answer and only one. That said, I decided not to tell most of my professors about being homeschooled until after the first test. I wanted to know what they thought of me relative to every other student, not relative to whatever expectations they might have had of a homeschooler. I didn't expect them to be prejudiced against me exactly, but I wanted to know for myself how I measured up. Most of them were pleasantly surprised when they found out, either because they knew some homeschoolers already and were glad to see another, or because they had never known one and had lots of questions. My education professors were especially curious. They were well aware of the existence of home-schoolers but naturally had met very few within the educational system. I quickly became the "resident expert."

Then there was the recurring question that homeschoolers face at every stage about social skills and adaptability. The only people I knew when I arrived at the university were my admissions counselor and my tour guide. That didn't last long. I couldn't afford to let it. Every single person goes through a transition from high school to college. I wasn't the only one. I came from a different place, it's true, but I was coming to the same place as every other freshman there. We all went through the process of meeting friends, professors, advisors, roommates, people who lived in our dorms, even finding people to eat lunch with. It was the same for everybody.

In the end, I think I came out pretty well off. There are so many new things to learn and experience and so many people to meet, and I intend to take advantage of it all. And yes, two years into the adventure of college, I know pretty much everyone.

"Education is learning what you didn't even know you didn't know."

Daniel J. Boorstin

The Final Product of
Homeschooling: A Friend

Brendan Hodge

As I write this essay, I'm a month away from my twenty-second birthday, and by the time it's published, I'll have graduated from Franciscan University of Steubenville, moved across the country, started my third full-time job, and gotten married (in roughly that order). Of my two younger siblings, also homeschooled, one will graduate from high school at the same time I graduate from college, and the other will graduate the year after. Soon my parents' house will be empty of children.

When I first heard of the opportunity to write an essay for this book, it didn't occur to me that I had anything to say. I barely think of my homeschooling experience anymore. No one asks me about it, I seldom tell anyone about it, and most of the time it really doesn't matter. I work full-time while finishing up my last two classes at college, and few people even ask about my college, much less my high school. I'm just the bright and slightly preppy-looking management trainee. So what could I possibly have to say for a book about homeschooling?

On thinking about it further, I began to wonder if perhaps that was exactly what I had to say. The night before I left for my freshman year of college, my parents took me out to dinner. At the end of the meal, my mother said, "Well, this is it. You aren't a child anymore. From now on, the decisions in your life are going to be your own. If we've done our job right, there's not much more we can teach you. And if we haven't, it's your problem now; there's nothing more we can do."

I was impressed by what my parents had to say. Since I was staying with an out-of-state friend for a week before moving to the campus, I used my new discretionary powers to watch several movies my parents had forbade me to see while still officially under their roof. This was not simply an act of youthful defiance. It was the beginning of the process, filled with both triumphs and failures, by which I found my own rules, my own standards, and my own way of living out the ideals my parents had helped me develop during our years of Catholic homeschooling.

What this comes around to is finding the objective of homeschooling. Obviously the immediate objective is to provide a solid academic and spiritual formation, superior to that which a traditional school could have provided. But beyond that, after the SATs, after the college applications, and even after the college graduations are over, what is it that parents and children seek to achieve together through homeschooling? In my book, the best end product is an independent, well-formed adult.

This can be a heart-wrenching thing for parents, and certainly for homeschoolers who have participated far more than most other parents in the formation of their children. Letting their children go can seem like dropping them off a cliff. Yet in a piece of peculiarly biblical irony, the only way to gain your children is to give them up. Turn them into adults, turn them loose, and they will come back, and be far more interesting than before.

As I write this essay, I'm visiting my parents for a week at Christmas. My fiancée is doing the same, each of us spending our last Christmas under the parental roof as children. Next year we will have our own household. We may visit our parents on Christmas

The Final Product of Homeschooling: A Friend

Eve, or share dinner on Christmas day, but the day itself and the season and the home will be ours. Yet while home visiting this last time, as the engaged son soon to be starting his own family, I find that I have a closeness to my parents I never could have achieved while under their command. Whether it's giving my mother advice about managing the family investments or trying to provide my sister with some guidance about choosing colleges, I find that I now come as a visitor and friend, not as a child.

My parents and I now have our respected differences. I still watch a lot of movies that my mom would never view, but I'm interested in working in the film industry, and she isn't. My fiancée and I might not bring our children up in the same way our parents brought us up, but that's because we're different people. Our marriage will be very different from that of either of our parents, but we're not marrying our parents. Still, Mom and Dad now stand high on my list of like-minded friends, higher than most other couples I know.

You can hold on. I've seen enough homeschoolers still in the nest during my time in college. Some of them are obedient in every detail, censoring their viewing, calling every night, asking whom they can date, and returning home for every vacation and sometimes permanently after graduation. Others go the opposite direction and manage to dig up what drugs and alcohol are available in the comparatively quiet waters of Franciscan University. Do the parents have much control over which way they go? I don't know. From the college end, it often looks as if they don't. But either life is, in my opinion, stunted. Neither the world, nor the Church, nor the family is in need of children kept in stasis — still returning to the family roost throughout their twenties or even thirties.

So what do I have to say about homeschooling four years after high school graduation? Next time you have the end-of-summer curriculum melt-down, and you're wondering why you're bothering in the first place, all of you, children and parents, sit back for a moment and think about what you want to produce: adult friends. When the schoolbooks are all gathering dust, and you can't remember how well you did in eighth-grade math, that is what you will still have.

I don't know for sure whether my fiancée and I will homeschool our children when they come. She definitely wants to; I'm not so sure sometimes. I suppose we will. That decision is still a long way off. But the one thing we already agree upon is what I have said already: the object of raising children is to produce adults and friends. And homeschooling is a better way than most to get there.

"The object of opening the mind as of opening the mouth is to close it again on something solid."

G. K. Chesterton

Homeschooling:
A College Student's Point of View
Daniel J. Davis

During my sophomore year at Michigan State University, for financial reasons I moved in with my aunt, uncle, and six cousins. The children are being homeschooled by my Aunt Maureen. I must admit that when I first heard that my cousins were not going to a *normal* school, I frowned at the idea. Thinking that the children would lack the social aspect of attending a Catholic elementary school with other students who had similar upbringings, I rejected this alternative method of education.

Living with the family for nearly a year now, I've learned that homeschooling involves much more than what my initial perception of this alternative schooling method would·be. Sometimes I come home for lunch to find other children, brought by their parents, participating in a history lesson that's much more than a simple lecture. Christian, Mary, and Laura, along with the other children in the history co-op, all constructed castles out of household supplies during their education of the medieval period that were equipped with working drawbridges and catapults. I was beginning to find out that my cousins do interact with other children in a school setting, which I think is important for the development of social skills necessary for life outside the home.

What I find particularly beneficial in my cousins' case is that they each have five other siblings they must get along with. They learn to deal with each other and work out differences on their own. By living in close quarters in a small house, the children learn to share their rooms, toys, books, and Mommy time. To accomplish this, everyone, including Mommy, must effectively communicate with each other. Sharing and communicating with one another are necessary life skills that I've witnessed my cousins develop over the past year.

One thing I've come to know in my own life is that people with strong family ties generally have an edge when it comes to decision-making. Throughout life everyone is faced with important decisions that will affect him or her for the duration of their lives. Growing up, I've seen that when people are raised in a Catholic family setting and have certain moral principles embedded in their hearts and minds, they have no problem standing up for what they believe when the time comes to make an important decision regarding their faith.

Often people question how homeschooled children will fare when they enter college. Having given this question much thought, and having befriended in the past year a few homeschooled persons who are now in college, I've come to some conclusions regarding this matter. My friend Christian was homeschooled during high school and now attends college. Just as any normal college student who has attended a private or public high school, Christian is a knowledgeable, sociable, well-rounded guy with a uniquely confident personality. What I find interesting in this case is that his confidence in his faith is unlike any other I've known. Disproving the homeschool naysayers' stereotype that when homeschooled children leave their *sheltered* lives for college, they will selfishly exploit all of the available opportunities for drugs, alcohol, and sex, Christian continues to lead the Catholic life that he was brought up knowing. If he hadn't told me he was homeschooled during high school, I'd have never known. I'd have simply assumed he was a naturally smart guy with unique leadership qualities.

Another benefit of homeschooling that stands out in my mind is the family dynamic within today's consumerist society. Now, perhaps more than ever, status is based on wealth and ownership of material items. Everywhere we go, we're inundated with ways to spend our money. The television, the Internet, billboards, and society set a standard for American consumerism. These mediums depict how we are *supposed* to live and what we should own to be accepted as a part of the ever-growing middle-class society. People often get caught up in materialism and see it as the source of happiness and status. The fact is, happiness can't be bought or sold. It comes from knowing where you come from and knowing where you're going.

What does this have to do with Catholic homeschooling? Well, part of knowing where you come from is having a family there to teach you that you're above all a child of God. Homeschooling facilitates family bonding, growing out of constant togetherness. This translates into the source of happiness; knowing what is important, what is meaningful, and knowing the difference between need and greed. If children don't have a family to grow and learn with, they will seek it from another source. Whether that other source be friends or material items, the important thing for children to learn at a young age is that friends will come and go, material things will break or get lost, but family and God are there forever.

All too often I witness families who are anything but a family. I recognize that there are instances when both parents must enter the workplace out of financial constraints. What I'm talking about is when parents leave their children to be raised by babysitters and day-care personnel for countless hours, in order to attain a certain level of wealth, and thus social status, selfishly squandering important time that could and should be spent with their children. This further enforces my argument that through homeschooling, finances and family togetherness can be saved.

Overall, my perception of homeschooling has changed immensely since living with my homeschooled cousins and meeting college students who have been homeschooled. Too many people patronize the public-school system as the only means to a respected education. Many private schools are excellent, but for many families, it's financially unfeasible to send their children to one. I've come to see that teaching your children yourself can be a rewarding vocation. Part of raising children is teaching them how to grow and learn, not only in their faith, but also in subjects such as English and history. Circumstances permitting, I think homeschooling is a highly respectable and excellent environment for children to learn and grow.

"Only virtuous people are capable of freedom."
Benjamin Franklin

A Love of Learning

Rosamund M. Hodge

I was homeschooled from first grade until the end of high school. It certainly wasn't a uniformly joyous experience. There were days, many days, when I didn't get anything done at all; days when I screamed and cried and declared that I simply *could not* go on; days when homeschooling seemed like one of the biggest mistakes of my life. Yet, looking back on the experience, I'm still incredibly thankful that my parents chose homeschooling.

Tumultuous as my scholastic career was, it probably would have been a lot worse if I had gone to a site-based school. Homeschooling offered me an amazing level of flexibility. If I got an inspiration for a writing project, I could drop everything and write for several hours straight. If we wanted to go on a family trip during the school year, it was easy: just pack a few books and go. Nor did this flexibility come at the price of academic limitations: I was able to take courses not only from my parents, but also from an online academy, the University of Nebraska, and the local junior college.

Granted, that flexibility has gotten me into trouble as well. One year I seriously over-booked myself, shouldering a course load that could be described as nightmarish at best. By the end of the first semester, I was approaching serious burnout. However, the same flexibility that had gotten me into trouble, got me out of it. I was able to drop or change courses with ease, thereby saving my sanity. Had I gotten into such trouble at a regular school, it would have been much more difficult to escape.

I also had a much more rigorous curriculum than I could have gotten anywhere but at a very exclusive private school. My parents cared about both academic excellence and making education interesting. Instead of boring, committee-written texts, they chose interesting, stimulating texts that often were written for college students. Even better, our history courses were largely made up of primary source material, which was far more fascinating than any textbook.

Finally, there are all the people I met through homeschooling. Yes, there's some truth to the canard of socialization: I met fewer people than I would have in a site-based school, and it was harder to meet them. But although the quantity was lower, I really believe the quality was higher. Homeschooling self-selects for independent people with a love of learning; the homeschoolers I met were fascinating people with the same sense of intellectual adventure. Some of them became close friends who will probably be with me for the rest of my life.

It's possible that I could have had these advantages without homeschooling. If I had gone to the right school, I could have had a rigorous education. I could have met wonderful people. I might even have been able to experience the same flexibility.

However, there's another reason I'm glad we chose homeschooling. At the risk of sounding clichéd, homeschooling is not just a method of education; it is a way of life. In my family, learning wasn't something you did for a set number of hours each day; it was something you did all the time, every day, simply as a matter of course. When I was about twelve, I became fascinated with the Indus Valley civilization and researched it for months. Just a couple of weeks ago, we sat around the dinner table discussing Jung, literature, and the difference between Nominalism and Realism.

My parents taught me that there is truth, real and objective and independent of our minds. They taught me that it's not only knowable, but worth knowing; that learning is honorable and valuable — and fun! They taught me that the past has wisdom and relevance for us today, and they taught me not to be afraid of those who mock learning.

Those lessons, more than any facts about empires or atoms, are the greatest legacy of my homeschooling. Every formal education comes to an end sooner or later; but the love of learning and the way of life my parents taught me will remain with me forever. And that's enough to make all the tribulations worthwhile.

"For the Lord gives wisdom,
and from his mouth come
knowledge and understanding."
Proverbs 2:6

Appendix A

Catholic Homeschooling Resource List

Catholic Publishers

It wasn't too long ago that Catholics getting started in homeschooling actively had to search out resources that were specifically Catholic. There were only a handful of businesses to fill the needs of the average Catholic home educator. Today that's changing. Many good companies have recognized our community's desire to permeate all school subjects with Church teaching.

ASCENSION PRESS
www.ascensionpress.com
Catholic books and adult faith-formation
programs, including the Great Adventure Bible study.
W5180 Jefferson St.
Necedah, WI 54646
(800) 376-0520

BETHLEHEM BOOKS
www.bethlehembooks.com
Children's books and historical fiction.
10194 Garfield St. S.
Bathgate, ND 58216
(800) 757-6831

CATHOLIC ANSWERS
www.catholic.com
Publishes *This Rock* magazine. Books
include apologetics and chastity titles.
2020 Gillespie Way
El Cajon, CA 92020
(888) 291-8000

CHRISTENDOM COLLEGE PRESS / ISI
www.christendompress.com
Catholic books, including the booklet
Home Schooling and the New Code of Canon Law.
11030 S. Langley Ave.
Chicago, IL 60628
(800) 621-8476

IGNATIUS PRESS
www.ignatius.com
Catholic books, videos, and periodicals.
Books include homeschooling titles
and religious curricula.
P.O. Box 1339
Ft. Collins, CO 80522-1339
(800) 651-1531

LEPANTO PRESS
www.olvs.org
Reprints of old favorites.
421 S. Lochsa
Post Falls, ID 83854
(208) 773-7265

Appendix A: Catholic Homeschooling Resource List

LOYOLA PRESS
www.loyolabooks.com
Henle Latin and Loyola Classics series.
3441 N. Ashland Ave.
Chicago, IL 60657
(800) 621-1008

MIDWEST THEOLOGICAL FORUM
www.theologicalforum.org
Publisher of the excellent Didache series
(high school religion textbooks).
1420 Davey Rd.
Woodridge, IL 60517
(630) 739-9750

NEUMANN PRESS
www.neumannpress.com
Beautifully bound Catholic reprints.
21892 County 11
Long Prairie, MN 56347
(800) 746-2521

OUR SUNDAY VISITOR
www.osv.com
Catholic newspaper, magazines,
books, pamphlets, and more.
200 Noll Plaza
Huntington, IN 46750
(800) 348-2440

PAULINE BOOKS AND MEDIA
www.pauline.org
Children's books and religious curricula.
50 St. Paul Ave.
Jamaica Plain, MA 02130
(800) 876-4463

ROMAN CATHOLIC BOOKS
www.booksforcatholics.com
Reprints of Catholic classics.
P.O. Box 2286
Ft. Collins, CO 80522-2286
(970) 490-2735

SCEPTER PUBLISHERS
www.scepterpublishers.org
Navarre Bible commentaries.
P.O. Box 211
New York, NY 10018

SOPHIA INSTITUTE PRESS
www.sophiainstitute.com
Spirituality, apologetics, scripture, prayer,
saints, sacraments, and homeschooling.
Box 5284, Manchester, NH 03108
(800) 888-9344

TAN BOOKS AND PUBLISHERS
www.tanbooks.com
Books and textbooks, both new and reprints.
P.O. Box 424
Rockford, IL 61105
(800) 437-5876

Homeschool Publishers

Catholics searching for high-quality materials for their homeschools should check out the following companies, which have been formed to address the specific needs of home educators and most of which are owned by Catholic homeschoolers.

ALAN JEMISON MUSIC
www.aljem.com
Music self-instruction.
P.O. Box 64
Ashton, MD 20861
(304) 258-5373

ALEXANDER PUBLISHING
http://members.aol.com/PlayOnKeys/
Playing On the Keys piano method.
Lynne Cimorelli
3941 Park Dr.
Ste. 20, #245
El Dorado Hills, CA 95762

CASTLEMOYLE BOOKS
www.castlemoyle.com
Spelling Power.
The Hotel Revere Building
P.O. Box 520
Pomeroy, WA 99347-0520
(888) SPELL-86

CATHOLIC WORLD HISTORY
TIMELINE AND GUIDES
SMAcademy@aol.com
Marcia Neill
4790 Irvine Blvd., Ste. 105
Irvine, CA 92620
(714) 730-5398

ECCE HOMO PRESS
www.eccehomopress.com
For the Love of Literature; American Catholic
historical fiction; Little Flowers and Blue
Knights Club materials.
632 Lantern Ln.
Ellettsville, IN 47429
(866) 305-8362 (toll-free)

INSTITUTE FOR EXCELLENCE IN WRITING
www.writing-edu.com
Teaching Writing: Structure and Style.
P.O. Box 6065
Atascadero, CA 93423
(800) 856-5815

LITTLE SAINTS PRESCHOOL PROGRAM
www.catholicpreschool.com
75 E. Mountain Way
Asheville, NC 28805
(800) 833-1585

Appendix A: Catholic Homeschooling Resource List

MEMORIA PRESS
www.memoriapress.com
Latina Christiana and
Traditional Logic.
4105 Bishop Ln.
Louisville, KY 40218
(877) 862-1097

STONE TABLET PRESS
www.stonetabletpress.com
Little Angel Readers.
3348 Whitsetts Fork Rd.
Wildwood, MO 63038
(636) 458-1515

WOOLY LAMB PUBLISHING
www.historylinks.info
History Links Unit Study/Integrated
Learning.
P.O. Box 411
Dickinson, ND 58601
(701) 260-2599

WRITE GUIDE, INC.
www.writeguide.com
Individualized writing courses via email.
470 E. Rempel Ave.
Palmer, AK 99645
(907) 746-7052

YE HEDGE SCHOOL
www.hedgeschool.homestead.com
Sentence diagramming and Catholic science books.
Mary Daly
24934 478 Ave.
Garretson, SD 57030

Books

Although there are hundreds of books available for home-schooling parents in general, there are only a few that are written specifically for Catholics.

A Catholic Homeschool Treasury: Nurturing Children's Love for Learning (Ignatius Press), by Rachel Mackson and Maureen Wittmann, eds.

A Mother's Rule of Life (Sophia Institute Press), by Holly Pierlot

Catholic Education: Homeward Bound: A Useful Guide to Catholic Home Schooling (Ignatius Press), by Kimberly Hahn and Mary Hasson

Catholic Home Schooling: A Handbook for Parents (TAN Books), by Mary Kay Clark

Designing Your Own Classical Curriculum: A Guide to Catholic Home Education (Ignatius Press), by Laura M. Berquist

Family Journal: A Homeschooling Mom's Companion (Catholic Heritage Curricula), by Rita Munn

Homeschooling with Gentleness: A Catholic Discovers Unschooling (Little Way Books), by Suzie Andres

Natural Structure: A Montessori Approach to Classical Education at Home (Catholic Heritage Curricula), by Edward and Nancy Walsh

Appendix A: Catholic Homeschooling Resource List

Please Don't Drink the Holy Water (Sophia Institute Press), by Susie Lloyd

Real Learning: Education in the Heart of the Home (By Way of the Family), by Elizabeth Foss

Curriculum Mail Order

Homeschooling mail-order companies that cater to Catholics are carving out their niche in this fast-growing market. Making curriculum and product purchases from these companies will help to alleviate any worry about buying books that contain anti-Catholic biases. In fact, these companies offer products that will aid you in teaching your children the beauty and fullness of Catholicism.

BY WAY OF THE FAMILY
www.bywayofthefamily.com
Offers discounts for large orders.
Offers Elizabeth Foss's *Real Learning.*
1090 Payne Ave.
St. Paul, MN 55101
(800) 588-2589

CATHOLIC HERITAGE CURRICULA (CHC)
www.chcweb.com
Offers new and unique Catholic
curricula and enrichment materials.
P.O. Box 125
Twain Harte, CA 95383
(800) 490-7713

CATHOLIC HOME-SCHOOLERS' BOOKSHELF
In addition to curricula — encyclicals,
Church documents, catechisms, and Bible study.
2399 Cool Springs Rd.
Thaxton, VA 24174
(540) 586-4898

EMMANUEL BOOKS
www.emmanuelbooks.com
Carries most of the curricula recommended
in *Designing Your Own Classical Curriculum*.
P.O. Box 321
New Castle, DE 19720
(800) 871-5598

HOMESCHOOL RESOURCES
www.homeschoolresources.biz
New and used books and texts.
Complete curriculum selection.
1500 W. Washington Ave.
Jackson, MI 49203
(517) 784-2640

OUR FATHER'S HOUSE
www.ourfathershouse.biz
Many hands-on and Montessori
products in addition to traditional
Catholic homeschooling curricula.
5530 S. Orcas St.
Seattle, WA 98118
(206) 725-0461

Appendix A: Catholic Homeschooling Resource List

RC HISTORY
www.rchistory.com
Connecting with History and other
history materials for Catholics.
P.O. Box 360
E. Bethel, MN 55011
(877) 832-5829 (toll-free)

SETON EDUCATIONAL MEDIA
www.setonhome.org
Texts published for Seton Home Study
School are available for individual purchase.
1350 Progress Dr.
Front Royal, VA 22630
(540) 636-9990

General Mail-Order Companies

Several well-established Catholic companies and organizations have recognized the positive impact that homeschooling has on the family. As such, more of these enterprises are offering popular homeschooling books and texts alongside their other merchandise.

ALL CATHOLIC BOOKS
www.allcatholicbooks.com
Discounted Catholic and homeschooling books.
5106 Roanoke Rd.
Troutville, VA 24175
(540) 966-2554 (FAX)

COUPLE TO COUPLE LEAGUE
www.ccli.org
Books on family life and homeschooling.
P.O. Box 111184
Cincinnati, OH 45211
(800) 745-8252

FAMILY LIFE CENTER
ST. JOSEPH COVENANT KEEPERS
www.familylifecenter.net
Books and cassette tapes on the
role of Catholic husband and father,
as well as on homeschooling.
22226 Westchester Blvd.
Port Charlotte, FL 33952
(941) 764-7725

ILLUMINATED INK
www.illuminatedink.com
Enrichment items for your homeschool:
Catholic crafts and games.
15825 160th Ave.
Bloomer, WI 54724
(715) 288-5925

LEAFLET MISSAL COMPANY
www.leafletmissal.org
Catholic gifts, books, sacramentals,
art, and more.
976 W. Minnehaha Ave.
St. Paul, MN 55104
(800) 328-9582

Appendix A: Catholic Homeschooling Resource List

MOTHER OF OUR SAVIOR
www.moscompany.com
Traditional Catholic gifts, supplies, and books.
P.O. Box 100
Pekin, IN 47165
(800) 451-3993

THE ST. JOHN FISHER FORUM
www.stjohnfisherforum.org
Large selection of Catholic books
for adults and children, including titles
popular with homeschoolers.
1572 Concord Rd.
Jacksonville, IL 62650
(888) 585-8825

ST. JOSEPH COMMUNICATIONS
www.saintjoe.com
Catholic cassette tapes, many useful
in teaching high school apologetics.
P.O. Box 720
West Covina, CA 91793
(800) 526-2151

STELLA MARIS BOOKS
www.stellamarisbooks.com
Homeschool books and texts in
addition to general Catholic books,
supplies, and music.
P.O. Box 11483
Ft. Worth, TX 76110
(800) 772-5928

Home-Study Programs

Catholic home-study schools offer a wide range of services, from full-service programs to partial enrollment to simply providing assistance to those who are putting together their own eclectic program. Several also sell books, texts, lesson plans, and testing services to non-enrolled families. See Appendix B for contact information and a summary of each school's services.

National Support Organizations

State and local support groups for Catholic homeschoolers are being formed and growing at an incredible rate across the country. At the lead are three national groups, each with a different mission.

CATHOLIC HOME STUDY
NETWORK OF AMERICA (CHSNA)
www.chsna.org
Provides information about state, regional, and national issues. When events require quick action, the Network sends fax alerts to state and local leaders. They also collaborate with other national homeschool groups, such as the Home School Legal Defense Association, to ensure that concerns and interests of Catholics are represented.
P.O. Box 2352
Warren, OH 44484

NATIONAL ASSOCIATION OF
CATHOLIC HOME & EDUCATORS (NACHE)
www.nache.org
Sponsors regional and national conferences. For those who are unable to attend, cassette tapes of conference talks are available at reasonable prices by mail order. NACHE publishes a quarterly newsletter, *Catholic Home*.

P.O. Box 2304
Elkton, MD 21921
(703) 553-9600

TRADITIONS OF ROMAN
CATHOLIC HOMES (TORCH)
www.catholic-homeschool.com
Provides assistance in starting and running local Catholic
homeschooling support groups — called TORCH chapters.
They publish a monthly newsletter filled with inspirational
articles, chapter news, and ideas for local support group
activities.
3307 Bigelow Ct.
Burtonsville, MD 20866

Magazines and Newsletters

Although there are no specifically Catholic homeschooling
magazines on the scale of *Practical Homeschooling* or any of the
other large Christian or secular titles, there are several good periodicals from which to choose. These are our professional journals;
it's a good idea to subscribe to one or two.

Catholic Home
www.nache.org
Quarterly newsletter. Contains both
family-oriented and home-schooling articles.
P.O. Box 2304
Elkton, MD 21921
(703) 553-9600

The Catholic Homeschool Companion

*Heart and Mind: A Resource
for Catholic Homeschoolers*
www.heart-and-mind.com
Quarterly magazine. Several regular columns by authors
such as Laura Berquist. Pullout unit study, reviews, and
other useful features in every issue.
P.O. Box 420881
San Diego, CA 92142

The Latin Mass
www.latinmassmagazine.com
Quarterly magazine. Contains a homeschool
insert with regular columnists such as Susie Lloyd.
Keep the Faith, Inc.
50 S. Franklin Turnpike, Ste. 1
Ramsey, NJ 07446
(201) 327-5900

Seton Home Study
www.setonhome.org
Monthly newsletter. Includes articles and features of
interest to both Seton families and non-enrolled families.
1350 Progress Dr.
Front Royal, VA 22630
(540) 636-9990

Traditions of Roman Catholic Homes
www.catholic-homeschool.com
Monthly newsletter (eleven issues). Geared toward
TORCH members, but has articles of interest to other
Catholic homeschoolers.
8 Orchard Dr.
Whitehouse Station, NJ 08889

Appendix A: Catholic Homeschooling Resource List

Websites

The Internet can be a valuable tool to homeschoolers. Catholics experiencing difficulty in finding fellowship with other homeschoolers can locate support on message boards or join an email listserv. A search at http://groups.yahoo.com/ will result in many Catholic homeschooling listservs, with topics running from classical education to unschooling to specific grade levels, and more.

The Internet can be used to find free curriculum, worksheets, unit studies, and ideas for homemade crafts. Parents nervous about teaching high school can sign up with online schools. The future growth of homeschooling might very well be aided by the growth of the Internet. The following is just a small sampling of Catholic homeschooling websites worth bookmarking. Follow their links, and you'll find a treasury of Catholic homeschooling on the Internet.

CATHOLIC HOMESCHOOLING SUPPORT
www.catholichomeschooling.com
Provided by Catholic Heritage Curricula. Free lesson plans, history timeline, articles, and more.

CHARLOTTE MASON IN THE CATHOLIC HOME
www.4reallearning.com
Sample nature pages, Charlotte Mason listserv, and recommended reading list.

FAVORITE RESOURCES FOR
CATHOLIC HOMESCHOOLERS
www.love2learn.net
Reviews and sample pages of popular homeschooling books and texts. History Index is especially great. Plus plenty of other useful information for Catholic homeschooling families.

HOMESCHOOLING TREASURES
www.homeschooltreasures.mackson.org
Rachel Mackson's website. Online magazine,
homeschooling links, curriculum suggestions, and more.

Blogs

Web logs, or blogs, are the latest trend in the Internet world.
Following are a few of the good ones that focus on Catholic
homeschooling.

DANIELLE BEAN
www.daniellebean.com

FLYING STARS
http://mrsnancybrown.blogspot.com

HERE IN THE BONNY GLEN
http://melissawiley.typepad.com

HOUSE OF LITERATURE
http://houseofliterature.blogspot.com

LOVE2LEARN
http://love2learnblog.BLOGSPOT.COM

STUDEO
http://studeo.blogspot.com

UNITY OF TRUTH
http://unityoftruth.blogspot.com

A MOTHER'S RULE OF LIFE
www.mothersruleoflife.com

Appendix A: Catholic Homeschooling Resource List

Colleges and Universities

Many colleges and universities recognize the benefits of actively recruiting homeschooled students. They attend our conferences and make accommodations to meet the special needs of homeschoolers.

After twelve years of homeschooling, some parents might be nervous about sending their children off to college. Finding an institution that continues the spiritual, as well as the academic, lessons learned in the home can be a difficult task. The following institutions are respected in the Catholic homeschooling community and welcome homeschoolers with open arms.

AVE MARIA UNIVERSITY
www.avemaria.edu

THE CATHOLIC DISTANCE UNIVERSITY
www.cdu.edu

CHRISTENDOM COLLEGE
www.christendom.edu

FRANCISCAN UNIVERSITY OF STEUBENVILLE
www.franciscan.edu

THOMAS AQUINAS COLLEGE
www.thomasaquinas.edu

NOTE: If the phone numbers, addresses, or website URLs listed in this appendix change, you'll find the updated information at www.catholictreasury.com.

Appendix B

Catholic Home-Study Schools

There are many homeschooling parents who desire the help and guidance of a good home-study school. For this reason I wrote to each of the following schools and asked them to give me a synopsis of what they have to offer Catholic home educators. I hope that having a brief description for each of the following schools all in one place will help you in discerning the best home-study school for your family.

THE ANGELICUM ACADEMY
www.angelicum.net
P.O. Box 4605
Rolling Bay, WA 98061
(800) 664-6209

The Angelicum Academy is a Catholic homeschool program based on the liberal arts and the classical great books of Western civilization (with optional, Socratic discussion seminars). Angelicum is a spin-off of the Great Books Academy (GBA) and looks to Thomas Aquinas College (TAC) in Santa Paula, California, as a model, as well as to the former Pearson Integrated Humanities Program at Kansas University.

The Great Books Academy has no religious affiliation. The directors of the GBA who are Catholic came to realize that an educational program that utilized the liberal arts and the great books could be more efficacious for Catholic students if it were based upon the shared starting points of a common creed as defined and clarified by the Catholic magisterial authority. So The Angelicum Academy was formed. Angelicum combines the great-books approach found at the GBA, with an intellectual assent to the teachings of the Catholic Church. Its essential purpose is to combine Catholic wisdom and secular learning. Consequently, the teaching Church, the Magisterium, becomes the shared starting point for the conversation at Angelicum.

KOLBE ACADEMY
www.kolbe.org
2501 Oak St.
Napa, CA 94559
(707) 255-6499

Kolbe Academy Home School is an orthodox Catholic and classical homeschool program for grades K-12. Using the Ignatian philosophy and method of education, Kolbe Academy helps the family train the student's memory, understanding, and will. The goals of Ignatian-directed education are to train the student to speak, write, and act.

Kolbe's classical academic program is flexible and adaptable to the needs of the parent and child. Week-by-week course plans are provided to guide parents in setting daily assignments. Assessment tests are available to determine student's appropriate grade level. Kolbe staff is available to assist in goal-setting and grading sample work. Books for all courses are available for sale, or may be purchased elsewhere. Quarterly tests with answer keys are available for core curriculum courses, although they can be individualized by the parent. These tests, along with sample work, are sent to the academy for inspection, with capsule reports returned to the parents.

A monthly newsletter includes news updates and home-schooling tips. Diplomas are issued upon completion of grammar school and high school. Detailed reports on student work are available on request, at any time. The student's cumulative folders, with report cards and transcripts, are retained.

MOTHER OF DIVINE GRACE SCHOOL
www.motherofdivinegrace.org
P.O. Box 1810
Ojai, CA 93024
(805) 646-5818

Mother of Divine Grace School (MODG) was founded in 1995 to assist parents who wish to educate their children according to the classical tradition, with Laura Berquist's book *Designing Your Own Classical Curriculum* as a guide.

MODG is a legal private school that offers a classical Catholic curriculum for preschool through grade 12. While most of the text recommendations are Catholic, not everything used is Catholic in origin, but all recommendations are compatible with the Faith. The curriculum parallels the suggestions in Dorothy Sayers's essay *The Lost Tools of Learning*.

The fundamental goal of such a curriculum is to teach children how to think and to learn the art of learning, the philosophy being that if they know how to learn, they will be equipped for life. Whether or not they learn all the subjects possible, they'll be able to learn any subject when it becomes necessary or desirable. MODG believes in following the child's own natural stages of learning, which correspond to the subjects of the classical Trivium: grammar, logic, and rhetoric.

MODG offers assistance to parents in forming their own curriculum with a little help getting started, practical tips, and some help with the evaluation of their children's work. This program is well suited to the family that wants to be in charge of its own school, but would like some help setting up its program and wishes to be enrolled in a legal school.

Daily syllabi and work evaluation are available. Although MODG doesn't grade all assignments — that's left to the parent — it does offer grading guidelines and will evaluate sample work. Consultants will help, too, in passing on organizational techniques.

OUR LADY OF THE ROSARY SCHOOL
www.olrs.com
1010 Withrow Ct.
Bardstown, KY 40004
(502) 348-1338

Founded in 1983, Our Lady of the Rosary School (OLRS) is an international Catholic homeschool organization that offers complete curriculums for students from preschool through grade 12. OLRS sees itself as an apostolate dedicated to saving the souls of children by giving them the opportunity to receive a truly Catholic education in the best possible environment — the home.

Their mission is to help parents teach their children the Catholic Faith in its entirety, using sound Catholic educational materials, covering all subjects.

OLRS provides parents with all the materials they need to give their children a sound, well-rounded Catholic education that will provide a thorough preparation for further academic growth and development in their own home. They furnish a highly integrated and sequential Catholic curriculum, complete with lesson plans, teacher manuals, and workbooks. They also provide exams, teacher assistance by phone or on the Internet, counseling, teacher correction of exams, report cards, diplomas, grade retention, and transcripts of student grades for college.

OUR LADY OF VICTORY SCHOOL
www.olvs.org
421 S. Lochsa St.
Post Falls, ID 83854
(208) 773-7265

Founded in 1977, Our Lady of Victory School (OLVS) uses the typical Catholic school format that was used successfully across the nation up until about 1960. They set educational standards for which they encourage their students to strive. They promote St. John Bosco's "Preventive System" of "Reason, Religion, and Kindness." They give traditional grades, including "F" when it's deserved.

However, they do not abandon the failing student or place him in an "educationally challenged" group. They place him at a grade level commensurate with his abilities, and they encourage him to advance from there. Pervading their educational program is their effort to teach students to strive to do their very best in all subjects, so that they can grow academically and morally. They want to arm their students with the tools through which they can process information, derive knowledge, and discover Truth.

OLVS encourages only the Latin Tridentine Mass, as promulgated by Pope St. Pius V, the traditional sacraments, the Rosary, novenas, and the study of traditional catechisms (e.g., the Baltimore Catechism). They encourage a strong personal love for the saints and the Roman Catholic Church of yesterday and today. With the help of parents, the children are encouraged to live and practice the Ten

Commandments. They're taught to dress modestly and to be respectful of their superiors, adults, and especially of priests and nuns with whom they might come in contact.

For non-enrolled families, they use the same program but the families do not send work in to OLVS and therefore do not receive progress reports or report cards.

OLVS has a special-needs consultant on staff who has a master's degree in the field and who helps develop a curriculum tailored for the special-needs student.

REGINA COELI ACADEMY OF THE LIBERAL ARTS
www.reginacoeli.org
6429 S. Woodland Hills Dr.
Tucson, AZ 85747
(520) 751-1942

Regina Coeli Academy (RCA) is the first all-online college preparatory program for Roman Catholics. Their highly qualified faculty provides evaluation of student achievement through a classical liberal-arts program. The academy's theology program, under the direction of Fr. Stephen F. Torraco, guides students through the Church's teaching in a four-year sequence based on the *Catechism of the Catholic Church*.

The purpose of the academy is to provide Roman Catholics with a rigorous online college preparatory curriculum that challenges the intellect and nourishes the spirit with the riches of the Catholic tradition. All courses are taught from a college preparatory level and provide opportunity for students, young or mature, to excel in specialized study or to enroll in a complete academic curriculum. They provide live classroom participation, interactive World Wide Web forum electronic mail, and evaluation of student work. It isn't unusual, after the completion of his courses, for the diligent student to be academically prepared to by-pass general education courses required by degree-granting institutions of higher learning. Preparation for the online distance-learning environment is afforded students from ages ten to thirteen via the Regina Coeli Junior Program.

Informational email list is available, which sometimes has tips or announcements of interest to the Catholic homeschooling family.

ST. THOMAS AQUINAS ACADEMY
www.staa-homeschool.com
P.O. Box 630
Rippon, CA 95366
(209) 599-0665

From preschool through twelfth grade, St. Thomas Aquinas Academy's classical homeschool curriculum is designed as one graceful whole, with a unit-study flavor, that easily adapts to many grade levels learning at the same kitchen table. They encourage a relaxed teaching style, tuned to the natural developmental phases of the child's intellect. Their goal is to help parents teach their child to learn, resulting in a competent, confident child with a lifelong enthusiasm for learning, ready for their lifelong vocation.

The classical liberal-arts curriculum is an independent-study program crafted for the homeschooling family, not a classroom program adapted for the homeschooling market. The curriculum does not depend on the availability of a Catholic library, nor does it presume a liberal-arts education on the part of the parent. There's no prior homeschooling experience required. Their advisory staff of veteran home-schoolers personally guides parents to and through a variety of texts and materials, according to student's needs and interests.

Although many of their materials do have unit quizzes, they promote a variety of methods to demonstrate mastery of a subject that are both fun and effective, rather than a standard quizzing format. Oral presentations, discussions, and hands-on projects are as important to their classical curriculum as are written work and unit testing.

St. Thomas provides an online bookstore for ordering convenience. They can also direct parents to the most expedient and least expensive resources and providers they can find. As an alternative to the usual one-size-fits-all lesson plans, they guide parents through yearly goal setting, and then help establish a pace and flow suited to a family's lifestyle.

SETON HOME STUDY SCHOOL
www.setonhome.org
1350 Progress Dr.
Front Royal, VA 22630
(540) 636-9990

Seton serves an enrollment of approximately ten thousand students, and several thousand more families through book sales and by furnishing materials to small Catholic schools.

As much as possible, Catholic texts are used in the subject areas: for example, the Faith and Freedom reading series and the Voyages in English series. The curriculum also includes Catholic history, music, and Latin texts. In addition, the Seton staff is constantly writing and rewriting Catholic textbooks and is currently updating religion courses to include input from the *Catechism of the Catholic Church*.

Seton offers grade placement tests and yearly standardized achievement tests, plus quarterly exams, progress reports, permanent records on file, transcripts (for transfers or graduation), and a diploma from Seton School. Parents send tests to Seton for grading, along with a quarterly report form, which includes grades for weekly assignments.

Counseling is available six days a week, usually from 8:30 a.m. to midnight (EST). The Seton staff strives to maintain a cordial, cooperative relationship with parents, and relies on frequent communication with parents to achieve the best in individualized instruction.

Parents are sent daily lesson plans, to assist families who don't have time to work on curriculum scheduling. These lessons are recommendations or suggestions, recognizing that some children learn more quickly, some learn more slowly, and some learn one or two subjects quickly but have trouble with other subjects.

NOTE: If the phone numbers, addresses, or website URLs listed in this appendix change, you will find the updated information at www.catholictreasury.com.

Resources for Homeschooling Children with Learning and Physical Disabilities

*Maureen Wittmann with Stacey Johnson,
Pattie Kelly-Huff, Melissa Naasko, and Janine Seadler*

In addition to these resources, several of the Catholic home-study schools have dedicated personnel to assist parents of special-needs children.

I was able to find most of the following book recommendations at my local public library. If your library doesn't carry these titles, request that they purchase a selection of them. Most libraries have forms, at the front desk and online, for patrons to make such requests.

Books

Asperger Syndrome and Difficult Moments: Practical Solutions for Tantrums, Rage, and Meltdowns, by Brenda Smith Myles and Jack Southwick (Autism Asperger Pub. Co.).

Creative Home Schooling for Gifted Children, by Lisa Rivero (Great Potential Press).

Dreamers, Discoverers & Dynamos: How to Help the Child Who Is Bright, Bored, and Having Problems in School, by Lucy Jo Palladino (Ballantine; formerly titled *The Edison Trait*). A must-read for parents of ADD and ADHD children.

Home Educating Our Autistic Spectrum Children: Paths Are Made by Walking, by Kitt Cowlishaw and Terri Dowty, eds. (Jessica Kingsley Pub.). A compendium of essays by parents who are homeschooling their children diagnosed with autism and Asperger Syndrome.

Homeschooling Children with Special Needs, by Sharon Hensley (Noble Pub.).

Homeschooling the Child with ADD (or Other Special Needs): Your Complete Guide to Successfully Homeschooling the Child with Learning Differences, by Lenore Hayes (Prima Pub.). A general guide to homeschooling children with learning disabilities. Concentrates heavily on the problems with public education in regard to special-needs children.

Homeschooling Your Gifted Child: Language Arts for the Middle School Years, by Lee Wherry Brainerd (Learning Express).

Peterson's Colleges with Programs for Students with Learning Disabilities or Attention Deficit Disorders, by Charles Mangrum II, Ed.D. and Stephen Strichart, Ph.D. (Peterson's). Peterson's is famous for their college guides. This book lists two-year and four-year colleges that make accommodations for learning-disabled students.

Precious Treasure: The Story of Patrick, by Elizabeth Matthews (Emmaus Road Pub.). The personal story of a mother's spiritual journey through her autistic son.

These two books can be ordered from www.joyceherzog.com or by calling (800) 745-8212:

Learning in Spite of Labels, by Joyce Herzog (Greenleaf Press).

Choosing and Using Curriculum for Your Special Needs Child, by Joyce Herzog (Greenleaf Press). Takes a very common-sense approach.

Appendix C: Learning and Physical Disabilities

Websites

Aut — 2B — Home
www.weirdkids.com/autism/aut2bhome.htm
Email listserv that provides support for parents
homeschooling autistic children. Website also provides
visitors with medical information, book recommendations,
and other online support.

Homeschooling Children Who Aut to Be Home
www.home.earthlink.net/~tammyglaser798/authome.html
This is the homepage of Tammy Glaser. Includes links to
other homepages of parents who homeschool their autistic
children, articles of interest, and more.

LD OnLine
www.ldonline.org
Website includes legal advice, teaching tips, Q&A
section, and a free monthly newsletter for parents with
learning-disabled children.

Services

AUDIBLOX
www.audiblox2000.com/
A program for learning-disabled children using
a system of cognitive exercises, aimed at the
development of foundational learning skills.
Barb Little: (701) 260-2777

AUTISM ASPERGER PUBLISHING CO.
www.asperger.net/
Publishes books and a newsletter on autism.
P.O. Box 23173
Shawnee Mission, KS 66283-0173
(877) 277-8254

ED CON PUBLISHING GROUP
www.edconpublishing.com
Publishers of the high-readability texts:
High Interest Classics.
30 Montauk Blvd.
Oakdale, NY 11769
(888) 553-3266

EDUCATORS PUBLISHING SERVICES (EPS)
www.epsbooks.com
Publishers of Explode the Code, an
excellent series of phonics workbooks.
P.O. Box 9031
Cambridge, MA 02139-9031
(800) 255-5750

JEMICY SCHOOL COMMUNITY OUTREACH
www.jemicyschool.org
Offers assessments, workshops, training courses,
and summer camps for dyslexic children.
11 Celadon Rd.
Owings Mills, MD 21117
(410) 653-2700

Appendix C: Learning and Physical Disabilities

THE LAB SCHOOL
www.labschool.org
Tutoring, evaluations, and consultation services.
4759 Reservoir Road NW
Washington, DC 20007
(202) 965-6600

THE LEARNING HOME
Helps parents in locating needed resources. President
Janine Seadler, M. Ed., provides consultation and
assessments for parents of children with learning disabilities, both locally in Maryland and long distance. She's in
favor of homeschooling, and trains and supports parents
who homeschool their learning-disabled (LD) child. She
believes in understanding both sides of the brain and how
the sides function to increase learning.
1611 Cynthia Ct.
Jarrettsville, MD 21084
(410) 692-0504

LINDAMOOD-BELL LEARNING PROCESSES
www.lindamoodbell.com
Provides training sessions. Website offers
information and definitions helpful in learning
about dyslexia.
416 Higuerist
San Luis Obispo, CA 93401
(800) 233-1819

RECORDING FOR THE BLIND AND DYSLEXIC
www.rfbd.org
Producer of audio textbooks. Individual members
have unlimited access to the audio library and
reference librarian services.
20 Roszel Rd.
Princeton, NJ 08540
(866) 732-3585

WILSON LANGUAGE COMPANY
www.wilsonlanguage.com
Publishes reading and spelling curricula, as well as
providing online training. They also provide a list
of trained tutors.
47 Old Webster Rd.
Oxford, MA 01540
(508) 368-2399

National Support

CHASK: CHRISTIAN HOMES AND SPECIAL KIDS
www.chask.org
Organization that helps Christian parents adopt
special-needs children. Website includes articles on
raising children with fetal-alcohol syndrome, AIDS,
blindness, ADD, spina bifida, Down syndrome, and
more.
P.O. Box 39
Porthill, ID 83853
(208) 267-6246

Appendix C: Learning and Physical Disabilities

THE INTERNATIONAL DYSLEXIA ASSOCIATION
(formerly The Orton Dyslexia Association)
www.interdys.org
This organization provides information on dyslexia,
is a source of printed material, and will provide leads
to resources and tutors in your local area.
8600 LaSalle Rd.
Chester Bldg., Ste. 382
Baltimore, MD 21286
(410) 296-0232

MUMS: NATIONAL PARENT-TO-PARENT NETWORK
(Mothers United for Moral Support, Inc.)
www.netnet.net/mums
A support and matching organization for families
of children with rare disorders or special needs.
150 Custer Ct.
Green Bay, WI 54301-1243
(920) 336-5333; (877) 336-5333 (parents only please)

NATHHAN: NATIONAL CHALLENGED
HOMESCHOOLERS ASSOCIATION NETWORK
www.nathhan.com
This Christian organization supplies information on
local support and resources. Articles at the website address
homeschooling children with ADD, autism, visual impair-
ment, deafness, spina bifida, and so on. Articles also address
the legal issues in homeschooling special-needs children.
Members receive a regular newsletter, HSLDA discount,
access to a lending library, family directory, and more.
P.O. Box 39
Porthill, ID 83853
(208) 267-6246

Appendix D

Foreign-Language Resources

Mary Glantz

The following list is intended to help you locate resources and materials that can assist you in exposing your child to another language.

I haven't personally used all of these sources, and so I can't endorse any one of them over another.

APPLAUSE LEARNING RESOURCES
www.applauselearning.com
Books, posters, games, music, videos, computer software,
room decorations, teaching incentives, dictionaries, maps,
puzzles, and magazines. French, Spanish, German, Italian,
Latin, Japanese, and Russian.
85 Fernwood Ln.
Roslyn, NY 11576
(800) 277-5287

AUDIO-FORUM
www.audioforum.com
Primarily self-instruction language programs in more
languages than you can imagine. If you want to learn
the language of your ancestors, this is the catalog for you.
1 Orchard Park Rd.
Madison, CT 06443
(800) 243-1234

CARLEX
www.carlexonline.com
Focuses on French and Spanish only. Offers books,
posters, music, videos, stickers, and other teaching aids.
P.O. Box 81786
Rochester, MI 48308-1786
(800) 526-3768

INTERNATIONAL BOOK CENTER
www.ibcbooks.com
If you live in the metropolitan Detroit area, this is a
fun store to visit because you can peruse through all
the materials before purchasing them. The International
Book Center carries many books, audiocassettes, CDs,
teaching aids, and dictionaries for preschool and up, in
French, Spanish, German, Latin, Arabic, Italian, Russian,
Japanese, Polish, Romanian, Dutch, Danish, Albanian,
Portuguese, and more.
2391 Auburn Rd.
Shelby Twp., MI 48317
(586) 254-7230

Appendix D: Foreign-Language Resources

TEACHER'S DISCOVERY
www.teachersdiscovery.com
Books, posters, games, music, videos, computer software,
room decorations, kits, teaching incentives, dictionaries,
and maps for the study of French, Spanish, and German.
2741 Paldan Dr.
Auburn Hills, MI 48326
(800) 832-2437

Books and Audio Cassettes
I've used all of these with success.

The Usborne First Thousand Words in French, by Heather
Amery and Stephen Cartwright (Usborne Publishing).
Audiotape and picture book.

A Bit of Everything (Un Peu de Tout), by Liza Sernett (T. S.
Denison and Co.). Games, activities, and cue cards for
introducing French to young children.

Passport Language Guides/French for Beginners, by Angela
Wilkes (NTC/ Contemporary Publishing). Audiotape
and book with conversational French.

Berlitz Jr. French (Aladdin Books, Macmillan Publishing
Co.). Audiotape and story book about Teddy the bear
for very young children.

Usborne First French, by Kathy Gemmell and Jenny Tyler
(Usborne Publishing). A series of three books without
audiotapes. The books contain simple conversations,
pronunciation guides, poems, and games.

Berlitz Kids/Adventures with Nicholas (Berlitz Publishing Co.). A series of storybooks and audiotapes that are geared toward different levels of fluency for the beginner student. Each set overlaps some material covered in the previous course and offers new material as well.

Let's Speak French (Hayes School Publishing). A series of three books that provide written exercises to challenge the more advanced student.

Speak French to Your Baby, by Therese Slevin Pirz (Command Performance Language Institute). An excellent resource for learning common expressions used by parents with their young children.

French in 10 Minutes a Day, by Kristine Kershul (Bilingual Books). A workbook designed to help the beginner student. Includes sticky labels to label things in the house, flash cards, a menu guide for ordering in a French restaurant and a basic translation guide that fits in a purse or pocket.

Foreign Language Courses on CD-ROM
Power Glide
www.power-glide.com
Spanish, French, German, Latin, and English as a second language. A free demonstration CD is available. Self-paced and no prior training needed.
1682 W. 820 North
Provo, UT 84601
(800) 596-0910

Rosetta Stone
www.rosettastone.com
Choose from nearly thirty languages. Uses immersion to
teach listening, speaking, reading, and writing skills. No prior
training needed. Tracks test scores.
135 W. Market St.
Harrisonburg, VA 22801
(800) 788-0822

About the Editors and Authors

Maureen Wittmann

Maureen and her husband, Rob, are parents to seven children, who have always been homeschooled. Maureen moderates three homeschooling email lists through Yahoo Groups: The History Place, Thrifty Homeschooler, and Pope Saint Nicholas V. She has a regular column, "The Thrifty Homeschooler," in the independent Catholic homeschooling magazine *Heart and Mind*. Maureen's other books include *A Catholic Homeschool Treasury* (Ignatius Press) and *For the Love of Literature* (Ecce Homo Press). Her articles have appeared in *Our Sunday Visitor, Latin Mass, Catholic Home Educator*, and others. The Wittmanns reside in Michigan.

Rachel Mackson

Rachel and her husband, David, have been blessed with three children, ranging in age from eleven to seventeen, all educated at home. The Macksons helped organize a local homeschooler group, *Celebrating Home Under Rome: Catholic Homeschoolers*, which now includes more than ninety families. Rachel leads a literature discussion group for high school students and directs an annual play, the most recent being a musical production of *The Pirates of Penzance*. Her website, www.homeschooltreasures.mackson.org, includes online articles and links for Catholic homeschooling resources. She is also co-editor and contributing author of *A Catholic*

Homeschool Treasury (Ignatius Press) and a graduate of the Plan II Liberal Arts Honors Program at the University of Texas in Austin. The Macksons reside in Michigan.

Bishop Carl Mengeling

Born and raised in Indiana, Bishop Mengeling was a member of the Diocese of Gary's first ordination class. He was ordained a priest in 1957 and served as an associate pastor and as pastor in various parishes throughout Indiana, including St. Thomas More Parish in Munster. He earned his Doctorate in Sacred Theology at the Alphonsianum University in Rome. Bishop Mengeling was appointed fourth Bishop of Lansing in January 1996.

Michael Aquilina III

Michael, now age sixteen, is the oldest of six homeschooled children. He is the author of *St. Jude: A Friend in Hard Times* (Pauline Books). He enjoys writing, photography, playing bass guitar, music, and ham radio.

Cynthia Blum

Cynthia and her husband, Ron, enjoy homeschooling their six sons, including a set of twins. A catechist for seventeen years, Cynthia serves the homeschooler support group in her area and is the assistant DRE for her parish. Blending classical disciplines, and the methodologies of Montessori and Charlotte Mason, Cynthia is the author of *Little Saints: A Catholic Preschool Program with Classical Disciplines*. For more information about the program, visit http://www.catholicpreschool.com, or see Appendix A.

Linda Bromeier

Linda is a professional educator with six years' classroom experience in remedial reading and learning disabilities. She has a master's degree in education from the University of Missouri at St.

Louis and is also the author and publisher of the Little Angel Reader Catholic phonics program. Linda is in her fifteenth year of homeschooling; co-founder of Gateway Academy, a Legionary of Christ School in St. Louis; first leader of St. Louis Catholic Homeschool Association; Catholic wife and mother of seven children.

Fredrick Cabell, Jr., Esq.

Fred and his wife, Laurie, are homeschooling parents of two teenagers and use a classical approach to homeschooling. Fred serves as chief counsel to Pennsylvania State Senator Jeffrey Piccola, and he and Laurie are incorporated members of *Regnum Christi*, a lay movement affiliated with the Legionaries of Christ.

Nancy Carpentier Brown

Nancy and her husband, Mike, have been homeschooling for ten years. Nancy is a freelance writer and contributing editor to *Heart and Mind* magazine (see Appendix A). She is a member of the American Chesterton Society (www.chesterton.org), an organization devoted to reintroducing the work of Gilbert Keith Chesterton. Nancy's column "The Flying Stars," appears regularly in *Gilbert Magazine* (www.gilbertmagazine.com). The Brown family lives in Antioch, Illinois.

Janet Cassidy

Janet and her husband, Mike, have enjoyed homeschooling their three children. Janet is a biweekly columnist for *The Catholic Times* of Flushing, Michigan, a freelance writer, and former radio host. She has a BA in Religious Studies from Madonna University in Livonia, Michigan. The Cassidys reside in Michigan.

Lynne Cimorelli

Lynne has eleven wonderful children and lives in El Dorado Hills, California, with her husband, Mike. They've homeschooled all of their children since birth. Lynne has a master's degree in piano performance from California State University, Sacramento, and has written a series of instructional piano books entitled *Playing on the Keys*. If you'd like more information on her books, you can reach her at PlayOnKeys@aol.com, or see Appendix A. She is music director for El Dorado Musical Theater, a children's theater company in which her children are very actively involved.

Kevin Conley

Kevin and his wife, Patsy, are the parents of seven children, who have been homeschooled from their earliest years. They're thankful to all of the Catholic homeschooling pioneers for the example they've set. They use the Kolbe Academy classical curriculum, and use Regina Coeli Academy, an online program, as a supplement for the older children. Kevin works as an actuary. They now reside in Raleigh, North Carolina.

Daniel J. Davis

Danny held bachelor's degrees in Political Economy and Political Theory and Constitutional Democracy from Michigan State University's James Madison College. His interests included religion, philosophy, literature, poetry, and analytical writing. Danny was looking forward to law school, advocating pro-life issues, work in government, and having a large family someday, when in August of 2003 he passed away into eternal life.

MacBeth Derham

A professional naturalist, MacBeth and her husband, Don, are parents to four children. Before her children were born, MacBeth worked as a field naturalist for a consortium of school districts. MacBeth has been using Charlotte Mason's method since her oldest was in first grade, and she co-moderates a Catholic Charlotte Mason online support group with more than a thousand members and maintains two websites: www.4reallearning.com and www.charlottemason.tripod.com. She's currently writing a book on outdoor education for homeschoolers.

Colin Fry

Colin is nineteen years old and is the oldest of eight children. After being homeschooled his whole life, Colin is now a college student majoring in history and getting his elementary teaching certification. Colin is active in Catholic apologetics, writing, and online debates. Other interests include studying Church history, collecting and promoting Catholic music, and playing wheelchair basketball.

Kim Fry

Kim is a mother of eight always-homeschooled children. The Frys spent the first twenty years of their married life traveling around the world with the Air Force. They now enjoy a lifestyle of learning on their ranch in Yoder, Colorado, where they raise dairy goats, chickens, vegetables, and children.

Cay Gibson

Cay is a homeschooling mother of five children living in Louisiana. Her husband, Mark, is an instrument technician. Cay has been published in several educational and religious magazines, including *Liguorian, Homeschooling Today,* and *Home Education Magazine.* She is also a regular columnist and contributing editor to *Heart and Mind* magazine (see Appendix A). Cay shares her passion for living literature in her book *Literature Alive!* which is available at www.houseofliterature.com and from By Way of the Family (see Appendix A). She is working on a companion guide for *Literature Alive!* and is writing a devotional book for Catholic mothers entitled *The Lacemaker's Shop,* which is based on the life of Venerable Zelie Martin, the mother of St. Thérèse of Lisieux.

Laurie Navar Gill

Laurie homeschooled her six children in suburban St. Louis for more than ten years. She taught writing and geography in co-ops for most of those years and has taught European history to high school students. She is the national trainer for the Catholic Kids Net K4J character-education program (www.catholickidsnet.org) and is co-author of the Celebrating the Faith in the Home series (available from Emmanuel Books; see Appendix A).

Mary Glantz

Mary and her husband, Paul, have been homeschooling two children for seven years. Mary holds an MBA from Michigan State University, and her work experience includes a variety of positions in mergers and acquisitions, strategic planning, and consulting. Her deep-seated desire to teach finally came to fruition when she and Paul decided to homeschool their children. They have found it a blessing and a joy, not to mention a constant challenge, to stay one step ahead of the children. Mary's hobbies include traveling, golfing, reading, bicycling, textile arts, and skiing.

Clare Glomski

Born and raised in Lansing, Michigan, Clare studied at home from kindergarten through grade twelve. She was always a good student, but it was hard to know just how good until she was named a National Merit Scholar in her senior year. She graduated *summa cum laude* from Quincy University with a bachelor's degree in elementary education with an added certification in middle school. She hopes to use education not only in a classroom of her own, but to help homeschool families excel.

Brendan Hodge

Brendan Hodge was homeschooled from sixth through twelfth grade and attended Franciscan University of Steubenville. He lives with his wife and two daughters in Whittier, California, where he works as part owner of a small I.T. services firm: www.bitsww.com.

Rosamund Hodge

Rose, the youngest of three children, was homeschooled from first grade through the end of high school. She's now attending the University of Dallas, where she maintains her interests in writing, literature, and all things Catholic.

Stacey Johnson

Stacey was born in Los Angeles, but primarily raised in northern Illinois. She converted to Catholicism when she was at the United States Military Academy at West Point, New York. Shortly after her first child was born, Stacey left the Army to become a stay-at-home mom, and began homeschooling for her first grade year. Now she and her husband, Michael, homeschool all four of their children. The Johnsons have found homeschooling useful for tailoring their children's education, especially since two of them have special needs.

Pattie Kelly-Huff

Pattie lives in Winthrop Harbor, Illinois, with her husband of twenty-four years, Scott, and their six children. They have been homeschooling for twelve years and follow a relaxed classical approach. Pattie has a master's degree in interpersonal and public communication and rhetorical criticism and taught at the university level before the children arrived. She balances her busy life as an artist working in sculpture, mixed-media collage, fiber art, watercolor painting; a portrait artist; and a jewelry maker.

Annie Kitching

Annie homeschooled while serving as director of religious education at St. Thomas Aquinas Parish in East Lansing, Michigan, where she has worked for the past twenty years. The two children mentioned in her essays are Aidan, age twenty-three, and Lydia, eighteen. In the past three years, the Kitchings have adopted Sergei (11), Anastasia (7), and Zhenya (6).

Sue Kreiner

Sue and her husband, Tim, have been blessed with eleven children and have educated them at home for more than fifteen years. They reside in Sunfield, Michigan, and are involved in the Works of Christ Community in Lansing. Sue is a certified doula, providing labor support during childbirth, and also enjoys catering special events.

Barbara Little

Barb and her husband, Mike, have homeschooled their six children for the past twenty years. Barb is co-author and publisher of the popular History Links series: www.historylinks.info. These history units are designed to provide integrated learning of history, language arts, and religion for the entire Catholic family (see Appendix A). She is also the importer and principal U.S. representative for the Audiblox program, www.audiblox2000.com, a cognitive training program developed for reading readiness and found to be highly successful in helping children overcome learning difficulties (see Appendix C).

Susie Lloyd

A Catholic Press Association award winner, Susie writes lighthearted columns on homeschooling and motherhood that can be found in *The Latin Mass, Catholic Faith & Family*, and other Catholic publications. She is also the author of *Please Don't Drink the Holy Water! Homeschool Days, Rosary Nights, and Other Near Occasions of Sin* (Sophia Institute Press). She and her husband, Greg, reside in Pennsylvania with their six daughters.

About the Editors and Authors

Nicola Martinez

Nicola is a wife, mother, and freelance writer of fiction and nonfiction. She homeschools her two daughters, works as a secretary-bookkeeper, and designs and edits various publications. In her spare time, she washes clothes, dishes, and occasionally, windows. She doesn't sleep much, but her life is wonderfully blessed by the Holy Spirit.

Carol Maxwell

Carol lives in the Wine Country of Temecula, California, with her husband, Scott, five sons, and a daughter (so far). The Maxwells are in their tenth year of homeschooling. Carol earned a bachelor's degree in English, has been published in Catholic magazines, and is in the process of writing books about real-estate investing and about leaving the workforce for full-time motherhood.

Daniel McGuire

Dan is a retired Marine Corps officer and a full-time doctoral student at Marquette University. He received a bachelor's degree in engineering from Virginia Military Institute and a master's degree in theological studies from the University of Dallas. He and his wife homeschool their seven children in Milwaukee, Wisconsin. Dan is also the author of the Blue Knights Boys Club program (published by Ecce Homo Press; see Appendix A), a six-year catechetical program for boys. His articles have appeared in several Catholic publications.

Melissa Ramirez Naasko

The Naaskos are a fairly new homeschooling family. Melissa loves the process of planning her curriculum and actually teaching her child, Joseph. Her younger son will begin instruction next year, and her infant daughter has a while to wait yet. Melissa and her husband, Benjamin, make their home in Colorado.

Marcia Neill

Marcia and her husband, Joe, are parents of four children and recent first grandparents. A homeschooler for fourteen years, Marcia is the director of St. Michael the Archangel Academy, an umbrella school for Catholic homeschoolers who reside in Orange County, California. She authored and publishes *Catholic World History Timeline and Guide* (see Appendix A) and was a contributing author to *A Catholic Homeschool Treasury*

Maureen O'Brien

Maureen and her husband, Steve, have four children. Natives of Rochester, New York, they currently call Decatur, Illinois, their home. Maureen left a career in healthcare administration when the Holy Spirit called her to minister to her family.

Holly Pierlot

Holly is a popular speaker on marriage and homeschooling topics, and the author of *A Mother's Rule of Life: How to Bring Order to Your Home and Peace to Your Soul* (Sophia Institute Press). She also runs the website www.mothersruleoflife.com, which helps mothers to organize their homes, classrooms, and spiritual lives. Holly and her husband, Philip, homeschool their five children on Prince Edward Island, Canada.

Gregory Popcak, MSW

Greg is a homeschooling father as well as a Catholic psychotherapist and author of six books on marriage and family life, including *Beyond the Birds and the Bees* (Our Sunday Visitor), and *For Better . . . FOREVER* (Our Sunday Visitor). He coauthored *Parenting with Grace* (Our Sunday Visitor) with wife, Lisa. He is the director of the Pastoral Solutions Institute, an organization that provides telephone counseling and seminars for Catholics struggling to apply their faith to tough marriage, family, and personal problems. He invites you to contact him at 740-266-6461 or through his website at www.exceptionalmarriages.com

Ed Rivet

Ed and his wife, Michelle, are parents of six children and live in Mason, Michigan. They began homeschooling in 1997, when their oldest child was nine. They are certified teachers of Natural Family Planning through the Couple to Couple League. Ed is the full-time legislative director (lobbyist) for Right to Life of Michigan. and holds bachelor's and master's degrees in public administration.

Janine Cerino Seadler

Janine is passionate about teaching children with dyslexia. She has firsthand family experience teaching dyslexic and ADD children. For the last seven years, she has been a consultant and tutor for homeschooling parents with learning-different children. Her expertise comes from her formal training as a certified reading specialist and extensive training from Wilson Language and The Jemicy Outreach Program. She works with her husband, Paul, a special educator, who does testing for their business, The Learning Home (see Appendix C). The Seadlers and their three sons reside in Jarrettsville, Maryland.

Monica Sohler

Monica and her husband, Paul, began homeschooling twelve years ago, when their oldest son, Joseph, was entering third grade, and now have two children in college, three still at home. The Sohler family numbers seven humans, plus a dog, a cat, two pet chickens, two budgies, a box turtle, two crayfish, and six pet mice.

Nancy Stine

Nancy is a homeschooling mother of five boys, ages five through twelve. She holds a degree in elementary education from the

University of Michigan. She taught junior high school before becoming a stay-at-home mother. Nancy converted to Catholicism before marrying her husband, Joe, and is growing in love and appreciation of both each year.

Joan Stromberg

Joan, married to Bob for over twenty years, is a homeschooling mother of eight children, ages two to nineteen. The children have always been homeschooled. Joan has written the Glory of America series, historical fiction about American saints. She has also written extensively on Catholic homeschooling and homeschooling support groups and is a regular contributor of American Catholic history to *Catholic Parent*. The Glory of America series can be purchased through the Stromberg's home business: Ecce Homo Press (visit www.eccehomopress.com or see Appendix A).

Mary Jo Thayer

Mary Jo and her husband, John, reside in Okemos, Michigan, and are parents of four children. Mary Jo was trained as a public-school teacher and claimed she would never homeschool. While in a master's program at Michigan State University, she underwent a transformation regarding home education. Mary Jo has also developed seminars for parents and talks for teens regarding the virtue of chastity, based largely upon Pope John Paul II's *Theology of the Body*. She may be reached at maryjo@speedlink.net.

Alicia Van Hecke (née Lawless)

Alicia grew up in a Catholic family of seven children. She attended Catholic elementary school before being homeschooled for all of high school, along with her two younger brothers. Alicia became Kolbe Academy's first homeschool graduate in 1988 and graduated from Thomas Aquinas College with a bachelor's degree in liberal arts in 1992. She and her husband, John, have been married for thirteen years and are raising and educating their six children. Alicia is also the webmaster of www.love2learn.net

Pete Vere

Pete was raised in Ontario, Canada. He holds a master's degree and a licentiate in canon law from Saint Paul University in Ottawa. Along with his wife, Sonya, and his daughters, he presently resides in Ontario, where he works as a canonist, writer, and Catholic speaker. In his spare time, he volunteers with the International Order of Alhambra — a Catholic fraternal organization that assists the mentally and cognitively challenged. He is the author of two books: *Surprised by Canon Law: 150 Questions Catholics Ask About Canon Law* (Servant) and *More Catholic Than the Pope: An Inside Look at Extreme Traditionalism* (Our Sunday Visitor).

Rachel Watkins

Rachel and her husband, Matt, have been married for twenty-one years. They have ten children, ages eighteen and under, and have been homeschooling for thirteen years. Rachel was diagnosed with multiple sclerosis when she found out she was pregnant with her second child. Rachel and Matt are board members of the National Association of Catholic Home & Educators (NACHE), active members of Traditions of Roman Catholic Homes (TORCH), and a teaching couple with the Couple to Couple League (CCL). Rachel is a freelance writer and the author of Little Flowers Girls Guides, a virtue-based program for girls ages five and up (Ecce Homo Press; see Appendix A). Matt and Rachel often speak on marriage and family issues and are regular Friday guests on the Heart, Mind, and Strength radio program with Greg and Lisa Popcak.

Robert Wittmann

Robert is a recognized leader in the national movement to expand school choices and opportunities. He has nearly twenty years' experience in the field of K-12 education as an administrator, researcher, and author. He currently serves as an educational consultant to charter schools. He is the author or co-author of three major education policy manuals, including *The Charter Challenge: A Handbook for Designing and Planning a Michigan Public School Academy* and *Redesigning America's Schools: Vouchers, Credits, and Privatization*. He is also the author of numerous education policy reports, articles, and opinion pieces. Robert and his wife, Maureen, homeschool their seven children in Michigan.

Steve Wood

Steve and his wife, Karen, have been married for twenty-two years, are the parents of eight children, and have been homeschooling for more than fifteen years. A graduate of Gordon-Conwell Theological Seminary, Steve served as an Evangelical pastor for a decade before being called to the Catholic Faith. He started Family Life Center International in 1992 and is also the founder of St. Joseph's Covenant Keepers, a movement that seeks to transform society through the transformation of fathers and families. Utilizing his book *Christian Fatherhood*, audiotapes and videotapes, television, radio, and conferences, Steve has reached tens of thousands of men in the USA, Canada, and overseas with a message of Christian faith and responsibility. He is the host of the live *Faith and Family* broadcasts on EWTN worldwide radio. A member of the American Counseling Association, Steve is also a Certified Family Life Educator. Steve's latest book is *The ABCs of Choosing a Good Husband* (Family Life Center Publications).